The New Rationalism

Albert Schweitzer at his desk, circa 1905. Photograph courtesy of the Special Collections Research Center, Syracuse University Library – The Albert Schweitzer Papers

The New Rationalism

Albert Schweitzer's Philosophy
of Reverence for Life

David K. Goodin

McGill-Queen's University Press
Montreal & Kingston | London | Ithaca

© McGill-Queen's University Press 2013
ISBN 978-0-7735-4108-5

Legal deposit first quarter 2013
Bibliothèque nationale du Québec

Printed in Canada on acid-free paper that is 100% ancient forest free
(100% post-consumer recycled), processed chlorine free

McGill-Queen's University Press acknowledges the support of the
Canada Council for the Arts for our publishing program. We also
acknowledge the financial support of the Government of Canada
through the Canada Book Fund for our publishing activities.

Library and Archives Canada Cataloguing in Publication

Goodin, David K., 1967–
The new rationalism : Albert Schweitzer's philosophy of reverence for
life / David K. Goodin.

Includes bibliographical references and index.
ISBN 978-0-7735-4108-5

1. Schweitzer, Albert, 1875–1965 – Ethics.   I. Title.

B2430.S374G65 2013   170.92   C2012-907109-9

Set in 10/13 Warnock Pro with Futura
Book design & typesetting by Garet Markvoort, zijn digital

Power makes no noise

...

True ethics begin where the use of language ceases.

Albert Schweitzer,
The Philosophy of Civilization

Contents

Abbreviations

Works by Albert Schweitzer

Works by Arthur Schopenhauer

The Fourfold Root of the Principle of Sufficient Reason	FFR
On the Basis of Morality	OBM
On the Will in Nature	WN
Manuscript Remains	MR
The World as Will and Representation	WWR
Parerga et Paralipomena	PP
"On Ethics"	PP-OE
"On Suicide"	PP-OS
"On Various Subjects"	PP-OVS
"On Law and Politics"	PP-OLP
"On Philosophy and the Intellect"	PP-OPI
"On the Antithesis of Thing in Itself and Appearance"	PP-OATI
"Der Intellekt überhaupt und in jeder Beziehung betreffende Gedanken"	PP-IBG

Works by Friedrich Nietzsche

Beyond Good and Evil	BGE
Birth of Tragedy	BT
The Case of Wagner	CW
The Gay Science	GS
Human, All Too Human	HH
Twilight of the Idols	TI
Untimely Meditations	UM
The Will to Power	WTP
Writings from the Late Notebooks	WLN
The Portable Nietzsche	PN
Truth and Lie in an Extra-Moral Sense	PN-TAL
Thus Spake Zarathustra	PN-TSZ

Preface

The journey that culminated with the publication of this book is long and complicated, and it would be far too self-indulgent for me to try to recapitulate it here. Suffice to say, this present work is a modified version of my dissertation for a PhD from McGill University in Montreal, Quebec, Canada. It represents, without exaggeration, several years and countless hours of research and writing – only a fraction of which now appears in the following pages. Even though I have made very liberal use of extended endnotes for important digressions into related topics and questions, I have attempted to streamline my discussion to make it straightforward and approachable for the reader. This required that much be left aside, at least for now. No single work on such an important and complex historical figure can ever be complete unto itself. This caveat should be kept in mind throughout as I present my findings.

I also want to underscore the fact that my research owes a tremendous debt to the prior scholarship on Albert Schweitzer. Even when I differ with that scholarship on certain points, my work could only advance because of the pioneering efforts of these other scholars. Undoubtedly, this book will in turn become a seed source for future critical appraisals by others who will seek to develop and possibly correct my own conclusions. In addition, I want to recognize the many individuals who contributed to my research, both directly and indirectly, throughout my graduate studies. My deepest appreciation goes out to my PhD supervisors, Dr Gregory

Mikkelson and Dr Torrance Kirby, without whom my dissertation would have never seen the light of day. Their encouragement and support of my project has made the impossible possible. I also want to extend my gratitude to my dean, Dr Ellen Aitken, for her confidence in me over the years. Deepest gratitude also goes out to Dr Maurice Boutin for his guidance throughout my program and to Dr Lisa Sideris for her assistance at the beginning of my studies at McGill. A number of other McGill professors also greatly furthered my work. These include, but are not limited to, Dr Peter G. Brown and Dr Colin A.M. Duncan. I also want to thank Dr Marilyn Scott for supporting my teaching at the McGill School of the Environment over the years. Very special recognition is extended to Dr Thomas Pliske and Dr James Huchingson for their guidance during my master of science program in environmental policy at Florida International University. I also want to recognize the following friends who have helped me refine and prepare my thought with respect to this present work: Robin Lutjohann, Steven Miscione, and Rebekah Hart. Finally, I wish to extend my gratitude to the anonymous readers of my manuscript during its pre-publication phase. Their comments were truly helpful and improved this present work greatly.

I dedicate this book to James K. Goodin (my father) and Robert K. Goodin (my brother).

The New Rationalism

Albert Schweitzer on the occasion of his Nobel Peace Prize. Photo by Yousuf Karsh, 1954. Courtesy of the Estate of Yousuf Karsh

Introduction

In the pages and chapters that follow, I examine the philosophy and ethics of the renowned twentieth-century scholar and humanitarian Albert Schweitzer (1875–1965). Specifically, I investigate how Schweitzer engages the writings of Arthur Schopenhauer (1788–1860) and Friedrich Nietzsche (1844–1900) to create what he refers to as an elemental nature philosophy that supports a mystical and ethical worldview – what he termed "Ethical Mysticism." These borrowed and transformed elements collectively constitute his Reverence for Life ethic. In this book, I attempt to explain the intellectual history behind Schweitzer's innovations, to reveal what this means for understanding Schweitzer's contributions to philosophy, and to lay this all out for the reader in the clearest terms possible.

By way of introduction I will first reflect upon what I believe makes Schweitzer's work noteworthy and actually quite refreshing. He is one of the few in Western thought who stands against the presumption that truth claims can only be established through ever greater articulations of highly esoteric philosophical argumentation. This approach is something Schopenhauer ridicules as a *Jeu de mots* – which is to say, nothing more than academic "word games" that merely satisfy a few specialists in the field but are utterly useless for real world ethics. Schweitzer faults Western philosophy for this same tendency. Real ethics, he came to believe, must be capable of being translated into what he calls "a living philosophy of the people."

This is an alienating starting place for many academics, and it certainly grates against my training and inclinations. It is also the very place where we must begin to appreciate what Schweitzer sets out to do. His turn away from philosophical technicality in order to speak directly to a non-academic audience fits into a particular tradition that has since been superseded by modern trends in philosophy, including phenomenology, existentialism, poststructuralism, and other theoretical approaches. Nietzsche, arguably, is the wellspring for these later developments, yet part of the reason for the sheer diversity in academic thought since his time comes from certain ambiguities in his books – a subject touched upon in chapter 3. I mention this now because Schweitzer has his own reading of Nietzsche, which causes his "hermeneutical turn" to not quite fit into any contemporary academic category. This is part of the reason Reverence for Life is so baffling to many philosophers today. And so I now take a few moments to discuss a hidden tradition that Schweitzer relies upon, a line of thought that goes all the way back to Immanuel Kant (1724–1804) through Nietzsche and Schopenhauer.

Nietzsche is an uncompromising de-constructor of *all* truth claims, not just those in religion. He also takes aim at the enduring principles that have secured Western philosophy from the time of the ancient Greeks. This includes the supposed primacy of the mind over both the physical body and the apparent reality revealed to the senses. The prevailing approach in philosophy had been to try to discover permanent and unchanging "truth" through the intellect's analytical reasoning powers – projects often working from a priori first principles, the parsing of linguistic concepts used to describe phenomenal reality, the utilization of syllogisms and logic to test their certainty, and the critical examination of the subsequent synthetic conclusions for inconsistency and other errors in reasoning. Nietzsche, however, rejects the validity of this and all such similar techniques for establishing truth, writing dismissively that he would "leave this distinction to the epistemologists who have got caught in the coils of grammar" (GS §354).

Nietzsche is not unique in this respect. Schopenhauer likewise states that the ethical systems "laid down by philosophers ... consist of abstract, sometimes even hair-splitting propositions with no foundation except an artificial combination of concepts" (OBM 170). This is not academic nay-saying. Schopenhauer believes that serious and harmful repercussions come along with this approach because, when such language games are used to create ethics for personal behaviour and civic responsibility, "their application to actual conduct would often ... have its ludicrous side" (ibid.). Schopenhauer instead turns to what he terms "intuitive" ethics. While this is fully described later, in brief, it means that the intellect and abstract reasoning are ancillary to a visceral foundation based in *pre*-rational responses to sensory perception. His ethical system is, in fact, based on compassion for another's suffering, and its actualization is manifested through Rousseau's famous dictum: "Achieve your wellbeing with the least possible harm to others" (185).

Schweitzer follows Nietzsche and Schopenhauer in that he has a similar mistrust of rationality as an exclusive philosophical foundation for truth and ethics. But, as beautiful as Schopenhauer's philosophy and ethical vision is, to simply write about an intuitive ethic is one thing, to actually make it a living social reality is another. This became for Schweitzer a life's mission. He would begin his Reverence for Life project by agreeing with Schopenhauer that the foundation of morality resides with pre-rational, intuitive truths. The most important of these inborn truths is a personal sense of conscience that heeds the call of compassion. Stated another way, Schweitzer believed that only the voice of Socrates' *daimon* could secure an ethical society, not any of the dry textual formulations scratched out on parchment from the pen of Kant, Hegel, or any of the other philosophers who had come to dominate academic discourse.

Society and the Self

Schweitzer reveals why he believed society needed to reject mainstream philosophical tradition in a sermon from 1919, delivered in his role as vicar at Saint Nicolai Church in Strasbourg. In the sermon, Schweitzer makes a confession to his congregation about an incident that occurred during a recent trip to Paris. He relates that it was "an ugly winter's evening" when his taxi approached the house at which he was to stay (*APR* 70). A man, upon seeing the taxi pull to a stop, ran up in hope of helping with the suitcases. Schweitzer recounts that, "as the car stopped, the misery of [his] existence caught me: torn, hungry, wet through [and through], and puffing [from the exertion]" (71). But before he could react, the appearance of the man triggered a confrontation with the porter for the house, who had also come out to meet the taxi. The porter did not deem the stranger trustworthy and made him leave at once. The entire encounter was over in moments. There was no time for Schweitzer to fully assess the situation, weigh all the consequences, and bring his faculty of reason to bear on the larger moral, social, economic, and political circumstances involved in what had just transpired before his eyes. Schweitzer told his congregation that, when it was all happening, he felt: "I could say nothing to the porter about [this], for he was only following his instructions and I was a stranger in the house and had no rights [to intervene]" (ibid.). But later that evening, while trying to enjoy dinner with friends, Schweitzer became inwardly troubled about the incident: "I could not excuse myself for having not followed that inner voice [of conscience and done something for the poor man]" (ibid.).

Schweitzer uses the confession to tell his congregation how people are caught between two equally powerful ethical forces. The first is the rational mind, which seeks order and consistency for our own actions and within greater society: it defers to societal laws, the dictates of philosophical reasoning, and the social norms for expected behaviour. The second is the inner-voice of conscience: it only obeys the boundless natural law of compassion. Sometimes the natural law and rational law coincide, and there is no problem. However, there are other times when we are forced to make compromises to practical necessity, such as when the porter chased off the homeless man, since such trade-offs are what organized society ultimately depend upon (79). But when this happens, one of two things will result. Either that second ethical force, the natural law, will begin to gnaw away at a person or we are forced to betray and cease to heed that inner voice altogether. This is the greater error, he indicates, for such a person has not only "killed personal morality, [but also] the truly human in themselves" (55). What Schweitzer is saying is that, in social ethics, there is an irreconcilable tension between practical necessity and an innate sense of universal compassion. He believes that Western philosophy conceals this terrible truth by turning to higher-world metaphysics and utopian thinking. This is a key problematic for Schweitzer, and it is one that he tries to address head-on.

Schweitzer realizes that civilized society demands laws that we hope are ethical and in keeping with our highest ideals. But any system of ethics can become *inhuman* when it externalizes morality and responsibility to logic, laws, social norms, and the like. Moreover, Schweitzer writes, "no one finds the way to [true] morality who ... [unquestioningly defers to the] commonly accepted rationality [promoted by society]" (71). The problem is that a person's conscience and societal laws are not always compatible. Nevertheless, while these ethical realities often "compete against each other," he says that "there is truth in both" (72). Here he is describing what is called an antinomy – two equally valid propositions that cannot be formally reconciled, ordered, or even prioritized: "The ethic of [an] ethical personality is personal, incapable of regulation, and absolute; [while]

the system established by society for its prosperous existence is supra-personal, regulated, and relative. Hence the ethical personality cannot surrender to it, but lives in continuous conflict with [society], obliged again and again to oppose it because it finds its focus too short" (POC 292).

The antinomic nature of these forces, however, does not spell doom for the hopes of an ethical society. Schweitzer actually uses them as a creative tension so that each mutually shapes the other: society by asserting its legal will on unruly citizen behaviour, and individuals by, in turn, correcting society through activism when it falls short with regard to ideals of social justice. At first glance this may seem merely a recipe for preserving the status quo and thus societal stagnation. But Schweitzer also holds out the possibility that real progress in civilization may emerge through these antinomic processes. Because society is itself an organization of individuals, it follows that, "in proportion as society takes on the character of an ethical personality, its code of morals becomes the code of [a truly] ethical society" (POC 294). In other words, the foundation of ethics, in its social expression, consists of those ethical agents who continually keep society on the right track by becoming the moral conscience society itself cannot manifest on account of its supra-personal rules and codified laws. Schweitzer believes that, in time, real social progress can emerge from this basis.

As seemingly straightforward and elegant as Schweitzer's solution may appear to be, I have come to the conclusion that there are certain serious underlying problems here and that these, in turn, explain why he could never complete the remaining volumes of his great work, *The Philosophy of Civilization* – the very volumes that were to spell out exactly how such an ethical society could come into existence and function. Still, despite these problems and the fact that his writings were left unfinished, Schweitzer's Reverence for Life ethic, as it pertains to *personal* morality, remains for us in a more substantial form. Its foundation, I believe, is not undermined by the lack of a complete picture of the civilized state. This is because Reverence for Life is first and foremost a virtue ethic for humanity. As I think the evidence shows, Reverence for Life still remains a trustworthy prescription for individual morality. Much of the content of this book is devoted to justifying this claim.

Early Scholarship

There was a time when Albert Schweitzer was very much maligned as a philosopher. The harsh judgment against his philosophy by his contemporaries began almost immediately. He was not unaware of this criticism, yet he chose to ignore it. Schweitzer believed that his work would speak for itself, but he never received critical recognition for his philosophy during his own lifetime. It is possible that he drew comfort from the fact that Spinoza, "whom hitherto everyone had attacked without making any effort to understand him," remained in obscurity until he was rediscovered by Friedrich Jacobi over a hundred years later (*POC* 190). Yet because Schweitzer never defended himself against his detractors, his unbreakable silence struck many as an admission of failure, that he was giving an unspoken acknowledgment that his philosophy was indeed fundamentally flawed. Others found his silence contemptuous and arrogant, that he had nothing but utter disdain for the academic life he had left behind. All this made him a magnet for any and every kind of slander. But a private letter from 1963 reveals that his silence was something else entirely (*Letters* 331):

> My strategy consists in never responding to any attack of any kind whatsoever. That has always been my principle, and I have stuck to it loyally. In the long run no one can fight against silence. It is an invincible opponent. Nor does anyone have to defend me. It is my lot to go my way without combat. It is my lot to pave the way for the spirit of reverence for life, which is also the spirit of peace. I am quite dumbfounded by the fact that I have been granted such a splendid calling; as a result, I go my way, spiritually unhindered. A grand, calm music roars within me. I am permitted to see the ethics of reverence for life starting to make its way through the world, and it elevates me beyond anything that anyone can reproach me for or do to me.

Schweitzer's humility in this statement is breathtaking, especially when considering that his detractors had not just maligned his philosophy but, in some cases, had called him a self-seeking hypocrite, an incompetent doctor, a racist, and even an Antichrist by those conservative Christians who were offended by his scholarly work on the New Testament. Yet his silence was not an implicit confession of his failures; rather, it reflected his long-suffering and characteristically Stoic love for humanity. As many of his readers already know, Schweitzer had a particular fondness for the Roman emperor and Stoic philosopher Marcus Aurelius (121–180 CE). A passage from Aurelius's (1966, 123; VIII.8) *Meditations* helps explain the real reason for his unbreakable silence: "You cannot hope to be a scholar. But what you can do is to curb [your own] arrogance; what you can do is to rise above pleasures and pains; you can be superior to the lure of popularity; you can keep your temper with the foolish and ungrateful, yes, and even care for them."

While Schopenhauer had preached that a person should maintain an inner state of being he called "volitional non-willing" and detach themselves from becoming involved with the daily struggles of other people, the Stoics instead counselled that "the aim we should propose to ourselves must be to the benefit of our fellows and the community" (176; XI.21). Schweitzer, who was otherwise a devotee of Schopenhauer, faulted him for not promoting a more engaged ethic of social responsibility. He reached back in time to recover a typically Stoic disposition and outlook for himself. Aurelius had advised his readers to help greater humanity with patient forbearance, arguing that the compelling example of their demeanour would eventually win over the most irascible opponent. Schweitzer evidently took Aurelius's words to heart. Consider, for example, the following passage (XI.18.173–4):

> Kindness is irresistible, so long as it be genuine and without false smiles or duplicity. The most consummate impudence can do nothing, if you remain persistently kind to the offender, give him a gentle word of admonition when opportunity offers, and at the moment when he is about to vent his malice upon you bring him around quietly with "No, my son; it was not for this that we were made. I shall not be hurt; it is you yourself you are hurting."

This socially engaged *cosmopolitan* philosophy of the Stoics is what attracted Schweitzer. His steadfast adherence to these Stoic principles explains his gentle impassability in the face of the unrelenting attacks on his scholarship and personal character. While the excellent biographies by James Brabazon have, in my opinion, dispelled much of the unpleasant shadow these wild criticisms once cast over Schweitzer's reputation, one of my aims is to investigate certain remaining questions concerning his academic works. I also intend to show that his philosophy is still capable of making important contributions to academia even today.

Methodological Considerations

I now draw this introduction to a close by providing a few words concerning methodology. Unlike Nietzsche's works, Schweitzer's works have no discernible progression of thought between early and later writings, with one very notable exception that will be discussed in the opening pages of chapter 1: the cornerstone concept of the Reverence for Life. Notwithstanding that key development, the framework for Schweitzer's intellectual worldview emerges whole and complete even in his earliest books such as the *Quest of the Historical Jesus* in 1905 – and it is thoroughly Schopenhauerian.

Despite the clarity this provides for a researcher, a complication for this investigation is Schweitzer's curious habit of seeding important elements of his philosophy in disparate and unrelated works, and not repeating himself elsewhere. For example, his essays on Goethe include important commentary on economic policy and moral personhood, and his dissertation on Kant's philosophy of religion includes an extended discussion of Schweitzer's own views on religious genius and aesthetics. And so on. He often assumed that any reader of his would have read everything he had previously written. This being the case, when writing about him a researcher needs to assemble Schweitzer's thoughts from across the entire spectrum of his disparate areas of expertise in order to form a complete picture – such as I have done in the following chapters. Schweitzer also presumed that his readers were familiar with the same sources he critiqued in his writings. Accordingly, where necessary, I provide extended discussion on these other figures and subjects in order to reveal the historical contexts and distinctiveness of Schweitzer's own thoughts.

In presenting Schweitzer's ideas, I try to avoid staying "above the text" with my commentary and reflection; instead, I seek to present my arguments through the primary literature itself. Too often secondary literature can introduce distortions of a historical figure's works; such distortions can get further amplified by other scholars who build on that foundation. This, I have come to believe, has already happened with the scholarship on Schweitzer, and it has greatly muddied the waters. It is for this reason that I decided to start afresh and, wherever possible, to present Schweitzer in his own words. This, I hope, will allow the reader to enter into an exploration of these texts and to perform his or her own "secondary analysis" of my conclusions along the way.

This brings me to the final complicating factor of preparing my book for publication: trying to anticipate its audience. Should it be written only for other scholars? Should it be even more narrowly focused and aimed at specialists within philosophy? Alternately, should the aim be for non-academic readers? In the end, I decided to try to make this material accessible to the widest possible audience. The opening chapters assume a general academic audience, and I explain the relevant background and philosophical concepts with these readers in mind. The subsequent chapters become progressively more technical, and certain passages are probably only accessible to specialists in philosophy. This is unavoidable, and I encourage lay readers to be patient as the greater part of this work should be open to them. I hope I have written something that will be equally enjoyable to both the specialist in philosophy and to the non-specialist. Whether or not I have succeeded, I leave for the reader to decide.

Summary of Argument

Schweitzer's approach to philosophy is to build his system around what he calls elemental truths. These are seen as permanent, unchanging truths concerning human nature and existence; they include the will-to-live theory and the universal cosmological Will, taken from the works of Schopenhauer. Schweitzer transforms these concepts in light of certain criticisms and modifications made by Nietzsche. In brief, I show that Schweitzer transforms Schopenhauer's theories, recasting them as purely biological phenomena in order to reconcile these philosophical postulates with the findings of empirical science.

The influence of Schopenhauer has been well documented in prior scholarship on Schweitzer. But exactly how Schopenhauer's will-to-live theory grounds Schweitzer's philosophy is either not well understood or is presumed to have been a strategic error on Schweitzer's part. It is thought that his reliance on Schopenhauer pushed Reverence for Life into unsupportable metaphysical excess and made certain of Schweitzer's claims about non-human life appear to be romanticized imaginings. My investigation demonstrates that the will-to-live theory is what Schopenhauer utilizes to escape the "lair of the skull" and to establish the independent reality of the empirical world. Only then does he engage in an analysis of cosmological causality, posit the existence of a universal Will, and claim the will-to-live as the Kantian essence of the things themselves. By using these techniques Schopenhauer seeks to prove that phenomenal reality exists apart from Cartesian consciousness. For this reason, Schweitzer *needed* the will-to-live theory: only Schopenhauer could provide him with a satisfactory linkage between rational consciousness and the outer, non-self world.

Schweitzer writes that he sought to create a "mysterious combination" of the philosophies of Schopenhauer and Nietzsche. He attempts to do this by combining the individualistic ethics of natural life affirmation in the works of Nietzsche with the altruism of ethical self-sacrifice in the writings of Schopenhauer. This produces a mystical worldview that envisions personal fulfilment actualized through ethical service to others. This is Ethical Mysticism. But Schweitzer still needs one more unchanging natural truth to anchor the Reverence for Life ethic. This is established through his New Rationalism project.

The phrase "New Rationalism" occurs only once in his 1936 article on the ethics of Reverence for Life. Nevertheless, it still represents, in my opinion, a fitting title for his project. In an earlier work, *The Philosophy of Civilization*, Schweitzer employs a similar phrase, "a rational theory of the world" (*denkende Weltanschauung*), in the context of upholding rationalism as the only way out of the crisis in civilization. He writes that, even though this philosophical movement of the eighteenth and nineteenth centuries had failed because it was incapable of dealing with the emerging "philosophical, historical, and scientific questions" of the times, only rationalism, if taken up anew, could anchor a lasting philosophy of civilization (*POC* 55): "All real progress in the world is in the last analysis produced by rationalism [*Rationalismus*]" (54). He therefore saw his task as reforging the "broken sword" of Kant's and Schopenhauer's Idealism (81). Schweitzer reclaims this discarded philosophy because, as he argues, only rationalism can become optimistic and ethical in the face of the nihilism that emerges from a strictly scientific worldview, and only rationalism can reach into the sphere of mysticism where a reverence for all life can be established. Schweitzer thus seeks to redress the errors of prior philosophers by establishing a new foundation for a rational worldview – one that differs from the flawed ontology originally developed by René Descartes (1596–1650) and upon which Kant and Schopenhauer had been largely dependent.

To this end, Schopenhauer's cosmological constant of the will-to-live was said by Schweitzer to also reside at the core of ontological self-awareness; the first fact of human consciousness would be defined as an individually unique synthesis of the Cartesian ego, Schopenhauer's will-to-live concept, and the historicity that comes to bear on a person through language, culture and circumstance. As such, Schweitzer's ontology and ethics would be inclusive of non-human life since all beings share equally in the will-to-live, yet he could also show how humans have a hermeneutically distinctive rational consciousness. In this one bold stroke, Schweitzer sought to dispel both the ethical anthropocentrism of Descartes and secure a solid foundation for his Reverence for Life ethic. It could then emerge as a cultural truth for all people everywhere, a philosophy of civilization for everyone.

Lastly, it should be noted that in the following chapters I use the term "pre-rational" to describe certain phenomena within the mind that arise from sensory intuitions of the world – for instance, the sense of awe and wonderment felt in wild nature. This is the sublime, and that surge of feeling comes before the intellect has a chance to put it into words. The pre-rational is thus *prior* to the rational. This distinction is important when discussing the subject of epistemology. In addition, I choose the term "pre-rational" to distinguish it from another term employed by Schweitzer, *das Irrationale*. He uses this term to describe mysticism, and it is probably best translated as "the non-rational." He means it in the sense of being confounded by an inexplicable excess of deep, profound meaning that goes far beyond mere intellectual understanding: "If rational thought thinks itself out to a conclusion, it arrives as something non-rational" (POC 80). It is the other side of the spectrum. The rational mind is bracketed by the pre-rational and the non-rational. The world is first felt, then intellectually comprehended, and finally exceeded in mystical appreciation. This final step is necessary because, as Schweitzer writes: "Anyone who undertakes the voyage to true ethics must be prepared to be carried round and round in the whirl [*Strudeln*] of the non-rational [*Irrationalen*]" (292). This is the experience of Ethical Mysticism. It is also how Schweitzer's elemental nature philosophy becomes a living philosophy of the people.

Chapter 1

The Crisis in Civilization

It was 1915 in French Equatorial Africa. Albert Schweitzer had only been in Lambaréné two years and was serving as a jungle doctor for people who did not have access to medical treatment in cities. He was now forty years old. At the age of thirty he decided that it was too selfish for him to remain in Europe and continue to write academic books and give organ concerts as he had done previously. Already possessing three doctorate degrees – one in philosophy, one in religious studies, and one in music – he now decided to enroll in medical school.[1] A man of deep religious conviction, Schweitzer felt the admonitions of Matthew 25 aimed directly at him.[2] He believed he had been vain and egotistical to remain merely a scholar and musician when the world needed so much more. The enigmatic figure of Jesus whom his own foundational work in 1905, *The Quest of the Historical Jesus*, had sought to fathom, silently reproached him to devote his life to the least of his brethren. Leprosy was still rampant in Africa, and lepers were in dire need of conscientious medical attention. There was no effective cure for the disease until the 1940s, and all a medical care provider could do was to try to redress its chronic complications so as to allow for the best quality of life possible.[3] In a moment of inspiration, which occurred while he was gazing at a magazine article about Africa, Schweitzer decided to seek the true meaning of Christianity by caring for those who needed it most. Seven years later he had his medical doctorate, said his goodbyes to family and friends, and set out for an African village located one degree latitude south of the equator.

That day in 1915, Schweitzer was in a small steamship travelling up the Ogowé River on an emergency medical mission to see a patient 260 kilometres away. It was now sunset on the third day of the voyage. To occupy himself, Schweitzer was once again lost in thought about the crisis in civilization that had brought forth the horrific battles that were then raging across Europe. Before the war Schweitzer had been penning a book that was to be entitled *Wir Epigonen* (*We Inheritors of the Past*), which was to be a critique of the concept of progress in modern civilization and was to show how an unseen and deep spiritual decay had undermined Western philosophical thought (*OLT* 146–7). But then the First World War broke out and the project was set aside as having come too late. Yet that day in 1915 Schweitzer was again thinking about the war and the spiritual crisis in civilization when his steamboat encountered a herd of hippopotamuses. Gazing at this incredible scene, Schweitzer had a sudden realization. He recounts this life-changing event in his autobiography (156):

> Lost in thought I sat on the deck of the barge, struggling to find the elementary and universal conception of the ethical which I had not discovered in my [earlier attempt at] philosophy. Sheet after sheet I covered with disconnected sentences, merely to keep myself concentrated on the problem. Late on the third day, at the very moment when, at sunset, we were making our way through a herd of hippopotamuses, there flashed upon my mind, unforeseen and unsought, the phrase "reverence for life." The iron door had yielded: the path in the thicket had become visible. Now I had found my way to the principle in which affirmation of the world and ethics are joined together!

Somehow, in seeing these families of behemoths making their way through the dark river water in the sublime light of dusk, the idea of Reverence for Life (*die Ehrfurcht vor dem Leben*) came to him. From then on, Schweitzer knew that the necessary change must come through what he called life- and world-affirmation. This meant an unflinching ethical focus on the present world instead of turning to "higher world" metaphysics and spirituality. He would call the latter ways of thinking life- and world-resignation because they looked past the immediately apparent reality in their search for some other answer to the injustices in the world.

This is one of the major problems Schweitzer had with mainstream philosophical and religious thought, but it was certainly not the only one.

The ethical ideals of the great philosophers and religious thinkers of the past had ceased to have any real meaning in the lives of contemporary people – those were culturally conditioned truths with no real claim to universality outside their historical contexts (*POC* 41). Worse, Schweitzer saw that the very idea of civilization had become only a "will to progress" in terms of material and technological achievements, and this left aside the goal of ethically perfecting persons and society (*OLT* 149, 153). He concluded that a new ethic had to emerge from "the mystery of existence" itself and that it had to be universally true for all people regardless of time, place, or cultural background. This required that his ethic be founded on an elemental truth, which, in philosophical parlance, meant that it had to be derived from a new first principle (*archē*). An elemental truth would allow for the specific articulation of the ethic to be interpreted and reinterpreted over time. Only in this way, Schweitzer thought, could it be "spiritually our own" (155). He also knew that this elemental truth had to be accessible to all, immediately evident, and intuitively confirmed. In the simplicity of the phrase "Reverence for Life" he found what had previously eluded him.

What would arise from this encounter on the Ogowé River would become Schweitzer's great work, *The Philosophy of Civilization* (1923). Curiously, in this book Schweitzer does not identify the Reverence for Life ethic as specifically Christian. In fact, Jesus is barely mentioned and usually only in passing. Schweitzer would reserve his impassioned defence of the Christian faith for another 1923 work, *Christianity and the Religions of the World*. This separation of publication aims was intentional. Schweitzer wanted Reverence for Life to be embraced by all cultures. To enable this, he established Reverence for Life as an elemental nature philosophy, not as something limited to Christianity. Only in its extended mystical meditations would Reverence for Life take on religious overtones, and only then could Christianity, or any other world religion, claim to find particular resonance with its elemental universal truths.

This is why Schweitzer felt he had to develop his philosophy as a two-part project: an elemental nature philosophy supporting a secondary manifestation he called Ethical Mysticism. He did this because he believed that "reason and heart must work together if a true morality is to be established" (*RFL* 112). The first part, the elemental nature philosophy, seeks to satisfy rational thought, and he creates it by conducting a critical philosophical and scientific inquiry into the basic truths of existence.

Much of this focuses on the writings of Arthur Schopenhauer and Friedrich Nietzsche. Schweitzer takes certain elements from their systems and refashions them for his own philosophy. This includes what he terms the New Rationalism, which is a different starting place for philosophy than the one established by René Descartes.

Schweitzer's project then moves from academic theory to the lived experience of ethical personhood – that is to say, it seeks to harmonize the reasoning of the analytical mind with the intuitive truths in a person's heart. Schweitzer creates Reverence for Life in order to substantiate a deep personal conviction in moral agency and even to support religious faith. This was the second part of his project called Ethical Mysticism. It is an enlightened and deepened worldview that informs and adds context to ethical decisions; it produces what Schopenhauer calls a "sublime character" for a person, allowing him or her to become ethically selfless and unconditionally altruistic (*WWR* §39, 206). And because this would become the true foundation for his ethic, Schweitzer's Ethical Mysticism does not require a person to belong to any religion. Few people are so spiritually inclined that they seek out a selfless life of Christian devotion to others, as did Schweitzer himself. Yet for such rare people, the worldview of Reverence for Life would also substantiate their faith with an intellectually sound elemental nature philosophy.

Put simply, Schweitzer's philosophy can support a religious worldview. But his is a *philosophy* of civilization, not a new religion. While Schweitzer once wrote about the "ethic of love" that he saw in the teachings of the historical Jesus (*OLT* 232), this ethic originates in an elemental truth first revealed in the human heart. Schweitzer establishes it through philosophical arguments concerning something called the will-to-live theory and through scientific findings on the evolution of humankind's social instincts. In this way, the ethic of love could be accepted by *all* religions, not just Christian ones, and even be embraced by people with no religious background at all – but more on this later. The conjoining of natural science, philosophy, and mysticism is a distinctive and unusual aspect of Schweitzer's ethic, and it is something that this work as a whole will try to put into perspective.

The Philosophy of Reverence for Life

Schweitzer considered Reverence for Life to be the summation of his life's work. Yet his ethic remains perplexing to scholars, a problem residing in its unclear philosophical grounding. Part of this problem results from the fact that Schweitzer completed only the first two volumes of what was to be a four-volume work on his Reverence for Life ethic – *The Philosophy of Civilization*. The two completed volumes present his analysis of the development of the Western philosophical and ethical worldview (*Weltanschauung*) and then introduce the Reverence for Life ethic as his response to the problematic established by his critical deconstruction of prior philosophical systems.

Advanced age and his humanitarian duties in Africa are part of the reason *The Philosophy of Civilization* was never completed, but it is clear from his autobiography (published in 1931) that he intended the example of his life to be the definitive word on his philosophy. Schweitzer would publish only a single article in 1936 to provide an additional explanation of the grounding for the Reverence for Life ethic, but this did not clarify the critical philosophical questions. And, while in 1952 he was awarded the Nobel Peace Prize for his medical mission in French Equatorial Africa (modern-day Gabon), which, for him, signified key public recognition of his Reverence for Life ethic, in academic circles the reception of his philosophy suffered from the incomplete picture offered by his published works.

And so we arrive at the fundamental problematic concerning Reverence for Life. How exactly does it relate to basic philosophical categories such as a theory of knowledge (epistemology), an explanation of existence (ontology), and – especially because Schweitzer describes Reverence for Life as a nature philosophy – how does it deal with Kant's challenge that we can never know anything *intrinsic* to the phenomena of the natural world?[4] With respect to these central questions on philosophical cosmology, the works of Schopenhauer and Nietzsche will be shown to have factored large in the development of Schweitzer's thought. My investigation here seeks to explore these correspondences with regard to understanding the philosophical underpinnings of Reverence for Life.

For the time being, cosmology can be thought of as synonymous with a worldview that places and orients a person in life. The technical dimensions of philosophical cosmology are addressed in upcoming chapters, where I argue that Schweitzer is particularly indebted to Schopenhauer for the cosmological description of the will-to-live, which, in Reverence for Life, becomes an elemental truth. I show that Schweitzer is also indebted to Nietzsche for his reimagining of Schopenhauer's philosophy in terms of biological phenomena as well as for his extension of cosmological thought into the sphere of economics. Economics is itself a form of applied ethics. Schweitzer's criticism of the Western worldview in *The*

Philosophy of Civilization took aim at the deleterious effects of modern economic life upon people with regard to their ethical development. He saw this happening both in Europe and in the colonial regions. Schweitzer came to believe that, for many people, modern economic systems had undermined the possibility of true moral personhood. Like Nietzsche, Schweitzer believed that a society's worldview becomes entwined with the economic circumstances of daily life, usually for the worse. I return to this subject later in this chapter.

Schweitzer never intended Reverence for Life to be merely a code of interpersonal conduct or an academic discourse. His ethic seeks to place people in life as moral agents and to embed them within a larger worldview that unites all people, all cultures, and all beings as one; he presents his philosophy as the necessary prescription for redeeming Western civilization from the colossal collective moral failure that led to the First World War. It is not an exaggeration to say that Schweitzer's project is nothing less than an attempt to establish Reverence for Life as *the* philosophy of civilization – an incredibly grand and bold undertaking on his part. And though he lived ninety years and accomplished much during his life, what was to be the very pinnacle of his achievements now languishes because of its lack of clarity in terms of philosophical grounding. And so we return to the central question: What exactly is Reverence for Life? To begin exploring this complex question, we need to take a closer look at the man himself.

The Man and His Works

Albert Schweitzer was a polymath with few equals in his time or any other. As already mentioned, he had obtained four doctorate degrees in fields of study ranging from the natural sciences to the humanities by the time he was forty years old. His particular contributions in each of these fields helped to define the cutting-edge of academic scholarship. In Africa he pioneered innovative medical practice in a remote jungle hospital (Richardson 2007, 137),[5] all the while finding time to contribute the occasional academic article to worldwide journals in each of his areas of expertise, researching and writing them in the hot African nights by the light of a kerosene lamp after a full day of surgery and hospital administration. I mention this to highlight the fact that, as a collective body of works and achievements, Schweitzer's contributions are nothing less than amazing. They are also quite intimidating to the researcher who studies him. Even when the scope of the investigation is confined to just his work in philosophy, as is mine, Schweitzer's critical writings on the great philosophers of the past are exceptionally comprehensive.

In *Out of My Life and Thought* Schweitzer jokingly curses the day he read Aristotle's *Metaphysics* and adopted his methodology of developing "the problem of philosophy out of criticizing [all] previous philosophizing" (119). This is his approach in *The Philosophy of Civilization*. He undertakes a critical analysis of Western philosophy from ancient Greece up to the present day, with the conviction that: "it is only the elements in [each of] them which can help the establishment of an ethical system that will interest us" (*POC* 24). Nevertheless, the style of the book departs markedly from that of Aristotle. Schweitzer had little interest in presenting a technical and systematic treatment of abstract principles and metaphysical concepts; rather, he provides commentary on the strengths and weaknesses of each figure and their thought. One reason for his taking this approach had to do with his specific audience. In the preface to the second volume of *The Philosophy of Civilization* he comments:

> Our philosophy would become more and more complicated. It lost the connection with the elementary questions – the ones that placed people in life and in the world. More and more it found its satisfaction in the working of philosophically academic questions and in the expert mastery of philosophical technique. More and more it would be held captive to these secondary and incidental matters. It is like this. Instead of composing real music, it frequently produced music only for the conductor's tastes, though often truly excellent music, still it was the conductor's music and not music for the audience. Instead of striving to establish thought and life in a practical worldview, through this philosophy, the only philosophy pursued, we came into the condition of having no worldview at all and consequently without a real foundation for civilization.[6]

The Philosophy of Civilization was written to be accessible to an educated laity, and this is why it consists mostly of commentaries on the history of philosophy together with a few sustained essays that were developed in relation to that critical deconstruction. His aim is to open up philosophy to everyone, something that he later reiterates in his autobiography: "I intentionally avoided technical philosophical phraseology [in *The Philosophy of Civilization*]. My appeal is to thinking men and women whom I wish to provoke to elemental thought about these questions of existence which occur to the mind of every human being" (*OLT* 199).

While this approach would reach a wider audience, it was not something trained philosophers were accustomed to recognizing as philosophy true and proper. However, we should keep in mind that Schopenhauer produced both academic and popular works and that he became very successful because of this. Schweitzer however only aimed for the simple persuasive truths he hoped would reach people in their daily lives. He never created an accompanying systematic work of dazzling complexity and subtlety for impressing an academic audience. This is both a strength and a weakness of his Reverence for Life project. This is what both charms the popular imagination and frustrates the scholar.

This is not to say his work was either simplistic or that his commentaries were not expertly rendered with surgical skill – quite the opposite in fact. Schweitzer's dissertation for his doctorate in philosophy, after all, is a critical and technical engagement of Kant's philosophy. Schweitzer was certainly capable of undertaking a Kantian approach in his written works, yet he chose to do otherwise. Schweitzer did not want his book to become a dusty academician's tome for descrying obscure intellectual ponderings about an abstracted theoretical world with only tangential relations to the real one in which people actually lived, worked, dreamed, suffered, and died. *The Philosophy of Civilization* was to be a book for daily reflection and inspiration to support a practical mysticism that placed everyday people in everyday life. This was to be a book open to everyone, a Reverence for Life ethic for all of humanity.

For the present-day scholar working with the same materials, however, certain challenges arise in reading these critical commentaries and translating them into their identifiable constituent elements for what Schweitzer argued was indeed an elemental nature philosophy with claims to universality. This as I have suggested will be found in how Schweitzer engaged the cosmological systems of Schopenhauer and Nietzsche in establishing his own Reverence for Life ethic, which is where this discussion turns to next.

Cosmology and Reverence for Life

Schopenhauer uses the phrase "the will-to-live" to describe the basic essence of human and non-human life, and he uses the phrase "the Will" to describe the cosmological force that is responsible for observable changes in the world. Schweitzer employs the same terminology in his own system and, further, sets forth an ethic of compassion that, like Schopenhauer's, is inclusive of non-human life. Yet there are major differences between the two with respect to social action. Schweitzer criticizes Schopenhauer for his ethic of world- and life-resignation (*Welt- und Lebensvernseinung*), which, he feels, calls merely for an individualistic and contemplative life. In contrast, Schweitzer came to see his humanitarian work in Africa as a means of actively setting his ethic into motion for greater social change. But the question of how Schweitzer employs and transforms Schopenhauer's cosmology remains, and this is where Nietzsche, the other great philosopher of the Will, becomes important for this investigation.

Schweitzer singles out and praises Nietzsche for both the cosmological naturalism of his famous Will to Power theory and for setting forth an attitude of radical life-affirmation. Nietzsche had a great interest in the natural sciences and claimed that he looked at science from the perspective of an artist (*BT*, "Attempt at Self-Criticism," §2). While scholarship is divided on the interpretation of his works, some have concluded that Nietzsche had re-envisioned Schopenhauer's cosmological Will for his own Will to Power theory, changing its metaphysical character to the sum of all organic and inorganic forces at each level of physical reality – dynamics that take place not only in microscopic biological processes within cellular tissue but also in macroscopic societal interactions between people in economic and political life. This, as I argue in chapter 3, is how Schweitzer interprets him. Through Nietzsche, Schweitzer finds a way to make the will-to-live theory compatible with modern science.

Here it should be recalled that Schweitzer also possessed an advanced degree in natural science as a medical doctor. In his autobiography he admits he had grown weary of how the truths within the humanities were established because it "is carried on in constantly repeated endless duels between the sense of reality of the one [scholar] and the inventive power of the other ... [and yet we are] never able to obtain a definite victory" in establishing a true verifiable fact (*OLT* 104). Natural science provides objective certainty and a way to dispel the ambiguity of opinion. Schweitzer, unlike Nietzsche, never doubts the veracity and importance of empirical science. Yet he also knows that the natural sciences are incomplete and unable to fathom the "mystery of existence" itself. He therefore concludes that the relationship between natural science and the humanities has to be complementary (104–5):

> Intoxicated as I was with the delight of dealing with realities which could be determined with exactitude, I was far from any inclination to undervalue the humanities as others in a similar position often did. On the contrary. Through my study of chemistry, physics, zoology, botany, and physiology I became more than ever conscious

to what an extent truth in thought [within the humanities] is justified and necessary, side by side with the truth which is merely established by [scientific] facts.

Schweitzer does not look past the empirical world of the natural sciences. He recognized that rational thought must always be correlated to what is found there and never become lost in the fanciful mindscapes emerging from the human imagination. At the same time the life-affirmation that he felt could only arise within the humanities must never lose its place. For this reason, he derives his Reverence for Life ethic and its elemental nature philosophy from empirical science by building on Charles Darwin's description of evolutionary social instincts and Schopenhauer's own engagement of natural science. Only then would it be translated into a philosophical worldview and social ethic. This last point also reveals why Nietzsche became so important to Schweitzer. He needed to redress what he saw as the metaphysical excesses of Schopenhauer as well as his ethic of contemplative detachment. Through what he calls a "mysterious combination" of the two thinkers (POC 248), Schweitzer developed the philosophical grounding and life-affirmation he needed for his own Reverence for Life project.

But metaphysical excess and ethical resignation were not the only problems Schweitzer found in Schopenhauer. He wryly writes of him that he was able to succeed where Kant had failed "because he did not possess Kant's moral depth" and thus could see more clearly and objectively the true problem of ethics (TAS 338–9). Schopenhauer wrote persuasively and passionately about an ethic of compassion that included all suffering, human and animal alike. Schweitzer deeply valued Schopenhauer's contributions to advancing Kant's philosophy and ethics into the natural world. But, at the same time, Schweitzer personally despised him, as the thinly veiled edge in the above quote reveals. The problem was that, as beautiful and wonderful as his moral philosophy was to read, and despite the penetrating truths Schopenhauer wrote about, he had preached one thing and practised another. Schopenhauer had a widely known and scandalous public image as a womanizing "Buddhist" who ate meat, lived like an aristocrat, and was a vicious anti-Semite at the same time. Even worse, there is a particularly infamous passage in Schopenhauer's *The World as Will and Representation* of which Schweitzer took special note: "In general, it is a strange demand to make on a moralist that he should commend no other virtue than that which he himself possesses. To repeat abstractly, universally, and distinctly in concepts the whole inner nature of the world, and thus to deposit it as a reflected image in permanent concepts always ready for the faculty of reason, this and nothing else is philosophy" (*WWR* §68, 383).

With specific reference to this passage, Schweitzer writes: "With these sentences Schopenhauer's philosophy commits suicide" (*POC* 243). Schweitzer considered Schopenhauer a hypocrite for preaching one thing for society and living by another less-than-moral standard in his private life. Schweitzer's decision to begin medical school in pursuit of his fourth doctorate at age thirty and then to devote the rest of his life to running a humanitarian medical mission in Africa was deeply influenced by what he saw as Schopenhauer's personal moral failings. Schweitzer lived his life as the anti-Schopenhauer. This is an important context for understanding Schweitzer. He would finish writing his ethic in deeds rather than just in printed words. For Schweitzer, this was not the failure of his philosophy but, rather, its ultimate testimony. He set himself before the public eye as a personal representative of his own ethic and tried to succeed where Schopenhauer had failed. This being the case, my investigation must consider certain biographical aspects of Schweitzer's life and assess those writings in which he expresses his views on ethical social action – particularly those involving economic life. Reverence for Life was not to be just an academic theory that advanced the work of his intellectual predecessors, and it was much more than a mere applied ethic. It is nothing less than an indictment of modern economic society, coupled with an exhortation for everyone to rise up and to make a real difference in the world.

The Decay and Restoration of Civilization

Schweitzer believed that the crisis in civilization arose from two root causes. The first was the failure of contemporary philosophy to tap into the spirit of the age and to connect with the common person in order to help him or her deal with the problems of their daily lives. Schweitzer knew that "the value of any philosophy is ... to be measured by its capacity, or incapacity, to transform itself into a living philosophy of the people" (*POC* 7). Modern philosophy had gone astray in this respect. Through the efforts of Hegel, Fichte, and others it had been drawn into speculative excess with unbridled power of invention over questions of "pure being" as a theory of the universe (4). Then, in a single stroke, the emergence of empirical science "reduced to ruins the magnificent creations of their imagination," leading the majority of people to dismiss rationalism and, with it, any optimistic convictions and moral meaning it could have provided (4–5). Into this cultural vacuum of values would step the economy itself as a principal means to give direction and meaning to the lives of the ordinary person. This was the second cause of the crisis in civilization. However, in order to fully reveal what Schweitzer means by this, I must devote most of the remaining space in this chapter to a discussion of his views on the adverse impacts of modern economic life on moral personhood.

The individual is front and centre in Schweitzer's prescription of the restoration of civilization. The actualization of the Reverence for Life ethic is dependent upon the person who is capable of inspiring others through the power of his or her ethical character. The greatest threat to the development of such ethical personalities, Schweitzer writes, comes from the circumstances of their daily lives. Unnoticed economic forces can both prevent the needed change and perpetuate the causes of social decline by progressively degrading the personhood of the citizenry. This threat was deemed to be of such great importance that Schweitzer felt compelled to write about economics in the very opening pages of *The Philosophy of Civilization*. He also wrote about economic life in the place where he maintained his hospital – the French colony that would later become the nation of Gabon. In both contexts, his commentary is much the same. Despite the different settings and actual form of the institutions, both cultures were suffering the same serious repercussions for the development of moral character and ethical agency due to the demands of making a living in modern market economies.

Schweitzer wrote that the very souls of people had become entangled in the economic institutions now controlling their lives (*POC* 18). This happened slowly and almost imperceptibly. But now conditions of life had dramatically changed for making a living and this has had a profound effect on personal identity. "For two or three generations [now] numbers of individuals have been living as workers merely, not as human beings" (11). Schweitzer means this quite literally. "Our society has ceased to allow all men, as such, a human value and a human dignity; many sections of the human race have become merely raw material and property in human form [e.g., labourers and corporate employees]" (15). He is not saying that people are simply working in a new setting, such as an industrialized factory rather than a village; rather, he is claiming that being an itinerant wage-earner in a modern self-regulating labour market has devalued human existence itself – something he was inspired to write about by the work of Nietzsche.[7] The problem was that a person was now only an employee who was easily replaceable, just like a soulless cog in the machines he or she worked on. Yet it is not just the factory worker and labourer who suffer this fate. "We are all more or less in danger of becoming human *things* instead of [true, self-determining] personalities" (334 [emphasis added]).

Schweitzer also became greatly concerned that public education was increasingly focused on training students for the job specialization needed for future employability. Because of this, both teachers and their students now lacked the breadth of knowledge and educational background that would allow them to be fully functioning citizens with critical thinking skills (*POC* 13).[8] He believed that this had further narrowed personal identity and injured the soul of modern people: their "mental horizon" was not a wide as it should have been (13). This left many of them incapable of thinking for themselves. It was now the case that a modern person increasingly "can only see himself as thinking in the spirit of some group or other of his fellows" (16–17). Public education and other social forces, he feared, were being used to subordinate people to economic institutions. They were being taught to see themselves through their eventual job titles – that then became who they were in their own estimation. Individuality was being lost. The very existential identity of humanity was being cast in terms of economic function.

Schweitzer believed that modern economic life had damaged the psyche of the human person in several other ways too. Increasingly, people were required to work long hours to provide for themselves and their families, leaving little possibility for the reading and reflection necessary for the development of strong ethical conviction (*POC* 13, 88). They were also too worn out to seek intellectual self-improvement or to strengthen the bonds of community with their fellows. According to Schweitzer, "family life and the upbringing of children [also] suffer[ed]" from the stress of making a living (334). All this exhaustion produced a great need for relaxation, and people turned to distractions that did not engage their minds. The various media, such as newspapers and periodicals, were taken over by "the spirit of superficiality" for the purpose of catering to this very need (14). An important avenue for creating critical thought was thereby closed off, further damaging society.

Another tragedy involved the very nature of modern economic relations. Schweitzer believed that a "serious psychical injury" occurred through specialized work that separated people from any direct connection to their fellows (*POC* 10). No longer were people getting immediate benefit from their labours. Economic exchange was now depersonalized in such a way that a person worked for wages and then had to purchase food and other commodities from another institution, not from a community of cooperative fellows as had been the case in former times (10). People were becoming entirely materially and psychologically dependent upon these soulless institutions (87–8). They had lost all immediate connection to greater humanity. Because of this, people were living "in a depressing, materialist state of serfdom" to the economic forces that now controlled their lives (333).

Perhaps the greatest danger of all this, Schweitzer believed, was to be found in the resultant damage to *ethical* personhood. Independence of thought was becoming progressively more uncommon; instead, people were becoming susceptible to group-think and merely echoed the common wisdom presented to them in the popular media (*POC* 17–18). The problem, Schweitzer writes, is that, "with the surrender of his own personal opinion the modern man surrenders also his personal moral judgment" (19). Such a "go-with-the-flow" person no longer thinks critically, and it becomes increasingly easy for him to excuse the "cruel, unjust, or bad behavior of his nation" (ibid.). No one was left to form the core of critical thinkers with strong communitarian sensibilities, educational background, and moral character to challenge the system. Society then unthinkingly ambles locked-step down "the path towards inhumanity" (14). Nietzsche had warned of the same thing. "Everything a man does in the service of the state is contrary to his nature ... This is achieved through division of labor (so that no one any longer possesses the full responsibility [for his decisions])" (*WTP* §718, 383). This is what Schweitzer saw happening in Europe in the wake of the First World War. Modern economic life had fractured the psyche and homogenized individuality, leaving society without a moral foundation other than the prevailing social trends (*POC* 20):

> The man of to-day pursues his dark journey in a time of darkness, as one who has no freedom, no mental collectedness, no all-around development, as one who loses himself in an atmosphere of inhumanity, who surrenders his spiritual independence and his moral judgment to the organized society in which he lives, and who finds himself in every direction up against hindrances to the temper of true civilization. Of the dangerous position in which he is placed [modern] philosophy has no understanding, and therefore makes no attempt to help him. [Philosophy] does not even urge him to reflect

on what is happening to himself. The terrible truth [is] that with the progress of history and the economic development of the world it is becoming not easier, but harder, to develop true civilization.

On top of all this, the people of the world had been profoundly demoralized by the First World War. Schweitzer writes that even those nations not involved in the conflict became deeply troubled over the idea of progress (*POC* 85). Modern science and technology had brought forth unimaginable death, not peace and prosperity. People awoke at the dawn of the twentieth century expecting utopia. They had been taught to believe that civilization was like a continuous blossoming of social progress, unfolding from the past into a better future for all (85). Instead, they entered a disturbing age of nationalistic and individualistic barbarity. Somehow there had been an unnoticed and terrible regression within the spirit of humanity. European high culture produced not enlightenment but unleashed mechanized, chemical, and airborne carnage upon the world (88). This is what civilization had become. Schweitzer asks his readers to resign themselves to these facts, saying that they must come to realize and accept that "material achievements ... are not civilization" (89). The common wisdom was that material, scientific, and technological invention was somehow connected to social progress, and this was a dangerous fallacy. In a supporting essay, he provides a diagnosis (86):

> The disastrous feature of our civilization is that it is far more developed materially than spiritually. Its balance is disturbed ... [I]n our enthusiasm over our progress in [scientific] knowledge and [technological] power we have arrived at a defective conception of civilization itself ... The essential nature of civilization does not lie in its material achievements, but in the fact that individuals keep in mind the ideals of the perfecting of man, and the improvement of the social and political conditions of peoples, and of mankind as a whole, and that their habit of thought is determined in living [in a] constant fashion by such ideals.

Civilization and economics are inseparable, and this terrible lesson became all too clear with the rise of Nazism. Schweitzer saw its spectre on the horizon. He even gave a public speech in Frankfurt in 1932 disparaging the Nazi economic policies that were bewitching the people (*Goethe* 56–7). And this is also why in his 1954 Nobel Prize lecture, Schweitzer would warn that "we [would be] guilty of contempt for history if ... we fail[ed] to take economic realities into consideration" when we tried to establish a lasting world peace. Reverence for Life was, from its onset, aimed at countering these causes for the decline that had befallen Western civilization – a catastrophe that would bring forth not one but two world wars.

Because of all this, Schweitzer set out to reform the political, social, and economic foundations of society. He did not define *exactly* what civilization should be like; he does, however, have a few recommendations regarding the distribution of wealth in society – a subject I revisit in the final chapter. Instead he mostly stipulated that real social progress could only be manifested through the promotion of intellectual, spiritual, and ethical personhood for each individual to his or her self-chosen end. A central concern in this project involves guaranteeing economic security within society (*POC* 10). Civilization requires people who are empowered to act with moral agency: as much as possible, each person must be free to pursue his or her desire for self-improvement in any way that he or she feels moved to explore. The individual must be the author of his or her own life because true civilization can only grow out of the collective manifestation of such self-actualized persons (320). In this sense, Schweitzer is a utilitarian because he sees society as "the sum of a number of individuals, not as an organized body" impressing authoritarian order into the masses (226). But this is most definitely not the "rational pleasure" utilitarianism of John Stuart Mill or the claimed naturalistic "biologico-sociological" foundation for economic market-based utilitarianism (227).[9]

Schweitzer's utilitarian vision is rooted in a worldview that promotes an individualized ethic of self-fulfillment actualized through social altruism (*POC* 299). People, he argues, had lost the primal cosmological connections to the land, and this had resulted in a psychic injury to those who now existed only as employees. This fracturing of prior relations to the land had created a placelessness within the human psyche, and this, in turn, had undermined civilization itself. Schweitzer hoped that his elemental nature philosophy could serve as the lynchpin for re-securing people not only within the natural world but also within their economic lives. Even if that life would still be found in a modern factory, the "sense of place" could still be restored *cosmologically* through the Reverence for Life ethic. Schweitzer believed that a person could reconnect to his or her fellows and all life through the New Rationalism that places his or her consciousness in contact with the universal will-to-live. Taking an interest in the life before them, and helping whenever they could, would allow people to reverence the infinite Will that dwells within them too (322). Schweitzer felt that this would be enough to give them the ethical orientation to be able to navigate their way in society. It would enable "the mass of individuals to work themselves out of the condition of spiritual weakness and dependence to which they have brought themselves [through being subjected to modern economic life]" (18).

Schweitzer in Africa

The life-changing event on the African river described at the beginning of this chapter actually had its genesis earlier in Schweitzer's life – the epiphany arose gradually from an accumulation of experiences and reflections about the problem of ethical society that go all the way back to his school days, and in particular to his readings of Schopenhauer and Nietzsche. And so, just like an archeological expedition, we need to continue peeling back the layers of history to discover what it was that inspired his Reverence for Life ethic. Schweitzer's views on economic life in Europe were deeply influenced by the changes he saw taking place in Africa as a result of colonialism. Therefore to provide additional context for the discussion just provided on *The Philosophy of Civilization* and economics, it is necessary to now go to his earlier published works, to speak of why Schweitzer was in Africa in the first place, and to detail exactly what it was that he experienced there. This discussion will also allow for a fuller picture of the man and his personality to emerge for the reader.

Schweitzer had chosen Africa for his humanitarian work out of a moment of inspiration after reading an article in the Paris Missionary Society magazine entitled *Les besoins de la Mission du Congo*, "The needs of the Congo Mission" (OLT 88). Yet, after setting his heart on the Congo, members of the overseeing committee warned him that his liberal theological positions would raise "serious objections" (97). Nevertheless, in July of 1905 he wrote a long letter to the Reverend Alfred Boegner, head of the Paris Mission, trying to sell him on the idea. He listed all his virtues, including his good health and his being a teetotaler, and tried to assuage any potential reservations Boegner might have had: "Please do not be alarmed by my activities in theological and philosophical scholarship ... Absorbed in my thoughts about Jesus, I have asked myself whether I could live without scholarship, without art, without the intellectual environment in which I now exist – and all my reflections have always ended with a joyous 'Yes'" (*Letters* 4–5). He was still rejected. Schweitzer remarked that it would have been an easy matter to have found an appointment through the liberal Swiss *Allgemeine Evangelische Missionsuerein*, but he felt that he had to honour that initial calling for the Congo region (OLT

97). This meant that he had to agree to go to Africa as a doctor since his scientifically minded liberal Christianity was considered unacceptable for missionary work (Wadlow 2007, 26).[10] He then enrolled in medical school to begin his long training to become a doctor. It was 1913 before he set foot in Africa.

Schweitzer was assigned to a mission at the native Galoa village of Andende near the colonial town Lambaréné, which takes its name from an expression in the local language meaning "let us try" (Wadlow 2007, 24). This remote outpost was established in the jungle interior around 1860 by a migration from the larger French coastal settlement of Libreville, so named because it had been founded in 1849 by freed slaves taken from a Brazilian cargo ship captured by the French (Trefon 2003, 42). The French and Galoa nevertheless also engaged in the slave trade in addition to their other economic exports of ivory, wood, and salt (Wadlow 2007, 25–6). Trefon suggests the motivation for the establishment of Libreville in the first place was the desire by the French to establish an indigenous labour force for greater colonial aims (42).

This region of Africa was originally discovered by the Portuguese in the fifteenth century, and they established their first settlement in 1521. By the time of his arrival, Schweitzer wrote that the local people had been devastated by colonial contact. "We have at present merely the remains of eight once powerful tribes, so terribly has the population been thinned by three hundred years of alcohol [used as a form of payment] and the slave trade" (*EPF* 6). Schweitzer found himself, quite literally, at the interface between two very different worlds: one consisting of the remains of traditional societies with subsistence livelihoods and the other representing European "high" civilization and its colonial agenda. As a witness to such events, he felt compelled to write about life in the colony and what he felt needed to happen for the greater benefit of the Gabonese people.

A Few Comments on Scope of Work

The subjects of colonialism, neocolonialism, and Schweitzer's place in history as an agent either for or against these politico-economic forces (he has been cast as both) are beyond the scope this book. Instead, I point the reader to Steven E.G. Melamed and Antonia Melamed (2003), who have prepared what is arguably the best and most definitive account of Schweitzer's relations with the Gabonese people. Schweitzer's legacy is wrapped in an uncomfortable history, and this has led many to consider him "persona non grata" as an academic thinker worthy to be spoken of anymore. Only recently has there been a resurgence of academic interest in him. The even-handed and unblinking assessment of Melamed and Melamed sets that complicated history into perspective. One of their key conclusions is that Schweitzer showed a capacity for cultural learning and sensitivity that started to emerge *after* he had written his early accounts of economic life for the Gabonese people. In time, Schweitzer was profoundly changed by his experiences in Africa and through his developing relationships with the people there. Melamed and Melamed underscore this point, reminding the reader that the very idea of Reverence for Life only came to Schweitzer in Africa. Yet his early accounts of Africa remain, and these are the ones that necessarily form the core my investigation.

Take, for example, the chapter in *On the Edge of the Primeval Forest* that deals with economic life. It was written in July 1914, just fifteen months after he arrived. While very much opposed to much of the colonial agenda and the rampant abuses that he saw, Schweitzer still used the typical colonial language of the day to describe the African people, and sometimes in harsh and judgmental ways – for example, writing that the locals were untrustworthy labourers who needed constant supervision. He also used language that today would be considered racist: for example, he referred to the people as "primitives." It has to be kept in mind, however, that this word did not carry the cultural baggage then that it does now. Schweitzer also spoke about the "primitive" Christianity of the Apostle Paul and the early Church to contrast it to later ecclesial developments. This was simply the standard academic vocabulary of his day. Similarly, Schweitzer used the term to contrast the traditional cultures of Africa with European society. To be sure, this reflects a cultural bias and value judgment. But the same can be said for today's accepted nomenclature. The very idea of a developing nation, or the United Nations' choice phrase "least developed country" (LDC), or even the word "development" itself, for that matter, all suggest that the current state of a society is not acceptable based on some value judgment. Such is the nature and danger of any type of academic investigation in these areas.

Because he lived such a long life (ninety years), in the 1950s and 1960s the elderly Schweitzer found himself caught up in the worldwide backlash of public sentiment against European activity in Africa. The outmoded language and economic commentary in his early writings would be used against him to impugn his legacy – ironically, in contradictory ways. The American civil rights activist W.E.B. DuBois (1868–1963) called Schweitzer "the last of the Great White Fathers" of Africa and claimed that, as a medical doctor, he had "assisted in perpetuating colonialism by making life tolerable under it" (Melamed and Melamed 2003, 182). However, others "labeled [him] a traitor to the white race because he preached and wrote that whites had exploited black Africa without giving enough in return" (186). Schweitzer was caught between these conflicting and politically motivated interpretations. Yet he remained silent during all of this, as was his lifelong practice in response to criticism of any kind. Fortunately, these perceptions of his humanitarian work have faded with the historical distance that has allowed for fresh perspectives and critical scholarship. Some of that history must be revisited in order to examine Schweitzer's views on ethical personhood with people living in a developing nation. Again, I suggest that the reader interested in a fuller treatment of Schweitzer's place in that complicated history begin with Melamed and Melamed (2003).

A People under Colonial Rule

The French introduced a cash economy in their African colony and imposed taxation upon the locals to force their assimilation and to prevent their reversion to traditional subsistence livelihoods (Trefon 2003, 39). One way of imposing this taxation was through indentured labour, whereby native "individuals … [were] forced by the army to leave their villages, often bound to each other with ropes, and set to cutting down trees that were exported to Europe" in lieu of cash payment for his or her owed tax (Wadlow 2007, 26). Schweitzer considered this to be nothing less than slavery under another name.

The colonial powers at this time were only interested in the export of lumber from the old-growth forests, particularly mahogany and another hardwood species known as okoumé (*Aucoumea klaineana*) that was used mainly for plywood. Schweitzer remarked that the local people would have been better served if an improved subsistence economy had been established instead. He noted that the region could support the cultivation of palm oil, coffee, pepper, cinnamon, natural rubber, vanilla, and cocoa. This would have provided a diverse economic base that could have supplemented some local needs as well. "But the chief business of Europeans is neither the cultivation of these things, nor the collection of rubber in the forest, but the timber trade" (*EPF* 4). This left the colony without a sufficient agricultural base for subsistence. It was "necessary, therefore, to import from Europe flour, rice, potatoes and milk, a fact which makes living a complicated business and very expensive" (5). While the cash economy and the creation of a wage-earning labour force allowed for new-found purchasing power, the local people were often required to exchange their labour in work camps that were largely dependent upon these expensive foreign foodstuffs. As a result, after the time they spent in these work camps in order to pay their annual tax, many people would "return home as poor as [they were when] they went away" (116).

Another problem and a huge drain on the new-found monetary wealth of the local people was cheaply produced imported alcohol, without which, due to its import duty, the colony itself would not have been profitable (*EPF* 125). Just as with his comments about the working people of Europe, the mental and physical exhaustion of long work hours inclined people to seek out unthinking distraction and relaxation. While in Europe it was the "picture show" or some vapid popular magazine (*POC*, 11), in Gabon these were not an option, and so the imported, plentiful, and readily available rum is what many people turned to instead. Schweitzer despised this as a great social evil. He was not opposed to the consumption of alcohol and, indeed, spoke favourably of the palm wine locally produced by the Gabonese for village festivals (*EPF* 125–6). But he believed the cheap foreign rum could destroy entire villages in time – something which was reported to him secondhand by the European traders as having already happened throughout the region (25).

This tragedy did not happen with the imposition of a colonial authority over the traditional societies. It started when the first commercial interests arrived in their lands; the colonial rule came afterwards to secure those private commercial interests (*TAS* 71). According to Schweitzer, colonial authorities focused on maximizing economic development for foreign companies: "as much of the population as possible shall be made available in every possible way for utilizing to the utmost the natural wealth of the country ... so that the capital invested in the colonies may pay its interest, and that the [European] motherland may get her needs supplied through her connection with them" (*OLT* 117). Benefit to the Africans was not a real concern, so strategies had to be developed to get the locals to cooperate with the colonial agenda. It would take the form of a two-pronged approach. Schweitzer noted a curious motto that summed it up. To motivate a person to work when previously such labour conditions never existed in their societies, it was necessary to "'Create in him as many needs as possible; only so can the utmost possible be got out of him,' say the State and commerce alike" (114).

The first approach was through taxes that had to be paid through labour, whether at the work camps or through their own ability to generate revenue through commerce. The second was to encourage "voluntary needs in him by offering him wares of all sorts, useful ones such as clothing material or tools, unnecessary ones such as tobacco and toilet articles [e.g., imported razors], and harmful ones like alcohol" (*OLT* 114). While Schweitzer could be said to be guilty of a subjective value judgment here about what people should want to do with their money, one of his assessments is not. He bemoaned the fact that traditional native industries were dying out, having "been destroyed by the goods which European trade has introduced" in their colony (124). Just as with his comments about modern economic life in Europe, people were becoming more and more dependent on impersonal institutions for subsistence instead of communitarian relations through native industries. Because of this, Schweitzer believed that the local people were not benefiting from the colonial relationship, and real development for the people was "going backwards instead of forwards" (124).

A Prescription for Self-Determination

To use the modern parlance in environmental ethics, Schweitzer certainly did not want to create human zoos by keeping traditional societies completely isolated from Western influence. He was not a neo-primitivist. The Gabonese were in dire need of access to modern medical care, and he felt it was unconscionable not to make European medical science available to people everywhere. This was in fact Schweitzer's stated motivation for going to Africa as a doctor (*OLT* 1–2). Such comments may have a certain air of paternalism about them, but Schweitzer's mission was really no different from that of such contemporary organizations as Doctors without Borders. Like them, Schweitzer held: "It was, and is still, my conviction that the humanitarian work to be done in the world should, for its accomplishment, call upon us as men, not as members of any particular nation or religious body" (3). He was not a missionary who was seeking to convert people or to "improve" them with Western ideas. Evidently, his outlook had matured since his initial desire, a decade earlier, to become an African missionary.[11]

Schweitzer was not opposed to making consumer goods available to people in developing nations. Luxury items, however, had become a means of disrupting existing social and political arrangements in these societies, leading to social strife. He remarked that the native informal economy had been aimed at reciprocity, collective interdependence, and social welfare. He also observed that tribal customs ensured that "there [were] no widows unprovided for and no neglected orphans" (*EPF* 127). But, with the introduction of foreign economic values and luxury goods, the social structures began to break down such that the tribal "chiefs beg[an] to sell their subjects [as slaves] for [foreign] goods" and to trade their land outright to foreign interests, leaving their people social "pariahs ... [and] landless laborers" (*TAS* 67, 71). Incipient consumerism had undermined the traditional social structures, leading to selfish individualism and greed. Similar psychological dynamics were identified to have taken place in Europe, which had similarly led to an ethical individualism that set society "on the path to inhumanity" (*POC* 14). Schweitzer's commentary on Europe was no doubt informed by his experiences in Africa.

The international market had unleashed non-traditional consumer goods and advanced Western weaponry in the colony, and this had irreversible effects on the Gabonese: "Already they have lost their freedom because of [international markets]. Their economic and social fabric has been transformed by it" (*TAS* 149). Schweitzer contended that economic development, which the people wanted, had to proceed under a different paradigm. "Real wealth for native peoples would be found in their producing, as far as possible, the necessities of life by their own agricultural and handicraft efforts" (150). He wanted to create a subsistence economy that was neither dependent on foreign markets nor isolated from them. As early as 1927, Schweitzer argued on behalf of human and economic rights for the African people, including the rights to freedom and self-determination in land ownership, the use of natural resources, the ability to freely choose work and place of residence, and the right to an education (188). His aim was to encourage the kind of economic development that would allow for the greatest self-determination for the Gabonese people.

Schweitzer practised what he preached. He did what he could to help the local Gabonese develop economically without losing the traditional communitarian character of their society. He opened two nursing schools to educate a new generation of healers who came from the locals themselves, "yet for unexplained reasons, these ventures did not succeed" (Melamed and Melamed 2003, 185). In the end, all he could personally do was train a few local nurses and orderlies, and lead by example on the inherent dignity of subsistence labour by joining in with the physical work of masonry and carpentry for the construction and maintenance of the hospital compound and facilities (*TAS* 70).

The Way Forward

Having arrived at this point, a clearer picture of the man and humanitarian has emerged. The centrality of economic life for the crisis in civilization has also been brought into sharper focus. However, to employ the archaeological analogy again, we still need to dig further to discover the origins of his Reverence for Life ethic. This is a journey that takes us to the academic roots that secure his work as a true philosophy in the strictest academic sense.

Here it is important to keep in mind that Schweitzer wrote that, even as a college student, he had grown "concerned that the history of [Western] thought was always represented as only a history of philosophical systems ... not as a history of the struggle to obtain a worldview" (*KP II*, vii). It is for precisely this reason, he concluded, that civilization itself had remained fragmentary and unsecured (vii). His project therefore sought another route. He would not proceed by presenting a systematic philosophical system in the way Kant and other philosophers had done: "[for] neither cautious academic theory nor ambitious fantastical metaphysics can give us a true worldview" (viii). Instead, his project focuses on establishing a worldview through elemental truths, and only then does it support a secondary metaphysics known as Ethical Mysticism: "[My philosophy does] not seek metaphysics, thinking it can reach a worldview that way, but on the contrary it seeks a worldview first, and then takes metaphysics out from it" (*KP II*, ix). This is an important distinction, and one that I revisit throughout this work. However, Schweitzer's innovative approach came with one very serious drawback.

Consider for the moment Schweitzer's very good friend, Albert Einstein. Virtually everyone has heard of the latter's general theory of relativity, and many can instantly recite its famous equation, $E = MC^2$, which describes the relationship between mass and energy. Its simplicity is its allure. But Einstein's famous formula is still backed up by painstaking mathematical development through a type of advanced theoretical physics that only very few specially trained academics can actually understand. The beauty of Einstein's work is that it appealed to both the laity and the specialist equally. This is a rare accomplishment. And this is what Schweitzer failed to do.

Put simply, Schweitzer did not "show the work" behind his beautifully simple ethic. Reverence for Life declares that "evil is what annihilates, hampers, or hinders life ... [and that] goodness, by the same token, is the saving or helping of life, the enabling of whatever life [one] can to attain its highest development" (*E-RFL* 230). Its beauty is its simplicity. This is an ethic that requires no scholarly initiation. It is a clear and elegant truism that anyone can remember and reflect upon in his or her daily life. But where is the accompanying philosophical backing that *proves* that this has the same credibility as, say, a Kantian treatise?

My aim is to show the academic merits of Schweitzer's work by pains-takingly working my way through the intellectual history behind the ele-mental truths he uses to underpin his philosophy. This project will show the other half of his work – which is to say, it will demonstrate the aca-demically rigorous grounding of the Reverence for Life ethic. Schweitzer's philosophy is deceptively complicated even though its message is simple. His breadth of knowledge and expertise was astounding, and he drew upon all of it for his philosophy of civilization. And he sometimes did this in unexpected ways. As a man possessing four disparate areas of exper-tise, his thoughts were naturally synergistic. Schweitzer was a savant and a mystic, and it all made intuitive sense to him. This present work will therefore attempt to untangle the enmeshed complexity of his thought for the reader in the clearest possible terms.

As previously mentioned, the particular question to be examined in the following chapters is how Schweitzer was influenced by the philoso-phies of Schopenhauer and Nietzsche, and how his own synthesis of their systems in the New Rationalism project relates to the problems of ethical personhood in economic society. It must be kept in mind, however, that I am not suggesting that other figures are not also significant to Schweit-zer's works and worldview. He freely drew inspiration from Johann Wolfgang von Goethe, Johann Sebastian Bach, the Chinese philosopher Chwang-tse, the Protestant theologian Martin Luther, and a whole host of other important thinkers too numerous to list. His books and legacy are inexhaustible wells for academic scholarship. Here, however, I focus on his philosophical cosmology, with regard to which, I contend, Schopen-hauer and Nietzsche are the most important intellectual forerunners for its development.

Much of what I argue in the following chapters either has not been identified in prior scholarship or has been presumed to have been a mis-taken or poorly grounded argument on Schweitzer's part. It is hoped that my work will set the stage for a re-examination of Schweitzer's work and launch renewed interest in him as an original and relevant philosopher within academia today. A central finding of this investigation concerns Schweitzer's New Rationalism. In particular, this aspect of his work may especially appeal to environmental ethicists since it opens the door to the idea of intrinsic valuation for non-human nature in a powerful new philo-sophical framework.

With all this in mind, my investigation will proceed as follows. In chap-ter 2, Schopenhauer's philosophy will be sketched-out before turning to the question of how Schweitzer was influenced by him. But even here it was by way of Nietzsche's writings that Schweitzer came to see Schopenhauer. Nietzsche transformed Schopenhauer's cosmology by re-casting his metaphysical- and religious-based theory of causality (etiology) as a biological phenomenon. This is Nietzsche's famous Will to Power theory. And while Schweitzer would retain the name will-to-live as used by Schopenhauer, his conception of it will be shown in chapter 3 to have followed Nietzsche in terms of naturalistic biology. Chapter 4 then presents an analysis of how Schweitzer critiqued and transformed the cosmologies of Schopenhauer and Nietzsche in his own writings. This is where Schweitzer's New Rationalism project will be introduced. Chapter 5 examines certain key academic questions raised by Schweitzer's philosophy. The first concerns whether New Rationalism can be considered metaphysical and what this means for its relation to contemporary hermeneutical and phenomenological theory. The second involves whether Ethical Mysticism is religiously or theologically based. Chapter 6 then moves on to present a discussion of Schweitzer's views of civil society, while the final chapter discusses the significance of my findings for environmental ethics.

It is hoped that my work on the foundations of Schweitzer's thought will assist those academics who seek to carry forward his philosophy of civilization. This book can be only one small step in that direction. Its aims are modest but significant. Before Schweitzer will be recognized in the academic domain of philosophy, he has to be shown to be a true philosopher who addressed those foundational questions expected of one. My project proceeds by revealing the intellectual history behind his Reverence for Life ethic, and discusses exactly what Schweitzer took and transformed from Schopenhauer and Nietzsche.

Chapter 2

Schopenhauer and Schweitzer

Until recently, the centrality of Schopenhauer to Schweitzer's philosophy was not well understood. Schweitzer mentions him only infrequently in his published works. Yet private correspondence tells a different story. In a letter Schweitzer wrote just three months before his death, he mentions that, as a schoolboy at Müllhouse Secondary School in Alsace, he studied under Wilhelm Deecke, who was "an enthusiastic follower" and a former pupil of Schopenhauer (Barsam 2002, 213).[12] And in another previously unpublished letter, Schweitzer responds to Jackson Lee Ice's question regarding his greatest influences. He gave only one name in reply: "I felt, even at the age of eighteen, that Schopenhauer's work ... was an event for me" (Barsam 2008, 55). Even so, these letters serve to underscore the infrequent occurrence of the name "Schopenhauer" in his books and articles. As mentioned in the first chapter, Schweitzer's decision to begin medical school for his fourth doctorate degree and then to devote the rest of his life to running a humanitarian medical mission in Africa was deeply influenced by what he saw as Schopenhauer's personal moral failings. Schweitzer would lead by example.

Due to Schweitzer's reluctance to, at times, directly associate his own name with that of Schopenhauer, my investigation into the relationship between these two men must proceed by different means. I begin by taking note of the curious dualism Schweitzer maintains between the scientific worldview and a person's lived experience in the world (i.e., life-view): "We must make up our minds to leave our conceptions of life and of the world *independent* of each other, and see that a straightforward under-standing between the two is reached" (*POC* 276 [emphasis added]). In this exceedingly enigmatic statement, Schweitzer is addressing an age-old debate.[13]

But, before we turn to that, it needs to be remarked that the academic domain of philosophy is heady stuff. To the uninitiated it can seem like a minefield of technical definitions and overly subtle nuance set in un-necessarily mind-bending articulations of careful phraseology concern-ing exceptionally obscure conceptual matters – it is little wonder that Schweitzer chose to express his philosophy in ordinary language! How-ever, this is one of the main reasons that he has not been taken seriously as a philosopher. The general assessment of academia is that Reverence for Life is in no way significant and that it fails to rise to the level of real philosophy. In order to prove that Schweitzer is not just an amateurish commentator, it is necessary to show that his system does indeed engage with key philosophical questions expected of a true philosopher. Be-cause of Schweitzer's reliance on Schopenhauer, the only way to do this is by getting into the technical nuances for Schopenhauer's will-to-live theory in the context of his overall philosophical argument. Only then can Schweitzer's distinctiveness be revealed.

Here it has to be kept in mind that Schweitzer earned a PhD in philoso-phy specializing in Kant. This was his training, and he was well versed in that highly specialized and technical argumentation indicative of Contin-ental philosophy. Schweitzer was no amateur here. It is a testament to his wisdom that he chose to write in ordinary language when trying to create what he called a "living philosophy of the people" (*POC* 7). This was a de-liberate decision on his part. However, that said, his philosophy of civil-ization is intended to be just that – a philosophy in the strictest academic sense. He just went about it in an unexpected way.

Schweitzer's approach was to create this philosophy out of what he called "elemental truths," which were taken from certain philosophers in the Kantian tradition. Foremost among these truths is the will-to-live theory, which he takes from Schopenhauer. This philosophical postulate is advantageous to Schweitzer for several reasons, including the fact that the ordinary meaning of "will to live" sums up much of its philosoph-ical definition rather nicely. No scholarly training is required in order to understand this elemental truth. Yet at the same time there is a deep in-tellectual history behind this philosophical concept. It is this aspect of Schweitzer's thought that has not been acknowledged in academia: his Reverence for Life ethic draws upon a specific intellectual history that he assumed his academic audience would immediately recognize and acknowledge as valid. But, for various reasons, such as the subsequent emergence and dominance of new trends in philosophy (including existentialism and phenomenology), this was not the case.

The aim of the following discussion is to show the depth of the intellectual history behind the will-to-live postulate in the clearest possible terms given the demands of the subject matter. It is hoped that academic philosophers will come to recognize exactly what Schweitzer was trying to achieve by drawing on Schopenhauer's will-to-live theory in his Reverence for Life ethic. I will therefore now turn to a detailed recounting of that history in order to set the stage for a new appreciation of Schweitzer to emerge. Only after this is done can the enigmatic statement about different conceptions of life and the world that was mentioned in the second paragraph of this chapter be made clear.

The Birth of Modern Philosophy

The defining dispute in the history of philosophy was between the "materialists," who held to the ultimate primacy of the physical world and natural body, against the "rationalists," who maintained that the mind had a special cosmological place over the apparent materialism of the visible world. This dispute may at times sound exceedingly esoteric and preoccupied with pseudo-problems that arise in unnecessarily technical and hair-splitting propositions of logic. But their concern was to establish certainty over mere opinion. No true theory of knowledge could ever be established unless a foundation was first exposed on the unfractured bedrock of absolute verifiable truth. In philosophical parlance this is called a first principle. Only with a completely defensible first principle can arguments be advanced with confidence about the validity of the subsequent claims. In trying to establish a new philosophy of civilization, Schweitzer felt he needed to engage these basic philosophical questions, and do so on their own terms.

In modern philosophy this debate can be traced back to René Descartes. He had sought a solution to solipsism – the fear that everything a person experiences may just be illusion, hallucination, or just some kind of waking dream that we mistake for real life. Just as a person recovering from an amputation of a leg may still experience the presence of that missing limb, so what our senses tell us may not actually correlate to something real. The mind is only connected to the world by the five physical senses, and perhaps they can all be fooled. What appears to be reality may not be really real. And if the senses cannot be trusted, what can? This type of questioning reveals how uncompromising the scepticism of philosophy was in trying to establish a first principle grounded in undeniable truth.

To this end, Descartes creates a thought experiment about a "grand deceiver" (ostensibly Satan) who could conjure up all things perceived by the senses in order to fool the rational mind. He then asks himself, can anything we experience be proven to be actually real without any doubt whatsoever? He concludes: No, there is absolutely nothing in our sensory experiences that can be established as certain. Worse, at least according to his logic, the objects perceived to be external to the mind are mutable and impermanent, and so no first principle can be established in the outside phenomenal world. In the final analysis, his uncompromising doubt distilled all claimed knowledge to just two irreducible premises: that he himself must be a limited finite being and that the "I" at the centre of consciousness, at a minimum, could be trusted to be real.

Descartes then turned to the question as to whether the outside world exists. He concluded that because the perceived reality is the subject for rational examination, it must be undergirded by a true intelligible nature. The external "sense world" thus exists only for the mind, and the mind alone. "I rightly conclude that my essence consists entirely in my being a thinking thing ... on the other hand, I possess a distinct idea of a body, insofar as it is merely an extended and not a thinking thing, it is [therefore] certain that I am really distinct from my body and can exist without it" (Descartes 2006, VI, 44). In other words, the mind's essence is thought, and bodies are only a spatially extended intelligible substance. For this reason, Descartes maintains that the objects of the visible world specifically exist for human thought and that all non-rational beings (i.e., plants and animals) have to be merely unthinking clockwork automata controlled by rational laws.

Schweitzer wrote that Descartes set philosophy "irretrievably on the road to the abstract" and drove an arbitrary wedge between human and non-human life that has plagued philosophy ever since (POC 309). He would seek to rescue philosophy from this misbegotten beginning, but he had to do it with their logic to be taken seriously. In large part he would do this by building on Schopenhauer's theory of knowledge.

Descartes' Legacy

Western philosophy became preoccupied with human consciousness. This is because Descartes used a first principle based on the recursive awareness of the self. He then systematically worked his way out of the solipsism of mere consciousness to describe the intelligible nature of the empirical world. Following critiques by Hume and others,[14] Kant took up this project anew and masterfully mapped the inner dynamics of the cognitive acts of knowing and understanding. Kant proved that spatial and temporal awareness are not contained in raw sensory experience but, rather, are the products of the intellect itself, which processes sensory information into recognizable ideas. Epistemology reached its high-water mark with Kant. No previously assumed premise or postulate survived his rigorous critical examination. Even the human "soul" had to be grounded in something actually provable, which, in this case, was consciousness itself (whose substance is a priori time as the ultimate object of the inner sense). But even here the soul was only demonstrable during a person's lifetime. Its permanence after the death of the body could not be positively established. The same went for God. Postulates such as the existence of an immortal soul and the Christian God were only possibilities arising from antinomies of logic. Yet, from this foundation, Kant proceeded to describe the empirical world in complete certainty of the veracity of his claims. But a problem was soon discovered.

First principles always determine the nature of all subsequent claims. By beginning with a first principle of rational consciousness, all resulting conclusions regarding reality were necessarily contingent upon an experiencing subject for their existence. Kant could not give the visible world complete independence from our perception of it. In the end, all he could say was that the outer world appears the way that it does due to the particular nature of the human brain, which renders sensory data consistently according to its inner constitution. The mind's "faculty of representation" thus determines the empirical character of the perceived phenomena. And so, what sense objects are in-and-of-themselves cannot be determined beyond their intelligible properties. Kant's work highlights the fact that the mind is only connected to the world by five senses. The mind creates its own "virtual reality" by constantly interpreting incoming sensory data by adding spatial and temporal qualities, thereby making it into something intelligible – a process based upon experience and the given properties of the brain's perceptual faculties. Consequently, it is easy to trick the mind with optical and auditory illusions.

Dissatisfaction with the Kantian approach led natural philosophers to begin anew with a different first principle. Continental philosophy had seemingly hit a dead end. The empiricists would instead take perception as a given truth, and they would do so uncritically despite Kant's work here. For example, Carl Linnaeus (1707–1778), who was the pre-eminent natural scientist of the eighteenth century, believed that empiricism allowed the scientist "to know the thing itself (*res ipsas nosce*)" and that the essence, the very "beingness" of plants and animals, could be revealed through examining their biological structures (Lindroth 2004, 4, 30). The empiricists embraced Newtonian physics and mechanical materialism for causal explanations, and by using inductive reasoning and scientific verification they made stunning advances in cataloguing the attributes of the phenomenal world. This is modern science as we know it. No longer would it be called "natural philosophy," as it had been in former times. Philosophers and scientists now moved in separate circles and would increasingly support incompatible truth claims about reality.

Schopenhauer and Science

Schopenhauer was the only Continental philosopher who broke free from the solipsism of consciousness and found a way to posit causality in the empirical world independent of human perception. He was thus able to create a true philosophy of science out of the Cartesian tradition. Yet he would never establish a leading tradition in philosophy, being occluded by Nietzsche and then by Martin Heidegger's interpretation of both Nietzsche and Schopenhauer, which set philosophy back on a track towards phenomenological abstraction. This is discussed more fully in the next chapter, but I mention it here because Schweitzer was one of the few to embrace Schopenhauer, and this is in large part why his cosmology now strikes many as peculiar when it is compared to the dominant paradigms in contemporary academia.

Schopenhauer's uniqueness is in how he redressed two key problems plaguing philosophy. The first was accounting for causality. This is one of the central issues that separated philosophy from empirical science because we do not have a physical sense that detects causality. It is instead a conclusion of the mind from the sequence of events and learned experience that ascribes a causal association for phenomena – for example, the porcelain cup that falls from the table and shatters on the floor is broken *because* of the impact. Kant had argued that such conclusions were not possible based merely on perception but became implicated by the mind, which ascribes causality to account for what is perceived.

The second key problem was the idea of a material substance as a substrate for the intelligible properties in the objects of perception. Kant termed this the "thing in itself" (*Ding an sich*; alternately, *noumenon* or the noumenal). While empiricists as far back as Linnaeus took the objects available to perception as the thing in itself in its entirety, Kant declared that the thing in itself was unknowable. Because he was confined by the Cartesian demands of uncompromising scepticism, Kant defended the claim that the mind was only able to discern the empirical world indirectly through the physical senses. While the objects of perception have many intelligible properties, such as weight, volume, texture, hardness, friability, and so on, the idea of a thing in itself to account for all these knowable characteristics of empirical objects could only be a supposition of the intellect. The thing in itself cannot be proven outside a set of intelligible properties, all of which support the original Cartesian claim about phenomena. What empiricists called substantive "mass" the philosophers in the wake of the Kantian tradition ridiculed as merely a myth of the mind.[15] Science and philosophy were at an impasse.

Schopenhauer, however, recognized the need for a theory of knowledge that accounted for the natural world apart from human perception and subjectivity. Schopenhauer did this by examining changes in the objects of perception that occur against the backdrop of the mind's faculties of Kantian space and time (i.e., the a priori). But to understand Schopenhauer, we must first discuss the French naturalist Comte Georges-Louis Leclerc de Buffon (1707–1788), upon whom he relied.

Causality, according to both Count Buffon and Kant, is an ascription of the mind regarding the objects of perception. Yet Buffon was able to demonstrate that a process of discernment exists that mitigates the human factor so that causes in the phenomenal world could be identified. Buffon (1969, 108) realized that, "because our senses, being themselves the effects of causes that we cannot know, can give us ideas of effects only, and never of causes," we are limited to asserting a physical truth as merely the probability of an observed outcome reoccurring from experience. The field of mathematics, on the other hand, proceeds from abstraction and extrapolated identity, and so "what we called mathematical truths … have no reality" apart from these relational definitions within mathematics itself (106). Yet, "these truths would always have been matters of pure speculation, mere curiosity and utter uselessness, if we had not found the means of associating them with physical truths [through the field of physics]" (107). This becomes the key link between the thing itself within the sense-world and the seemingly irreducible rationalism of the mind. Causality, a rational deduction, can also be identified as an empirical reality that is independent of experiencing subjects; physics determines mathematically the causal relations in the sense-world because "what is involved here is combining and calculating the probabilities in order to judge whether an [observed] effect depends on one cause rather than another" (108). Thus, the probability of whether one cause or another (e.g., temperature or pressure) is responsible for an observed change can be calculated to a mathematical certainty, allowing causality to be determined apart from subjective perception.

Physics, chemistry, and other natural sciences have been able to determine the properties of the natural forces in those fields of study. But the causality for living beings had not been examined the same way. This is what Schopenhauer does. He describes the natural force operating here as the Will (*Wille*). The Will is not self-causal agency in intention or volition but a generic name for the cause of change from one physical or mental state to another. The Will is supra-personal and indeed a nonhuman force operating within the mind, and it was also responsible for the physical and chemical changes in the outer world detected by science (*WWR* §17, §18). For Schopenhauer the Will was both causality and the thing itself subsisting phenomena. This, then, is Schopenhauer's solution to the Kantian dilemma. Delving one step further towards the true inner nature of phenomena (i.e., the noumenon), Schopenhauer declared that phenomenal reality is *The World as Will and Representation*.

The second part of his famous book title, "Representation," is a reference to what are known as Plato's Universals. These are metaphysical ideas for the species of the natural world.[16] Schopenhauer examines phenomena in historical time and asks himself why it is that the same phenomenal forms keep reoccurring. He recounts an illustrative example of noticing a cat playing in his yard. It occurs to him that myriad individual cats have existed throughout history and that all these cats were essentially the same. "I know quite well that anyone would regard me as mad if I seriously assured him that the cat, playing just now in the yard, is still the same one that did the same jumps and tricks there three hundred years ago; but I also know that it is much more absurd to believe that the cat of today is through and through and fundamentally a different one from that cat of three hundred years ago."[17] Individual cats have arisen and passed away through causality, and yet, "in all these forms we recognize only the different aspects of the principle of sufficient reason [of existence] that is the ultimate principle of all finiteness, of all individuation, and the universal form of representation as it comes to the knowledge of the individual as such" (*WWR* §30, 169). He concludes that a metaphysical "Idea" of a cat must control the appearance of each new manifestation of a kitten born into the world. This conception of Platonic Universals for every species in nature (a very primitive forerunner to the modern idea of DNA) allowed

Schopenhauer to go further than Kant in describing empirical reality. The natural world could then be presented as a storehouse of different Platonic Ideas trapped in physical substance that exist independently from perception and that change in appearance as objects move from potentiality to actuality in time through the cosmological Will.

The activity of the evolutionary Will was described by Schopenhauer as mindless and meaningless striving, yet not entirely random or aimless. The Will, in joining with a Platonic Idea, creates a discrete body under *principium individuationis* (the law of specification), forming a nexus (*Weltknoten*) of space and time brought together as an individual will-to-live. And just as the evolutionary Will strives for objectification of Platonic Ideas in phenomenal reality, it is the character of the individual wills-to-live to also struggle against one another in order to express their embodied Ideas in the world of nature. By drawing on this cosmological claim of the Will as the Kantian thing in itself, and by positing Platonic Ideas as the intelligible substrate of empirical reality, Schopenhauer is able to do what Kant could not. He is able to use philosophical argumentation to establish the independent reality of the external world.

Schweitzer and Schopenhauer

It was through Schopenhauer that Schweitzer found a starting place for reconciling philosophy with empirical science. The will-to-live is a philosophical postulate that is in agreement with the empiricists' claim that the empirical world actually does exist – which is to say that it is not some kind of "social construction" or waking phantasy. Schweitzer needed Schopenhauer to rid philosophy of these Cartesian biases. Only through Schopenhauer could non-human life and the abiotic features of the natural world be given independent existence and independent causality. Admittedly, to the sensibilities of most people today, this is the most obvious of all possible claims; but for philosophers, both now and then, it was quite radical and remains controversial. Some contemporary philosophers even argue that empirical science is illegitimate and that the natural world has no reality outside socially constructed, human rational consciousness.[18]

That said, Schweitzer had no sympathy for the metaphysical idealism found in Schopenhauer's use of Platonic Ideas. As a medical doctor, Schweitzer was only interested in the will-to-live concept to explain how cosmological processes bring about the existence of the observable phenomena in empirical reality. This was the linkage he was after. Through Schopenhauer he was able to bring this one elemental truth from philosophy into agreement with modern biology by relating it to the scientific "cell-theory of matter" to account for biological processes (*POC* 196).[19] The impasse was now broken, and the way was open for bringing the Cartesian world of rational consciousness into dialogue with empirical science. Put in its simplest terms, the will-to-live for Schweitzer was not metaphysics but physics. As for the question of exactly how Schweitzer was able to sanitize Schopenhauer from his greater metaphysical claims and make it an entirely "this worldly" philosophy compatible with natural science, this will have to wait and be discussed in the next chapter when I turn to Nietzsche.

Schopenhauer and the Thing in Itself

With this overview in mind, we can now turn to a more in-depth analysis of Schopenhauer. The preceding discussion reveals the centrality of the cosmological Will in the works of Schopenhauer. This, in turn, points to a more interesting question because the Will for Schopenhauer was also the Kantian thing in itself. The question before Kant was whether a knowing subject could gain knowledge of the thing in itself that lay behind the objects of perception. Kant concluded that the thing in itself was unknowable.[20] But Schopenhauer could not accept a philosophy of the mind as his starting point for describing existence. Particularly offensive to him was Hegel's philosophy of *Geist* (Mind as the universal Spirit of the world) since the same chemical and physical forces operating in the physical matter of the natural world also controlled the functioning of the "grey matter" of the brain – and surely, he thought, this must defeat any claims that a first principle could be based within the intellect (*PP-OVS*, §1B, 213). And because he considered that "the intellect [was] physical not metaphysical" (*PP-OATI*, §5, 59), his problematic became whether the intellect (a projection of the organic brain, which, in turn, was a projection of the thing in itself) could discern its true nature. To go further than Kant regarding the nature of the thing in itself (*noumenon*), even though it lay behind the serial projections of body and mind, Schopenhauer turned to the analysis of the Will as it was revealed in the embodied will-to-live.

At this point in the discussion it must be remarked that Kant would not go as far as Schopenhauer. He was more cautious regarding claims to truth. In his epistemology, even the existence of a reality external to self-consciousness could only be granted a provisional and indeterminate existence: "That there is something real outside us which not only corresponds but must correspond to our outer perceptions can likewise be proved to be, not a condition of things in themselves, but for the sake of experience. This means that there is something empirical, that is, some appearance in space without us, that admits of a satisfactory proof" (Kant 1950, 84, §49). Experiencing subjects require *something* to experience that exists apart from themselves, yet the empirical is always mediated through the spatial and temporal faculties of the mind. And, while the object of inner sense (self-consciousness) demonstrates the actuality of the "soul" (the experiencing self), which exists in time, the soul cannot be said to exist apart from the mind's faculty of representation. Moreover, the form of outer phenomena is determined by the nature of our senses and cognitive faculties, and so Kant, unlike Schopenhauer, cannot give "Ideas" existence apart from perception. This is where he stands at starkest distinction to the great Prussian. Kant steered clear of the excesses of speculative metaphysics, but Schopenhauer stood at the edge of the noumenal nothingness and dreamt of Nirvana.

Schopenhauer, Evolution, and Buddhism

Schopenhauer adapted Jean-Baptiste Lamarck's (1744–1829) theory of evolution in order to ground cosmology in natural history.[21] For Schopenhauer, the Will is Lamarck's vital force (*élan vital*), which "quickens" (in the Aristotelian sense) each organism: it is the true procreative source for each new life (WN 265). This Lamarckian- and Aristotelian-inspired theory of evolution would, however, become entwined with Buddhist metaphysics. This is where Schopenhauer's philosophy takes a sharp turn and becomes decidedly unscientific.

Schopenhauer presents the cosmological Will as an evolutionary force that progressively brought forth the *objectification* of reality, beginning with the "most universal forces of nature," such as gravity and magnetism (WWR §20, 107–8; §24, 123; §27, 142, and 149–51). Phenomenal reality then emerged through a chain of its own causes to become matter, whereupon the species of nature, as defined by their Platonic Ideas, then appeared (WWR-2 §26, 130–2). Humankind, not surprisingly, is claimed to be the pinnacle of evolution.[22] Yet there is still an evolutionary inter-dependence here: the higher forms of life *had to develop* from the earlier, more primitive life-forms (WWR-2 §28, 153), for "unless the serpent eats a serpent, he does not become a dragon" (WWR-2 §27, 145 [Schopenhauer citing Francis Bacon]). The definitive moment in evolution was the emergence of non-human animal consciousness,[23] whereupon "the *world as representation* now stands out at one stroke with all its forms, object and subject, time, space, plurality, and causality" (*WWR-2* §27, 150 [emphasis in original]). Put simply, Schopenhauer argues that the act of subjective perception in consciousness actually makes phenomenal reality objectively real. His position here, not coincidentally, is very similar to that found in the doctrine known as the Twelve-Fold Chain of Dependent Arising (*pratītyasamutpāda*) in Buddhist metaphysics, with the exception that Schopenhauer's doctrine of reincarnation is rolled out through geological time to become a progressive evolutionary history of the world.

Not surprisingly, then, matter in Schopenhauer's cosmology has ephemeral existence. Atwell (1995, 68, 152) concludes that matter is the "third thing" between cause and effect and that it is a phenomenal substance that the differentiated wills-to-live struggle over to maintain their temporal forms (cf. *WWR-2* §27, 147). For Atwell, Schopenhauer's matter only exists as a corollary in the becoming and passing away of phenomenal bodies. Nevertheless, Schopenhauer strictly maintains that there are only two ultimate principles of existence: the causal Will and the Platonic Ideas that undergird phenomenal representations. For this reason, empirical substance is said to exist as a set of intelligible properties, and what appears to be physical matter is only an impermanent *secondary* reality emerging from the objectification of the outer world through perception. Sensations then arise to be received by the intellect through causality from the other corporeal wills-to-live, which are themselves only objective forms of their own inner subjectivity. Matter is thus only a by-product of causality through the other wills-to-live. This being the case, Schopenhauer argues that "matter is through and through causality" (*WWR-2* §26, 135). Nevertheless, despite his elegance, as a medical doctor, Schweitzer simply could not accept a theory of the universe that was based on such highly speculative Buddhist-inspired metaphysics.

Salvation and Compassion

Schopenhauer can find meaning in an ultimately meaningless world of suffering through a single tenuous thread: compassion. This is the keystone that unites his ethics and his doctrine of salvation (soteriology). Schopenhauer claims that compassion is the sole non-egoist motive for it takes the other as its foremost concern. Accordingly, he says, it is the only valid first principle for ethics (*OBM* §19.1, 168–9). All other ethical principles are either subject to antinomies of logic or can be undermined by passions of the personal will. As Schopenhauer writes: "Boundless compassion for all living beings is the firmest and surest guarantee of pure moral conduct, and needs no casuistry. Whoever is inspired with it will assuredly injure no one, will wrong no one, will encroach no one's rights; on the contrary, he will be lenient and patient with everyone, will forgive everyone, and help everyone as much as he can, and all his actions will bear the stamp of justice, philanthropy, and loving-kindness" (OBM §19.4, 172).

Compassion emerges from a transformation of the egotistical self through contemplation on the universal will-to-live, which yields a sublime personal character and an ethical worldview. And it is through compassionate acts, "whereupon the distinction between I and Not-I disappears," that a pathway to divine salvation opens up (PP-OE §2, 134). Compassion breaks down the sense of separation that makes the personal self *seem* like it is entirely different from the other. Compassion arises by way of a pre-rational sublimity through the perception of suffering. The sublime is a different way of knowing, something that Schopenhauer calls "intuitive pure knowing." This is a different kind of knowledge and he sees it as superior to the analytical intellect because such "*intuitive knowledge* can guide our actions and conduct directly ... this explains why the real life of the scholar, whose merit consists in an abundance of abstract knowledge, is so inferior to the man of the world whose merit consists in a more perfect intuitive knowledge" (MR 296 [emphasis in original]). An "intuitive pure knowing" would become a key inspiration for Schweitzer's understanding of negative (apophatic) theology (see chapter 4).

Notably, Schopenhauer uses the Christian claim of there being "no greater love" than self-sacrifice for the sake of another (John 15:13) as an example of his ethics: "what could possibly express more clearly the consciousness that this [self-]destruction is only the destruction of a phenomenon and is therefore itself phenomenon, while the essential being of him who faces destruction remains unaffected: it continues to exist in the other" (PP-OE §6, 141). In other words, the self and the other share a single undivided unity through the universal Will (i.e., the Kantian thing in itself). The two lives are separated only by the secondary and impermanent conditions created by perception, which objectifies phenomenal reality. But compassion dissolves the *principium individuationis* (the law of specification) that ties together the *Weltknoten* (the will-to-live described as, literally, a "world knot"). The experience of compassion then imparts a sense of transcendent sublimity – the foretaste of Nirvana itself.

Acts of self-sacrificial altruism may allow the "person" to achieve Nirvana. But there are two other indirect consequences. The first is that such acts of conscience serve to generate greater awareness of the power of compassion in those who witness or hear of them. In other words, a sympathetic response of sublimity can be generated in others. This can facilitate an incrementally expanding ethical consciousness in humankind that improves all of society. Schopenhauer also believes that this would eventually bring non-human life into ethical consideration.[24] Schopenhauer, the passionate anti-vivisectionist, cannot surrender the phenomenal world to unfeeling others. All life is ethically considerable since every form of existence has the same basic essence as the self. This then is the second repercussion. Individual acts of compassion can, in time, help free others and even the whole phenomenal reality from *samsara* (endless reincarnation) through the power of "grace" (*WWR-4* §70, 407–9). "Grace" is Schopenhauer's term for a specific qualitative imputation of the unitary universal Will upon an individual will-to-live. Grace does not come by way of a deity. Presumably, it is the echo of the self-sacrificial compassion, asceticism, and aesthetic revelation imparted by moral agents who have already achieved Nirvana.

For Schopenhauer, ethics remain entwined with and rooted in the will-to-live: ethics are mediated through the body, not the Kantian rational soul. It is paradoxical that abhorrence of and mental anguish over bodily suffering becomes the basis for an "ethical mysticism" (to borrow Schweitzer's phrase) aimed at denying the reality of the self and the phenomenal world for the betterment of all. The paradox is resolved when suffering is presented as a necessary experience to unite the self with the other (*PP-OS* §1, 78). Compassion over suffering dissolves the sense of otherness and individuality that maintains *samsara*, and "since all suffering is a mortification and a call to a resignation, it has potentially a sanctifying force … [but] only when suffering assumes the form of pure [intuitive] knowledge, and then this knowledge, as a *quieter of the will*, produces true resignation" (*WWR-4* §68, 395–7 [emphasis added]). This final move towards world- and life-resignation was particularly distasteful to Schweitzer, and he would turn to Nietzsche to find a theory of world- and life-affirmation to balance Schopenhauer's otherwise immensely beautiful ethic.

Discussion

Schweitzer drew upon Schopenhauer's will-to-live theory as his basis to begin to relate empirical science with Continental philosophy and ethics. He assumed that this was a settled matter and that academics would accept Schopenhauer's revolutionary work on philosophical causality as a given truth. This was a strategic error on Schweitzer's part because the domain of philosophy moved on to newer theories that re-established the Cartesian nature of the phenomenal world as its true reality. This is not to say Schopenhauer's will-to-live theory to explain biological development is fundamentally flawed, especially in light of how Schweitzer modified it, only that contemporary academics have failed to appreciate his philosophy precisely because of these modern trends.

In addition to the will-to-live theory, many elements of Schweitzer's thought can be identified in the preceding analysis, including an ethic based on compassion, an attention to evolutionary theory, an interest in interpreting world religions in light of philosophy, and also the idea that altruism can inspire others to transform all of society. Schweitzer, like Schopenhauer, also emphasizes the place of the physical body in ethics (over the role of the Kantian intellect) by contending that it is only compassion for suffering that can guarantee a lasting foundation for a moral society.

But Schweitzer was no simple follower of Schopenhauer. Much of his philosophy was *far* too metaphysical for him, particularly its Buddhism inspired theory of perception. Reverence for Life would also not present a prescription for divine redemption (soteriology). Schweitzer's was to be entirely a "this worldly" ethic.[25] And so in order to rid Schopenhauer's cosmology of its greater metaphysical and religious associations, Schweitzer turns to Nietzsche's reformulation of Schopenhauer's theory of causality. But first, as promised at the start of this chapter, Schweitzer's enigmatic statement about different conceptions of life and the world must be revisited. This distinction is important for understanding Reverence for Life, and Schopenhauer's will-to-live theory is the key to deciphering it.

Monism and Dualism

Somewhat unexpectedly, Schweitzer created a dualism between the lifeview of rational consciousness and the scientific understanding of the world. "We must make up our minds to leave our conceptions of life and of the world *independent* of each other, and see that a straightforward understanding between the two is reached" (*POC* 276 [emphasis added]). I am now in a position to clarify what he means.

This straightforward understanding would become the very foundation for his new philosophy of civilization. To put it simply, Schweitzer needed at least one shared element between philosophy and science in order to break through the Cartesian wall that had separated these two ways of looking at reality. This opening would come through Schopenhauer's will-to-live theory, which exists in both domains (natural science and Continental philosophy). But this one point of reconciliation does not produce a harmonization. It is merely one small area of overlap between otherwise exclusive disciplines. That was enough. Schweitzer wanted to keep the domains independent because both outlooks on reality have particular claims to legitimacy and particular roles to play in his philosophy of civilization. He therefore only links them at the will-to-live.

Schweitzer felt that he needed to keep natural science and philosophy independent of one another. The problem was that for Schweitzer the worldview of natural science, by itself, was ethically nihilistic. World- and life-affirmation arose from the life-view of rational consciousness, which is the exclusive province of philosophy. Because of this, Schweitzer had to keep something of that Cartesian consciousness alive in his new philosophy of civilization. To this end, he describes the will-to-live as the place in a living being where biological instinct, rational consciousness, and a mysterious third category, "the capacity for divination," are fused together (E-RFL 228).[26] The way was now open to allow true life-affirmation to emerge out of the dualism between rational consciousness and the scientific worldview through that mysterious third category – a subject that will be discussed at length in chapter 4.

Now this is where Schweitzer's philosophy becomes very complicated indeed. In an interesting twist on his assertion of the necessary dualism between science and philosophy, he presents the life-view of Ethical Mysticism (i.e., the secondary metaphysic built on primary elemental truths) as a mystical *monism* of the universal will-to-live. Now the question must be asked: How can Schweitzer explain this transition to monism? He explains it in this key paragraph from *The Philosophy of Civilization* (KP II, xiv):

The vital element for our life-view is not our [scientific] knowledge
of the world, but on the contrary it is in the certainty of the
predisposition that is given in our will-to-live. The infinite immortal
spirit confronts us in Nature as a mysterious creative power. In our
will-to-live it is experienced as world- and life-affirmation and as an
ethical predisposition. Just as it is given in the certainty of our will-
to-live, so too our relationship to the world can be likewise found
if we seek to recognize this connection in rational thought: this is
worldview. The [Reverence for Life] worldview comes out of the life-
view [of Ethical Mysticism], not the life-view [*Lebensanschauung*]
out of the [scientific] worldview [*Weltanschauung*].

Schweitzer sometimes uses the term *Lebensanschauung* in contrast with *Weltanschauung*, as he does here. The former refers to an ontological understanding of life derived from a priori rationality, while the latter refers to an understanding of life based solely on a scientific view of the world, evolution, and life-processes. Other times, however, Schweitzer uses *Weltanschauung* in a more general sense that is inclusive of *Lebens-anschauung* – for example, such as when referring to the worldviews of Reverence for Life or Ethical Mysticism. Both senses are used in the preceding passage. In brief, Schweitzer asks his readers to accept the Reverence for Life worldview that envisions the natural world as a mysterious manifestation of something closely resembling Schopenhauer's cosmological Will: "the ultimate insight is the recognition that the world, in how it appears to us, is in every respect a mysterious appearance of the universal will-to-live" (*KP II*, xii). As for how he arrives at this monism, Schweitzer uses inductive reasoning to form a general principle within rational consciousness. This is called an *epagoge* in philosophical parlance. The *universal* will-to-live is adduced from the observable behaviour in every animal, every plant; each life struggles to maintain and maximize its vitality whether it is a weed growing from a concrete joint, the desperate struggles of a wounded animal, or human enterprise. Thus from each empirical example of individual "being" emerges the first principle of ontological "Being" through the *epagoge*. This is also how the scientific will-to-live concept is brought into the domain of rational philosophy. Schweitzer can then analytically parse this principle of Being to conclude that the phenomenal self is merely a particularized manifestation of the universal will-to-live within the empirical world, and just a singular aspect of a supra-personal Will operating in nature as an evolutionary Creative Force.

It is through this inductive process that the individual will-to-live concept is extended to become a monism of the universal will-to-live. The sum of all wills-to-live, thereby, forms a common basis for understanding the true nature of existence of every life: human and non-human alike. This is not romanticism. Schweitzer has only taken the particulars of sense perception, and by using inductive reasoning, posited a general principle of Being – an *epagoge* to universality. It is scientific type reasoning applied to rational concepts. Admittedly, a scientific approach through inductive reasoning to a universal concept is not the same as "science" in the modern understanding of the term. But it is also not the fanciful and imagined metaphysics that some have understood the universal will-to-live concept to be. It is something in between.

Consequently, this general principle of Absolute Being does not have the same ontological priority as do empirical objects for Schweitzer. It is merely an inferred reality beyond immediate perception. He therefore warns not to aim Ethical Mysticism at "an unreal creation of thought ... [since from] self-devotion to the [intellectually created] Absolute there comes only a dead spirituality" (*PO*, 304f). The *epagoge* cannot fully overcome the dualism between the scientific worldview and the rational consciousness of the Cartesian tradition, as was announced at the start of this section. The monistic life-view [*Lebensanschauung*] of Ethical Mysticism is merely a contemplative state of consciousness that intentionally does not allow itself to become subsumed by either the nihilistic worldview of science or lose itself in fanciful metaphysics born of rationalism. Rather, it exists in continuous dialogue between the two, always open to new spiritual revelation and scientific discovery.

These shifts between dualism and monism in the works of Schweitzer are admittedly confusing. This distinctive feature of Schweitzer's philosophy can only be introduced here. It will be revisited in the next two chapters as we continue with our investigation. The point being drawn out will then become more clear. But first, certain questions have to be investigated further. It was mentioned that aspects of Schopenhauer's philosophy were unacceptable to Schweitzer, including his metaphysical excess and philosophy of resignation. This is why Nietzsche would become especially important for Schweitzer.

Chapter 3

Nietzsche and Schweitzer

Nietzsche was the first philosopher to wrestle with Darwin's theory of evolution. In trying to understand the ramifications of evolution for the Western worldview, he became deeply concerned with what it meant for both ethics and the human place in the universe. Schweitzer would be drawn into these same problems and troubling questions through the writings of Nietzsche. Moreover, it was Nietzsche who provided him with the answers he needed in order to create his Reverence for Life ethic. This is reflected in a letter dated 19 February 1964 (*Letters* 336–7):

> Nietzsche compelled me to keep being concerned with the problem
> of ethics and the emergence of an ethical civilization. Thus, by the
> fall of 1915, I developed the notion of an ethics of reverence for life.
> It dawned on me that European philosophy deals purely with half
> an ethic. All it demands is kind behavior and mercy toward other
> people. A complete ethics, however, requires kindness and mercy
> toward all life, for any living creature can suffer. Kindness knows
> no limits. It is boundless. Only a profound and complete ethics is
> able to create an ethical civilization. Through studying Nietzsche
> I came to realize that an ethics focusing solely on [hu]mankind is
> incomplete and cannot really be justified. Schopenhauer was right
> when he said, "Preaching ethics is easy, justifying ethics is hard."

Only a complete ethics can be justified. There is no justifying the semi-ethics of European philosophy.

A central concern for Schweitzer was where any system of ethics could draw its ultimate authority. If ethics were merely the province of rational beings capable of language and social contracts, then ethical duties and responsibilities would be limited to people alone: this is what Schweitzer calls the "semi-ethics" of European philosophy. Alternately, if ethics were somehow embedded in the natural order of the world, then they should be brought forth out of human nature automatically just by natural instinct alone: philosophers would not have to appeal to enlightened self-interest to create ethical societies. Because of this, there was a great fear that ethics were only arbitrarily founded and socially convenient without any ultimate authority at all. Worse, the new Darwinian science seemed to complicate these questions immensely. Consider the following passage in Nietzsche's *Beyond Good and Evil*: "Do you wish to live in conformity with nature? O noble Stoics, what fraudulent words! Imagine a being that is like Nature is, prodigal without measure, indifferent without measure, without intentions nor consideration, *without pity or justice*, simultaneously fruitful and sterile and uncertain!" (Hadot 2006, 198 [emphasis added]).

The history of evolution certainly did seem to be "without pity or justice" for individual life forms that had to struggle for existence, devour one another, compete for opportunities to procreate, and yet eventually succumb to suffering and death. Not only individuals but also entire species have fought vainly against extinction before disappearing forever. This is precisely why Schweitzer felt he had to turn to a monistic and mystical interpretation of the universal will-to-live. Like Nietzsche, Schweitzer had come to believe evolutionary science was at "face value" ethically nihilistic. This is something he had learned from Nietzsche, and it is why he would come to a very similar conclusion (*KP II*, xii):

My solution to the problems is this – that we must resolve to forego in every way the optimistic-ethical interpretation of the natural world. If one takes the world as it is, then it is impossible to adjoin to it a sense in which the aims and goals of human enterprise, or humanity itself, can become meaningful. Neither world- and life-affirmation nor an ethic can be established out of what our [scientific] knowledge can reveal concerning the true state of the world. A purpose to evolution cannot be discovered for us, nor can a sense of importance be obtained for our actions.

This passage comes two pages before Schweitzer offers the mystical and monistic life-view as a way to overcome the harsh reality of the scientific worldview. But how can he have it both ways? Schweitzer claims that it is improper to imagine a purpose to evolution or to claim that humans can find their ethical ideals mirrored in nature. Then, two pages later, he upholds the centrality of the will-to-live as the foundation for a mystical worldview that sees reality as the result of an infinitely creative evolutionary Will. Is this a contradiction? No. The answer to how he can uphold both ways of looking at the world is something he learned from Nietzsche. This innovation, which will be discussed next, would become the means to bring together his new philosophy of civilization.

Nietzsche, in his struggles with evolution and its implications for human society, turns against the *strictly* scientific way of viewing the natural world. He instead interpreted the harsh realities of Nature the way artists interpret their subjects in order to create meaning in their works of art. He spells this out in the preface to *The Gay Science* (cited from Hadot 2006, 285):

No, this bad taste, this will to [purely scientific] truth, to "truth at all costs," this adolescent madness in the love of truth – we've had enough of it: for that, we are too experienced, too serious, too joyous, too weather-beaten, too profound. We no longer believe that the truth is still the truth, if its veils [of mystery] are taken away from it – we've lived too long to believe that … A hint to philosophers! We should have more respect for the modesty with which Nature hides behind enigmas and colorful uncertainties.

Schweitzer would likewise seek to balance out the strict scientific worldview (with its mechanical necessity and ethical nihilism) against the human need to find meaning for our lives. He would similarly bring this about through an "artistic" interpretation of reality which Schweitzer instead described as mysticism – specifically, Ethical Mysticism. Notwithstanding and despite the difference in terms, both sought to create a culturally defined truth that was informed by science but not limited to its reductionist and mechanistic logic.

Schweitzer believed that only a culturally defined truth could uphold a sense of purpose and meaning for life. Truth had to preserve the mystery of existence for mystical reflection: it had to be kept partially "veiled," to use Nietzsche's expression. But how could he claim such a culturally defined truth as being in any way legitimate? This would come about through what is called in philosophical parlance the "synthetic a priori" which means (in this context) combining self-evident rational concepts into a new value system.

But to explain exactly how this is accomplished, Nietzsche's philosophy must be laid-out in his own terms. Even then, it must be noted that Schweitzer did not accept all of Nietzsche's views uncritically. This is particularly the case with Nietzsche's near complete rejection of scientific facts in his later works. In addition, and of particular relevance to this chapter, Schweitzer would differ with Nietzsche on how to interpret Darwin's views about the evolution of humankind's social instincts. He instead secured Schopenhauer's compassion in Darwinian science as another critical component in his foundation for the philosophy of civilization. Yet Schweitzer needed to universalize his ethic of compassion by showing how it is grounded in both natural science and in Cartesian consciousness. This would come about in his New Rationalism project.

The following discussion establishes these relatively simple and straightforward conclusions, but it will necessarily have to proceed through a very technical engagement of philosophical questions using the vocabulary Nietzsche himself employed. Only in this way can Schweitzer's work be revealed to be a philosophy in the same sense as are the works of Kant, Schopenhauer, and Nietzsche. Schweitzer's works have never been appreciated as philosophy in an academic sense – that is to say, as a comprehensive system of thought complete with a theory of knowledge and an ethical first principle. Obviously, this has hampered the appreciation of his ethic in academia. To redress this problem, Schweitzer will be shown employing certain distinctive features of Nietzsche's work even though he himself usually expressed his philosophy in ordinary language aimed at a non-academic audience.

As readers not familiar with his works will soon discover, some of Nietzsche's views come across as rather odd and, at times, even quite outlandish. But none of this detracts from the fact that Nietzsche is arguably the most influential philosopher of the modern era. Such well known figures as Martin Heidegger (1889–1976) and Michel Foucault (1926–1984) base much of their own systems directly on the same texts that I outline in this chapter. Even the field of environmental ethics has been deeply influenced by Nietzsche. It is now an accepted truth that empirical science is itself a culturally conditioned practice that is not as neutral or as objective as it presents itself to be.[27] This claim originated with Nietzsche. These are also the same texts that would influence Schweitzer in his decision to likewise reject the unspoken nihilism of empirical science. And just as Nietzsche urged, Schweitzer's Ethical Mysticism presents an interpretation of natural science that upholds a life-affirming and mystical worldview.

Nietzsche and His Works

Friedrich Nietzsche died at only fifty-five years of age. Even more tragic, for the last eleven years of his life he had been reduced to a near vegetative state after having had a complete mental breakdown. Though a prolific writer, his works cannot be considered complete – at least if measured against what he could have written had he lived as long and productively as did Kant and Schopenhauer. What is worse, a particularly important work, *The Will to Power*, was never completed. What remains of it from his manuscripts (*Nachlaß*) consists entirely of fragments and preliminary drafts. Another complication is the inherent difficulty of discerning the intent of Nietzsche's thought because of his particular stylistic approach and the divergent opinions in subsequent scholarship concerning the same. His essays often take the form of biting commentary on contemporary figures, and he even creates fictional narratives and poetry in order to present his philosophy. His writing style is flamboyant, often exceedingly obscure, and at times deliberately obtuse. Unlike Kant, Nietzsche certainly did not lay out his ideas in a straightforward and systematic manner. For all of these reasons, Nietzsche is possibly the most difficult modern philosopher to understand.

But one thing *is* clear. Nietzsche saw himself as undertaking something entirely new in philosophy. His works are designed to reorient the reader's expectations and to prepare the ground for the emergence of a different understanding of humanity, culture, and the world. He began this project through an uncompromising deconstruction of every truth claim regardless of whether it was founded in science, philosophy, or religion. For this reason, Nietzsche has been thought of as a "prophet of the postmodern" – which is to say, as the first philosopher to reject not only the idealized foundations of these domains but also all essentialist dogma pertaining to a singular unified human nature (i.e., the Kantian soul, which presupposes the necessary existence of God) as a basis for ontology (Gemes 2001, 337–8).[28] But it cannot be uncritically assumed that it was Nietzsche's intent to portray the problem of "being" as it has been developed by subsequent postmodern philosophers. To wit, Gemes notes that, while the postmodernists celebrate the "death of the subject" and decentred subjective disunity, Nietzsche actually sets unity as a goal for individuals and culture (339; see, for example, *um ii*, §4). It is only the Cartesian-Kantian soul (whose uniform substance is a priori time) against which Nietzsche specifically argues.

Of the early interpreters of Nietzsche, William Mackintire Salter (1853–1931) is perhaps the most perceptive and prescient. His works were written prior to Heidegger's distinctive interpretations, which would change the academic perception of Nietzsche. Salter understood Nietzsche as an a posteriori epistemologist who considered the natural body to be constituted as groups of sensations united under a centre of force (Salter 1915, 442, 453). Consciousness emerges as a secondary manifestation from this Will to Power nexus. The mind then comes to perceive the sense world not as its true Heraclitean reality but, rather, as rational constructions akin to its own nature, for which permanence and solidity is ascribed. Therefore, "a 'thing' is only a certain sum of activities bound together by a concept or image [within the mind itself]" (444). As such, there is no true substance behind the sensory world: there is only the Will to Power of cosmological forces grouped into bodies that are ever-changing in their internal constitution as they vie for dominance. "Hence, in general, the world we commonly picture is a false one, not real: we fancy that it exists quite independently to us, that we simply find it – and we are mistaken. We may correct our images in this way or that, may make one interpretation of the world succeed another, but we do not get beyond images and interpretations" (444).

However, today the dominant tradition is decidedly Heideggerian. Hannah Arendt (1988, 12), for example, follows Heidegger's interpretation and claims that all external phenomena described in Nietzsche's works are to be taken as "symbols" for the inner experience of beingness, such that "the rift between the thinking or willing ego and the world of appearances collapses." Like Salter, she too does not concede the apparent reality as it is revealed to the sense as objectively real, but her epistemological reasoning differs entirely from Salter's. The *a priori* existential is the sole basis for ontology here. The differences between Salter and the Heideggerians are, in some senses, very subtle; nevertheless, they are still diametrically opposed. How to interpret Nietzsche is therefore quite a thorny question, and one over which many academics have chosen sides. But what is of interest here is how Schweitzer understood Nietzsche. The larger questions regarding epistemology are revisited in chapter 5.

Evolutionary Reality

By turning to the new evolutionary science of Charles Darwin, Nietzsche sought to undermine the Cartesian belief that the mind has special and privileged access to ultimate truth. Through Darwin's writings, Nietzsche came to believe that the human mind was particularly ill-suited to perceiving truth for the reason that "consciousness is the last part of the organic [evolution] and consequently also the most unfinished and weakest part of it" (GS §11, 158). The human species appeared very late in evolutionary history. Because of this, rather than presenting the human mind as the crowning achievement of evolution, Nietzsche argues that the intellect is merely an accidental and ancillary offshoot of primate evolution and that this reveals a deep defect in our species.

Nietzsche says that animal consciousness evolved as a response to the "instinct of fear," which allows all animals, in varying degrees, to live within a rational world of Cartesian consciousness (GS §355, 301).[29] Only in this way can they make spatial inferences to track prey, to remember and anticipate danger from a sense of place, and to identify the identical from similar sensory objects. Yet, according to Nietzsche, as "the most endangered animal" (GS §354, 298) primordial humans had to evolve further than simple animal consciousness. Through language, we invented a conceptual world for our consciousness (HH §11, 56). Speech, he writes, "*developed only under the pressure of the need for communication ...* consciousness is really only a net communication between human beings" (GS §354, 298). And so, "conscious thinking *takes the form of words, which is to say signs of communication ...* [this is] the way reason enters consciousness" (GS §354, 299 [emphasis in original]).

The upshot of Nietzsche's argument is that, because the reasoning powers of the human mind evolved in this way and are nothing more than an offshoot of that "fear-based" conceptual world created through language (HH §19, 57), we cannot claim that Cartesian logic and pure reason have access to a higher-world reality (TI, "'Reason' in Philosophy" §5, 482–3). Yet human consciousness still exists, in part, within that conceptual world of language. For Nietzsche, this means that the true essence of reality is hidden from perception by cognitive veils of language and rationality that distort our worldview.[30]

Nietzsche contends that the body's biological instincts intervene to regulate the intellect in order to keep it from excess: the mind is necessarily correlated to the body through instincts and physiological drives such that what it perceives as truth is actually "*the kind of error* without which a particular kind of living creature could not live" (*WLN* 34 [253], 16 [emphasis in original]). If this were not the case, Nietzsche claims, the human species would have "perished through its perverse judgments and waking phantasies, [with] its superficiality and credulity, in short its consciousness" (*GS* §11, 158). What he is saying is that through natural selection the biological Will to Power (his term for Schopenhauer's will-to-live) shaped the human intellect to function within the reality of the natural world and to see certain truths that were not necessarily true, but only evolutionarily useful in protecting the frightened human "herd" animal.

What is worse, Nietzsche argues that when reason and abstract concepts are turned to the analysis of physical reality, "all that we [can] actually know about these laws of nature is what we ourselves bring to them – time and space, and therefore relationships of succession and number" (*PN-TAL* §1). He thus concludes that we live in a "trimmed and simplified world on which our *practical* instincts have worked" (*WLN* 14[93] 250 [emphasis in original]). The human mind has no access at all to actual *Truth* – that is, truth with a capital "T." The only reality is the biological Will to Power as an evolutionary force bringing forth and maintaining life under naturalistic necessity.

For this reason Nietzsche believes that "the total nature of the world is ... to all eternity chaos, not in the sense that necessity is lacking but in that order, structure, form, beauty, wisdom, and whatever other human aesthetic notions we may have are lacking" (*GS* §109, 201). Put simply, he believes that the idea of shape and form for the objects of our world (say, for example, an apple being "apple-shaped") is a necessary illusion of our perception rather than a true objective reality. While hard to fathom, he seems to believe that the human mind superimposes perceptual expectations on sensory experience and that this allows us to see certain realities (i.e., those that are roughly correlated to our evolutionary advantage) but not others. To use the same example, he appears to be claiming that people evolved to notice edible fruit but not the complex biochemical gas exchanges that occur between the trees, soil, and biota (as some insects do) since that sensory information did not serve the hominids.

In his opinion, life was merely complex groupings of natural forces as cohesive organizations of a Will to Power nexus surviving in a complex world of other similarly constituted power relations. In this respect, Nietzsche is even more nihilistic and pessimistic than Schopenhauer with regard to the arbitrariness of existence. Even the truth claims of science would not be spared his ruthless, unforgiving critiques.

Nietzsche's Later Writings

According to Nietzsche, "science also rests on faith; there is simply no science 'without presuppositions'" (GS §344, 281). For him, objective scientific facts divorced from human subjectivity are not possible. Each hypothesis set forth by a researcher was for him merely a personal conviction that must gain acceptance from the scientific community to become an objective theory (280). He believes that the initial conviction of the researcher relies upon a biasing of data resulting from the aforementioned evolutionary dynamics within perception. Because of this, "physics too is only an interpretation and arrangement of the world (according to ourselves! if I may say so) and *not* an explanation of the world" (BGE §14, 15 [emphasis in original]). Babich (2004, 147) argues that Nietzsche pushes these points to "hyperbolic extreme" because he fears science has become a new kind of authoritarianism over the domain of truth (147). In this way it was becoming "the true legacy of Plato's academy" with the elevation of math as the sine qua non for knowledge – a new type of idealism created in abstract concepts (141; cf. TI "How the 'True World' Finally Became a Fable," 485).

For Nietzsche, science is merely an expression of a "will to truth" against the uncertainties of life. He was concerned that science was rising to a type of mythology with its own idealized realities disguised as empirical facts (GS §344, 283). Thus, he argues that science itself is "a *metaphysical faith*" (283 [emphasis in original]). He also fears that science is aiming for an objectivity that would transcend all subjectivity – in effect, it is attempting to dehumanize knowledge. For these reasons, Nietzsche believes that science represents a "will to death" because it denies the reality of human subjective experience and affirms a world order that differs from the one actually experienced in the fullness of life (282).

Real truth, however, can never be inhuman because "delusion and error are conditions of human knowledge and sensation" (GS §107, 163). Evolution created the human intellect to see the world through cognitive veils that distort our perception of reality; the falsification of the empirical world through culturally defined values and beliefs is therefore not improper because too much "*honesty* would lead to nausea and suicide" (163 [emphasis in original]). Nietzsche says that the lived experience of a person's life is inherently aesthetic due to the cognitive rendering of sensation and the falsification of knowledge to suit the circumstances of our lives. Taking as his example the ancient Hellenic world, which was filled with a rich and diverse pantheon of religious myths and speculative cosmology, he writes: "Those Greeks were superficial – *out of profundity!* ... Isn't it precisely in this sense that we are [also] Greeks? Worshipers of forms, sounds, and words? And precisely in this sense – artists?" (Hadot 2006, 285; *GS*, Preface §4 [emphasis in original]). Science must never become the dead ideal of the empiricists; rather, it must stay true to what it actually is – a life-affirming "gay science" that recognizes itself as a human craft (*techne*) and an artful practice (*die Kunst der Auslegung*). His solution is simple. We must always interpret science through the lens of the artist because only in this way can we find real meaning in our lives.

Nevertheless, it is now clear that with the publication of *Beyond Good and Evil* (1886), and the second edition of *The Gay Science* (1887), Nietzsche's position on the body has shifted noticeably from his earlier works. He now warns that we "should not erroneously *objectify* 'cause' and 'effect' like the natural scientists do (and whoever else thinks naturalistically these days –) in accordance with the dominant mechanistic stupidity which would have the cause push and shove until it 'effects' something; we should use 'cause' and 'effect' only as pure *concepts*, which is to say as conventional fictions for the purpose of description and communication, *not* explanation" (*BGE* §21, 21 [emphasis in original]). The truth is that "*we* are the ones who have invented causation, succession, for-each-other, relativity, compulsion, numbers, law, freedom, grounds and purpose; and if we project and inscribe this symbol world onto things as an 'in itself,' then this is the way we have always done things, namely *mythologically*" (21 [emphasis in original]).

With these words, Nietzsche sets himself apart from earlier claims on the biological primacy of the body and positions himself in direct opposition to Buffon's grounding of the sciences, whether he was aware of him or not. This creates a problem for Nietzsche that is never fully resolved – that is, how does he account for the world of appearance epistemologically? He proclaims the non-self world to be Will to Power in its entirety, and the Will to Power has causality as its very nature. Yet his comments in *Beyond Good and Evil* specifically locate the causality of phenomena residing within the self, a very Neo-Kantian position. In earlier works, such as *Thus Spoke Zarathustra* (1883–85) and *Truth and Lie in an Extra-Moral Sense* (1873), Nietzsche presents the mind itself as an emergent phenomenon of physiological forces and as shaped by evolution. His overall argumentation thus becomes circular without a clear grounding for the exact nature of the Will to Power as to whether it is first and ultimately cosmological or whether it is wholly psychological and Kantian (cf. *GS* §54, §57, §58, and §112). The latter is the conclusion of Martin

Heidegger who interprets Nietzsche from the last period of his works and dismisses the physiological passages as merely metaphor for inner experience.[31] Heidegger and some of those who followed in his tradition, including the strict social construction theorists, dismiss the truth claims of natural science based on Nietzsche's questionable and sometimes entirely indefensible conclusions about science, which, it must be recalled, were written at a time when he was becoming increasingly compromised by mental illness.[32]

Rationality and Life-Affirmation

An important question is how can Nietzsche say that his view of life is better or truer than those promoted by religion. When discussing all such cultural truths (the synthetic a priori), including his own, Nietzsche concludes that they are "false judgments" (*BGE* §4, 63). Yet, at the same time, he maintains that these judgments "are the most indispensable for us ... [because] without granting as true the fictions of logic, without measuring reality against the purely invented world of the unconditional and self-identical, without a constant falsification of the world by means of numbers, [hu]mankind could not live" (63). This is the key to Nietzsche's philosophy of perspective (i.e., "perspectivism"). While such truths are always false, their falsity is not necessarily a basis for dismissing them. This is because they may still be culturally advantageous, life-affirming, and even "species-cultivating" (63). Culture itself is an accumulation of such judgments (*HH* §107, 79):

> Everything is necessity – thus says the new knowledge; and this
> knowledge itself is necessity. Everything is innocence: and knowl-
> edge is the path to insight into this innocence. If pleasure, egoism,
> vanity are *necessary* for the production of moral phenomena and
> their greatest flower, the sense for truth and justice in knowledge;
> if error and aberration of the imagination were the only means by
> which [hu]mankind was able gradually to raise itself to this degree
> of self-enlightenment and self-redemption – who could venture to
> denigrate those means?

Nietzsche's life and works aimed to achieve this very project. He attempted to save culture from ethical nihilism through synthesizing concepts into a new cultural narrative that was confirmed by, but not limited to, natural science. He interpreted science as a cultural critic and artist, and in this way he sought to direct the path of accumulated cultural resentment (*ressentiment*) into an "overcoming" in order to create a future defined by Supermen (*Übermenschen*, alternate translation: "transcendent humanity"). These would be the ones with the power to write a new history for humankind unfettered by the limitations of the culture into which they had been born. The *Übermenschen* would have the power to start a new direction for civilization.

Nietzsche on Schopenhauer

Life is arbitrary and meaningless. Nietzsche learned this from Schopenhauer. But, in rejecting a Buddhist escape to Nirvana's bliss, he can only present to the reader one certain and nihilistic reality. There is only the Will to Power, consisting of myriad natural forces. The human intellect is an expression of this evolutionary biology, but it cannot be said to be its pinnacle. Rather, Nietzsche depicts humans as the most pathetic and misbegotten species to have ever accidentally emerged in nature, and he contends that our minds are the most flawed of any creature. For Nietzsche, the human intellect only exists to perceive error and to create imagined realities so that our species can survive as a marginally viable and frightened herd animal.

We, however, call these imagined realities and cultural truths our sense of humanity. And what we choose to value in art and culture can actually *become* truth – certainly not as necessary and unchanging scientific facts but as culturally defined truths. We make this so through a collective cultural willing for it to be so. Our unique and misbegotten brains have the power to create these conditional truths: this is where life-affirmation rises like a glorious phoenix from the ashes of Nietzsche's scorched-earth approach to philosophy. He sought to promote a "self-overcoming" of the evolutionary Will to Power in order to create a type of consciousness entirely free to choose its destiny and the *power* to make truth claims for a better society. These are the *Übermenschen*. And while Schweitzer does not join Nietzsche in rejecting empirical science, he does embrace his central message about the possibility of creating new cultural truths out of naturalistic possibility.

Schweitzer on Nietzsche

Schweitzer reads Nietzsche as, at first, recognizing "the ideal [of] a scientifically deepened Positivism" in finding life-affirmation based on scientific findings (POC 243). But Nietzsche eventually turned against his own views in his later works. Schweitzer writes about this in a particularly noteworthy passage: "But Nietzsche cannot get rid of the antagonism between the spiritual [*Geistigen*, alternatively: intellectual] and the natural. Just in proportion as he emphasizes the natural does the spiritual [*Geistige*] shrink back. Gradually, under the visible influence of the mental disease which is threatening him, his ideal man becomes the 'superman,' who asserts himself triumphantly against all fate, and seeks his own ends without consideration for the rest of [hu]mankind" (246).

Schweitzer believes that Nietzsche rejects the natural world in his final works in favour of a radical and individualistic life-affirmation for people alone – and, at that, only the *Übermenschen*. This change occurs not only because of the unresolved tension between the natural world and rational consciousness in Nietzsche's early writings but also because of his worsening emotional and mental problems. This, for Schweitzer, was a tragic twist of fate. Nietzsche's failing mental health derailed the potential breakthroughs he could have made for philosophy, particularly with respect to establishing a naturalistic basis for ethics.

Schweitzer determines that Nietzsche's "original belief was that he could conceive the higher life-affirmation as the development to a higher spirituality of the will-to-live" through the Will to Power theory (POC 246). But, in the end, Nietzsche would merely promote an ethic of "a more or less *meaningless* living out life to the full" (246 [emphasis added]). A very harsh assessment. The wonderful grand naturalism of Nietzsche's philosophy would decay together with his great mind into a mere ecstatic self-affirmation and psychological self-overcoming – meaning found in madness. An ethic for humanity as a whole and for the world in which we live slipped away from him. Nevertheless, Schweitzer was still deeply inspired by Nietzsche's individualist focus as the starting point for ethics, as well as his naturalistic conception of the cosmological Will for its "*religious* reverence for life" (247n8 [emphasis added]).

Schweitzer also agrees with Nietzsche that evolutionary science was a dead end for those trying to find meaning for humankind in natural history. Nature often seems capricious and unethical since what lives and who dies is often as arbitrary as it is a matter of naturalistic necessity. Worse, there is no ideal for human social values to be found in nature that cannot be countered by another interpretation promoting ruthlessness and selfish opportunism. For Schweitzer, there is nothing in nature to which an ethic can be anchored – except for a line of thought he discovered in the works of Charles Darwin.

Charles Darwin and Social Ethics

This chapter now moves on to a discussion about the second key inspiration Schweitzer would take from Nietzsche. Through him, Schweitzer became attuned to the problem of trying to reconcile philosophy and ethics with Darwin's evolutionary theory. Yet despite Nietzsche's influence, Schweitzer would come up with his own interpretation concerning the evolution of the human intellect, and he found a way to claim compassion as a scientific truth for his Reverence for Life ethic. But first I must outline what it was Charles Darwin actually wrote.

For Darwin, explaining the emergence of social instincts in the human species through natural selection was a problem. He concluded that incipient reasoning powers led some of our hominid ancestors to learn that aid given to a fellow may be returned in exchange, whereupon this behaviour, if reciprocated, would become habituated within the immediate social clan. This inclination and habitual behaviour yields a competitive advantage: these traits would be favoured for generational inheritance to offspring. But – and this is key – these traits would only be passed down if a clan was in competition with other groups for the same subsistence resources. The cooperative clan would have to be able to supplant others through greater success in rearing offspring, actively excluding others from limited resources, and/or engaging in outright warfare to eliminate those groups that did not possess such cooperative inclinations. Only in this way, Darwin (1882, 129–31) concluded, could social instincts have become a defining characteristic of the emergent human species.

Only later, Darwin writes, with the emergence of fully human beings, could these social instincts become strengthened through psychological pressures. The opinions of others in the clan could then be brought to bear on the individual and thereby further reinforced and codified into social norms and taboos. The point here is that social instincts are no longer being perpetuated by natural selection: they have become decoupled from direct evolutionary advantage for the individual. It is now a social selection within intra-clan dynamics that determines both survival and reproductive success for the individual within that community. Further habituation of these inherited propensities led to the psychological phenomenon of social instincts being felt and experienced as a duty to one's "inmost soul" and other "sacred" abstractions (131). Social instincts could now become self-actualizing rather than simply being imposed by others in the clan. This is how Darwin explains the emergence of humankind's peculiar preoccupation with a seeming anti-natural compassion for the infirm and aged in our populations. It is also how he explains marital monogamy's becoming a social ideal (131–45). Nevertheless, he warns that, even though it is *certain* that such civilized behaviour as caring for the imbecile, the sickly, and the maimed, along with developing vaccines and medicines to help those of weak constitutions, had all been "highly injurious to the race of man," this inherited sympathy represents "the noblest part of our nature" (134).[33]

In his reading of Darwin, Schweitzer ascribes to a very atomistic interpretation of evolution. Animal life only survives at the death of another, and plants draw their sustenance from the decaying biomass of all that carnage from those who have since succumbed to their earthly graves. Indeed, "the world is a ghastly drama of the will-to-live divided against itself" (*POC* 312). Nature is like a pointillist painting marked out in individual instances of suffering and death. Patterns of beauty and harmony only emerge when one steps back and observes from a distance. But Schweitzer does not give himself permission to do this. "The beauty of nature is darkened by the suffering [we] discover everywhere within it" (281). He looks unflinchingly at the reality of predation and finds that death and procreation are the twinned teleologies of life when considered from a strictly atomistic Darwinian perspective. Schweitzer therefore claims only the naturalistic will-to-live and Darwinian sympathy as the foundation for his philosophy, not all of capricious nature.

Schweitzer's reading of Darwin is informed by the evolutionary views of both Schopenhauer and Nietzsche. Schopenhauer takes support from Jean-Jacques Rousseau to show that the true basis for ethics is a type of compassion that draws humans into social groups and, further, that this is the natural foundation of society. Nietzsche, however, embraces the worldview of Thomas Hobbes, which holds that the first societies were drawn together only by fear and for selfish advantage. For Nietzsche, it is the ruthless Will to Power that overcomes the "nasty, brutish and short" existence of early humans – not Rousseau's *pitié* (*WTP* §1017, 525). Nietzsche believes that human existence had become decoupled from nature. Society became self-referential, and this, for him was unnatural and therefore improper. Schweitzer on the other hand, like Darwin, finds humankind's true humanity in this curious social instinct that was as natural as it was a product of rational consciousness. The fact that ethical sympathy was decoupled from natural selection yet still naturalistic made it exactly what he was looking for to secure his philosophy of civilization.

Schweitzer, therefore, writes of Darwin's *Descent of Man*: "we possess devotion to others as descendants of herds which maintained themselves in the struggle for existence while others succumbed, because the social impulses were developed in them the most strongly and the most universally" (224).[34] Humans possess a natural instinct to form social groups that served an evolutionary advantage. Yet this natural inclination is not self-actualizing in our species under natural laws alone but requires rational thought to manifest itself fully. Through Darwin, Schweitzer asserts that "altruism therefore is now regarded as natural and at the same time as something which has come into existence though [rational] reflection" (255). This sentence is key. Schweitzer sees the very task of philosophy as taking the altruistic potential within this natural instinct and "bring[ing] this to completion" as a social reality (255).

Schweitzer would try to do this by actualizing Darwin's social instinct through the life-view of rational consciousness. World- and life-affirmation would come from a naturalistic truth supporting an elemental morality that existed in both the domains of philosophy and evolutionary science: compassion. But this alone would be an incomplete ethic. Schweitzer still needed to provide additional ethical orientation to make compassion into a viable social ethic. Yet because Darwin's evolutionary social instincts became a rational thought process for the evolving hominids, Schweitzer now had a theoretical basis to extend ethical compassion beyond the immediate family to all of humanity, and even to the natural world, through conscious reflection. Schweitzer believed that the circle of ethical consideration had to be widened to include all life, not just for the sake of non-humans but in order to firmly secure it in a person's ethical character – a lesson he took from Schopenhauer and Nietzsche. In many ways, Schweitzer anticipated the American wildlife ecologist and environmental ethicist Aldo Leopold, who also wrote that extending ethics to animals, plants, and the land too was an evolutionary possibility for our species.[35]

For these reasons, Schweitzer claims that Reverence for Life is, simultaneously, a rational, natural, and even universal ethic. He also describes it as an absolute and spiritual ethic. Yet because the natural world is capricious and cannot serve as a mirror for our social ideals, Schweitzer takes only Darwin's social instincts and Schopenhauer's will-to-live theory to secure an elemental ethic that is compatible with science. He then turned back to Cartesian consciousness to create a mystical, monistic, and life-affirming interpretation of the natural world. But this life-view never subsumes the scientific worldview. The scientific worldview is the dominant reality and the idea of a universal will-to-live is always thought of with a certain air of unreality about it – such beliefs are always deemed to be merely possibilities and mysteries, never scientific facts (*POC* 308).[36] To use Nietzsche's metaphor, Reverence for Life views nature with its "veils of mystery" still intact. Yet Schweitzer also feared allowing rational thought to go too far in speculative excess. The will-to-live of rational consciousness is therefore kept elemental and only in its extended life-view does it become a type of mysticism. This allows the dualism of the head and heart (i.e., scientific knowing versus the mystical wanting in lived experience) to coexist in a delicate harmony within the monistic life-view of rational consciousness. The deeper significance of this is explained in the next chapter.

Conclusion

To recap the findings of this chapter, and returning for the moment to Schweitzer's own words that began this discussion, he had stated outright that it was thoughts on Nietzsche that set the stage for that day in 1915 when the Reverence for Life ethic emerged as the answer for the crisis in civilization. The preceding discussion on Nietzsche's philosophy, with its wrestling with evolutionary naturalism and its resulting implications for ethics, allows us to say specifically what it was that Schweitzer would take and reject from Nietzsche.

Schweitzer accepted the idea that there are two kinds of truth: one scientific and one cultural. This would be retained in Schweitzer's philosophy. But, unlike Nietzsche, he never rejected scientific facts as being false or biased. For Schweitzer, culturally meaningful truths always had to be correlated to the best available science. That said, society still needed a cosmology that upheld the value and special dignity of life – all life, human and non-human alike – that natural science seemingly could not do by itself. This is why Schweitzer offers a mystical and poetic interpretation of Schopenhauer's universal will-to-live theory for his own Reverence for Life ethic, as was described at the end of chapter 2.

But Schweitzer still needed two more things to make this cosmology complete. Somehow he had to substantiate the claim that compassion was both a scientific fact and dependent upon rational consciousness. This would come out from his reading of Charles Darwin. He reached a different conclusion regarding the naturalness of compassion than did Nietzsche, and this brought him back to Schopenhauer and his elemental morality of *pitié*. Nevertheless, for Schweitzer this morality would not be grounded in Buddhist metaphysics as it was for Schopenhauer but in Darwin's own views, which held that social instincts were both evolutionarily naturalistic and at the same time still required rational reflection for their actualization. This then was the second constituent element he needed for his ethic.

But Schweitzer still needed one more thing to establish a complete foundation for his philosophy of civilization. He needed a different starting place for philosophy than the one created by Descartes. This would be the New Rationalism, a project that was inspired in large part from Nietzsche's own views on philosophy, culture, and naturalistic possibility. From a purely philosophical point of view, this is perhaps the most innovative aspect of Schweitzer's entire corpus of work, and it is what sets him out as a truly original philosopher in his own right.

Chapter 4

The New Rationalism

To briefly revisit the findings of the last two chapters, Schweitzer saw triumphs and flaws in both Schopenhauer and Nietzsche. In each he found something to secure his Reverence for Life ethic. Not only that, he saw a certain complementarity between their very different philosophical systems. To put it simply, Schweitzer believed that both *nearly* had it right but that each had fallen victim to particular errors. He spells out his assessment in *The Philosophy of Civilization*:

> Nietzsche and Schopenhauer ... are the only thinkers in this continent who philosophize in elemental fashion about the will-to-live, [yet make the mistake of] ventur[ing] to follow the paths of one-sidedness. Each completing the other, they pronounce sentence on ethics of European philosophy by bringing into daylight again the elemental ethical thoughts contained in life-negation [Schopenhauer] as in life-affirmation [Nietzsche], thoughts which philosophy was keeping buried. Arriving as they do at the [error of the] non-ethical by thinking out to a conclusion [in one-sidedness], one in life-negation, the other in life-affirmation, they corroborate together the statement that the ethical consists neither of life-negation nor life-affirmation, but in a mysterious combination of the two. (*POC* 248)

This was Schweitzer's project. He would seek to produce the "mysterious combination" of these two lines of thought in his Reverence for Life ethic.

From Nietzsche he would take a natural life-affirmation that honours the person in the world as a true personality but that does not abandon social ethics as he did. To do this, Schweitzer would, like Nietzsche, maintain cultural truths over the nihilistic facts of natural science. Yet he also believed that philosophy must always be informed by and correlated to science. Schweitzer would therefore seek out those elemental scientific truths that would keep the life-view of Reverence for Life from speculative excess – specifically, these were the will-to-live theory and Darwinian social instincts. Schweitzer also agreed with Nietzsche that the human species could find a path that differed from the one exemplified by the chaotic struggle within the natural world. Humanity is both of nature and beyond it: we have the power to choose.

But Schweitzer also saw Schopenhauer's life-negation as valuable. It was a way to have a higher calling beyond the naturalistic instinct of self-preservation. A balanced view on life-negation and life-affirmation would therefore become a vital part of his Ethical Mysticism. For Schweitzer, altruism emerges from a deep meditation on the personal will-to-live, which brings forth a mystical realization and an ethical impulse to help other life achieve its highest possible development even, sometimes, through self-sacrifice. This is a most curious transformation of Nietzsche's egotism. Even Schweitzer admits that, in a sense, "it is not through kindness to others that I am gentle, peaceable, forbearing, and friendly, but because by such behaviour I prove my own profoundest self-realization to be true" concerning the will-to-live (POC 315). In precisely this way, Schweitzer seeks to combine Nietzsche's deepened egotism with Schopenhauer's image of the self as the "mirror of the world" (WWR II, 380). In effect, Ethical Mysticism takes the impulse towards selfishness and aims it outwards so that it is vicariously fulfilled through others. It thus becomes a type of virtue ethics, which is something that has been previously noted by commentators such as Mike Martin (2002, 2007).

How he would achieve this great cosmological synthesis comes, somewhat expectedly, through a particular kind of philosophy called hermeneutics. This branch of philosophy examines the social person in society. Originally hermeneutics only dealt with the problem of interpreting the ancient texts of extinct cultures, but it has since grown to become a philosophy of contemporary cultures too. This is what Schweitzer did with his own hermeneutics. As will be shown here in this chapter, he began with a hermeneutical framework to address the problem of trying to come to an understanding of the historical Jesus in the New Testament scriptures, and then later he adapted this same hermeneutic philosophy for understanding people across contemporary world cultures and for linking all life in the biosphere in a common "essential" (ontological) way. Schweitzer did this by creating a new first principle for consciousness that was different than the one developed by Descartes. Schweitzer's project, which he called the New Rationalism, was deeply informed by Schopenhauer's doctrine of the universal Will.

As a trained natural scientist (a medical doctor) Schweitzer had no use at all for Schopenhauer's Platonic Universals. But he did accept the doctrine of the Will as a common link between individual will-to-live lifeforms. This was because using the will-to-live as a way to explain the physiological development of all life is a philosophical claim in harmony with natural science. For this reason, Schweitzer can assert that "the will-to-live is everywhere present, even as in me" (E-RFL, 230). Nevertheless, while empirical science can investigate the physical facts of life, "like all science ... it can lead me only to the mystery of life, which is essentially in me, however near or far away it may be observed" (230). The deeper significance of this statement will be explored in a moment. But, in general, Schweitzer is saying that natural science can lead us to the recognition that the same physiological processes take place in all life and that this biology is essentially the same no matter the species. Yet the "mystery of being" cannot be known this way, nor, for that matter, can it ever be the subject of rational knowledge. This mystery has to be experienced through a different way of knowing, a *pre*-rational kind of knowing, an intuitive pure knowing – by way of something Kant calls the "sacred shudder" (*Schauer*) felt in the presence of the power of nature (Hadot 2006, 270). In ordinary language, this is called the sublime.

Schopenhauer writes that all the individual wills-to-live are united through the unitary cosmological Will. He also argues that the feeling of the sublime brings this connection with other life to our conscious awareness. This is "intuitive pure knowing" mentioned back in chapter 2. For Schweitzer, compassion over another's suffering is one such intuitive path to this experience; for example, witnessing another sentient being in deep pain can bring about a "sacred shudder" known as empathy. Likewise, people who have been deeply wounded (physically or spiritually) can grow to be newly sensitive to pain in others. They are sometimes so moved that they become very compassionate people as result. Schweitzer's contention that there exists a "brotherhood of those who bear the mark of pain" refers to the transformed and sublime character of such persons. In this way the experience of compassion creates (or rather reveals) an *essential* bond between different people, drawing them back to their simple and common humanity. Compassion restores humanity to a proper relation with itself, and potentially it can bring humankind into ethical harmony with the entire natural world.

But more importantly, at least to this particular investigation on philosophical questions, compassion was the means by which Schweitzer saw a pathway opened up to the inner essence of another life. The question for us here is: How does he justify this claim in academic terms? This is a particularly thorny question since essence in this context is a reference to what is called the "thing in itself," which Kant declares is absolutely unknowable. Schweitzer's solution to this age-old problem in philosophy is breathtakingly innovative. He would do it through a hermeneutical analysis of existence.

By way of introduction to this new way of thinking about the nature of existence, it needs to be kept in mind that Schopenhauer's universal Will is unitary, which means that it is always undivided even though it is present in separate wills-to-live; different life is "one being" at a deeper metaphysical level. Also, while the will-to-live theory was seen by Schweitzer as a way of describing empirical physics, the unitary cosmological Will (i.e., the *universal* will-to-live) as a common essence of life was substantiated by him through three separate approaches: (1) an epagoge of the individual wills-to-live, (2) the pre-rational intuition of the sublime, and (3) the hermeneutical analysis of existence.

But first, it should be kept in mind that one upshot of having the Will unitary was that Schweitzer could claim historical distance would not block essential humanity from experiencing itself: an intuitive connection could be created between discrete manifestations of the will-to-live even across the horizon of time. This primal and pre-rational connection with other life is justified by the hermeneutic that he reveals in the last chapter of his famous study on the historical Jesus. To describe it, however, it will be necessary to discuss the particular context in which he presented it. This means going into a detailed recounting of his discussion on the historical Jesus in the New Testament scriptures. Only then can Schweitzer's hermeneutical New Rationalism be brought out in its own context immediately afterwards. One thing to be attentive for in the following exposition of Schweitzer's scholarly research is the profound influence of Schopenhauer even here when discussing Christianity.

The Hermeneutical Analysis of Being

"Those who are fond of talking about negative theology can find their account here" (*QHJ* 478). Schweitzer, in the final chapter of his critical study of New Testament scholarship, begins to write about the historical Jesus in terms of negative theology. This move struck many as unexpected since the preceding analysis had been aimed at revealing how prior scholarship had romanticized the life and theology of the historical Jesus to suit the expectations of each researcher. Schweitzer claims that, because Jesus does not greet us as an author, there is an impenetrable barrier that prevents the present-day scholar from being able to know this person using the tools of historical science. While much can be learned about late Jewish eschatological thought, the researcher simply cannot fully place him- or herself in the mental worldview of this enigmatic figure. Schweitzer sought another means not reliant upon rational analysis and historical science. This would be by way of negative theology.

Before proceeding, I need to clarify what is meant by negative, or apophatic, theology. "Apophatic" has a range of possible meanings. It can signify a corrective used to transcend the limitations of positive statements concerning the divine or the deity: it is a way of showing deference to the ineffability of God. And so, saying that God is "love" would not be appropriate because the divine essence lies beyond this declarative statement, which is derived from human relational experience. Apophatic theology thus attempts greater inclusivity by finding words and expressions appropriate to the divine as well as by offering a way to give a methodological nod to the impossibility of this task. The apophatic thereby safeguards the humility of the exegete.

The apophatic can also refer to something fundamentally more than simply an exegetical methodology. Particularly in the Orthodox East, it is stressed that it is not right to say that God is unknowable – rather, He is "beyond the unknowable" (*hyperagnostos*), to use the phrase employed by Pseudo-Dionysius, Maximos Confessor, and Gregory Palamas. The point to be taken here is *not* that God is simply something that can never be fully captured in language but, rather, that the essence (*ousia*) of the Godhead is in no way similar to that of human thought. God is not *Geist*, nor is He the God of Descartes, Who is revealed to the rational mind as His corresponding Image. For Orthodoxy, God is in no way similar (*homoousios*) to ordinary human beings. The distance between Creator and creature is only bridged through Jesus (*Theandros*), not through the Kantian intellect. But this is another subject altogether.[37]

I mention it here to underscore the fact that Schweitzer's use of negative theology does not match either of these two standard conceptions of the apophatic. It is something else and something new. In certain ways, he anticipated the apophatic hermeneutics of a present-day scholar in this field, Jean-Luc Marion (1946–present). A brief mention of Marion's thoughts is therefore useful to set the stage for appreciating Schweitzer's own negative theology. A fuller engagement with Marion and hermeneutics is offered in the next chapter, which looks at the questions of metaphysics and mysticism in the works of Schweitzer. But a more central problem must be dealt with first.

Negative theology attempts, in the words of Marion (2002, 132), to use particular language constructions that serve "to deconstruct [the concept of] God and nevertheless to reach God [at the same time]." It is a language game – or to use Jacques Derrida's appraisal, "the apophatic has always represented a sort of paradoxical hyperbole" (133). Nevertheless, such unusual textual constructions are necessary to encapsulate "concepts" that are not themselves concepts but, rather, modes-of-being and kinds of awareness that cannot be reached directly by the rational mind. In short, the apophatic attempts to overcome the intellect itself in order to capture more of the human experience in words than the mind is capable of fathoming without such rhetorical devices. This is what makes the apophatic so fascinating for hermeneutical philosophers. They are not necessarily trying to come up with a new theology. Most are seeking to understand the nature of consciousness and how linguistic ontology affects our perception of the world. Marion is an exception here. He begins from this basis, but then he dares to also establish a new "postmodern" theology. In this, Marion is particularly interested in something called super-saturated phenomena. He uses this terminology to draw attention to the fact that certain objects of perception can exceed the ability of the intellect to fully comprehend them except through a cognitive reduction to mere rational concepts. Negative theology is thus, for him, an important historical precedent and a means of trying to capture more of that super-saturated meaning available in the world than philosophy could do otherwise. And because the "excess [of intuition from super-saturated phenomena] conquers comprehension and what language can say" (160), it is necessary for Marion and other hermeneutical philosophers to proceed through the almost Zen-like paradoxical phraseology that is so indicative of negative theology. I, too, have to turn to the same type of textual constructions when I discuss Schweitzer's apophatic hermeneutics. Some patience may be required on the part of the reader when it comes to deciphering these hermeneutical expressions.

However, as the following discussion reveals, Schweitzer does not actually seek to develop a theology in the traditional sense (e.g., Incarnational Christology). Rather, he sets out to explore the pre-rational nature of intuition and what this means for understanding both the historical person known as Jesus of Nazareth and ourselves as ethical beings. More specifically, Schweitzer uses his philosophical engagement with the New Testament to establish the foundation for his New Rationalism project, a foundation complete with a new ontological understanding of human consciousness. It is therefore a true apophatic hermeneutic. It will however take this and the next chapter to fully spell this all out for the reader.

Hermeneutics and the Historical Jesus

Schweitzer would attempt a very distinctive and innovative approach to redress the problem of understanding historical texts. But he was not naïve. He knew that it was not possible to enter the mental worldview of a person who lived two thousand years ago. Jesus belonged to a culture entirely different form Schweitzer's own time. His solution to bridging the distance between these different historical and cultural worldviews was through Schopenhauer's unitary Will.

Schweitzer writes that "each world-view comprises elements determined by its own time and elements undetermined by time" (QHJ 481). What he is saying is that each configuration of a will-to-live is particular to the individual; the resulting worldview of that person's will-to-live is defined by its culture and historical time period. Nonetheless, because all wills-to-live are connected through Schopenhauer's unitary Will, Schweitzer believes that no will-to-live is entirely alien to one's own, "for the same [W]ill, manifested in however varying circumstances, always creates world-views which comply and coincide with its own *essential* nature" (481 [emphasis added]). In other words, Schopenhauer's unitary Will constitutes a common essence for all life.

Because of this, Schweitzer believed that a person of today can still relate to the personal strivings of Jesus on a deeper intuitive level such that, "He can be known without much being known about him, and the eschatological element in his teaching can be grasped, even if the details are not always understood" (QHJ 480). Put simply, people are people – that essential humanity will always be relatable through an immediate sympathy and compassion even if this pre-rational sympathetic understanding is not accompanied by a full intellectual explanation of their historical circumstances. Accordingly, he writes, "to know Jesus and to understand him requires no scholarly initiation" (480). How this is possible comes from a particular ontological claim that grounds his New Rationalism project.

Schweitzer did not simply borrow from Schopenhauer. He sought to advance his philosophy in a new way through what he called the New Rationalism. Schweitzer began with a new understanding of consciousness born from a different starting place than the one established by Descartes. He attacks Descartes' "cogito ergo sum," calling it "the stupidest primary assumption in all of philosophy!" (*E-RFL* 228). Further saying, "he built an artificial structure by presuming a person knows nothing [initially] and doubts all, whether outside himself or within" (228). For Schweitzer, consciousness is not a blank slate of pure a priori time or a simple essence as Kant held. Instead he asserts: "When I seek the first fact of consciousness, it is not to know that I think, but to get a hold of myself ... [whereupon I discover] the simple fact of consciousness is this, *I will to live*" (227 [emphasis in original]).

This is a deceptively simple phrase. It is not a statement about incipient desire and orientation in a culturally conditioned worldview. It is much more than just that. The first principle of Schweitzer's ontology is a dialectical synthesis of the Cartesian self-aware ego with Schopenhauer's cosmological will-to-live: it is an "I + will-to-live" formula that explains intentional consciousness. He is describing what Heidegger would later call the "there-beingness" (*Dasein*) of life, albeit in an elemental expression.[38] Yet, in contrast to Heidegger, Schweitzer presents the inner essence of each person as a unique and complicated nexus consisting of biological factors, cultural historicity, *and* a single thin thread of the unitary Will that unites all life *as life*. This is how Schweitzer seeks to bridge the gap between cosmology and consciousness. This is the New Rationalism.

As just mentioned, Schweitzer presents something that resembles Heidegger's *Dasein*. In both cases, self-consciousness is an intentional projection emerging from historically conditioned origins that presuppose *Dasein* as a being-in-the-world, a being with concerns (*Besorgen*) and emotional attachments (*Fürsorge*). Heidegger similarly relies on pre-rational intuitions that define an individualized *Dasein* as *Dasein* – in his case, the feelings of unease (*unheimlich*) and dread (*Angst*). The key difference is that Schweitzer does not close off *Dasein*'s origin entirely but leaves that one thin thread of the cosmological Will to trace our way back to common essential humanity through the pre-rational intuition of compassion (*Mitleid*). Heidegger's *Being and Time* was published in 1927, while Schweitzer was writing about an ontological being that existed as a culturally conditioned projection of its own historicity back in 1905 – albeit in a book about the New Testament. His definitive "I + will-to-live" formulation for this being in time was first set forth in 1923 and then again in 1936 with an expanded discussion. There is no evidence that the two authors ever read each other's works, which is itself a bit of a mystery since Schweitzer did claim that he kept abreast of all the significant academic developments taking place in Europe even while living in a remote African jungle. Nevertheless, without clear evidence to the contrary, their hermeneutical systems should be considered to have been developed independently.

Now, returning to the main subject, for Schweitzer the being that emerges in the recursive self-awareness at the heart of consciousness is the "I + will-to-live" nexus: a biologically, culturally, and historically conditioned worldview. In *The Quest of the Historical Jesus* he writes: "a world-view consists of a [W]ill penetrating and shaping the body of available contemporary thought-forms [of language and culture]," and thereby an individual being becomes implicated and self-identifying with historically and culturally determined factors (481). Every worldview includes both the variable elements arising from its historicity and biology in addition to the permanent, unchanging constant of the unitary universal Will. In direct opposition to his famous cousin, the existentialist philosopher Jean-Paul Sartre (1905–1980), Schweitzer holds that historicity does not entirely subsume essence.[39] Essential humanity remains even if existence presupposes a particular and historically conditioned existence as the ultimate object of inner sense – that is, the "I will to live" is the first fact of consciousness. The common thread uniting all instances of particularized being is the unitary cosmological Will. It always remains accessible to the experiencing subject, even occasionally across the horizon of time into the past if we have access to some textual trace of former lives (e.g., biographical memoirs, ancient epistles, a civil war diary, etc.). While the essence of that other being cannot be fully experienced through the cognitive and rational mind, something of his or her life can still be felt behind the words through pre-rational intuitions such as the sublime of compassion.

The Hermeneutical Horizon

A certain passing resemblance exists between Schweitzer and the hermeneutics of Friedrich Daniel Ernst Schleiermacher (1768–1834). But Schweitzer does not claim to be able to know an author better than he knows himself, yet he does rely on a certain type of psychological transference to understand a historical figure. Nevertheless, as just discussed, Schweitzer's hermeneutics culminate in an apophatic horizon over which the rational mind cannot cross. Only the pre-rational Will remains to fathom the dark abyss, intuiting something of the self-same human presence behind the textual words. His aim is that, as he writes in *The Quest of the Historical Jesus*, "once accord has been reached between will [of self] and will [of the other], the essence of the world-view is immediately made apparent" (484). But no conceptual knowledge comes of this. There is no interpretive claim to be made. There is no objective consequence for the researcher in the interpretative project of bringing ancient texts to a contemporary worldview – at least not directly. Schweitzer presents no technique for the exegete. This is a hermeneutics aimed at *mystagogy* (a personal initiation into a mystery). And so he ends his book with a most unusual paragraph:

> He [Jesus] comes to us as one unknown, without a name, as of old,
> by the lakeside, he came to those men who did not know who he
> was. He says the same words, "Follow me!," and sets us to those
> tasks which he must fulfill in our time. He commands. And to those
> who hearken to him, whether wise or unwise, *he will reveal himself*
> in the peace, the labours, the conflicts and the sufferings that they
> may experience in his fellowship, and as an ineffable mystery they
> will learn who he is ... (QHF 487 [emphasis added])

This is exactly what Schweitzer did when he undertook his humanitarian mission in Africa – he was following after the historical Jesus in order to try to understand him in ways historical scholarship could not. He was seeking to experience a union with Jesus through ethical service to the least of his brethren. While presented in the context of hermeneutics, his goal is not an imagined psychological transference to give the researcher an ability to know an author better than he knows himself. Nor does it appear that Schweitzer seeks divine illumination in order to give humanity words that encapsulate a spiritual knowledge gained through direct mystical experience. The capacity for divination, which he wrote about in his 1936 article entitled "The Ethics of Reverence for Life," seems to be limited to revealing an *ethical* essentialism through the sublime of compassion. This is Ethical Mysticism.

Religion and Elemental Morality

Schweitzer's Jesus could perform no miracles. In fact, Schweitzer goes on to write: "The Jesus of Nazareth who came forward publicly and as the

Messiah, who preached the ethic of the kingdom of God, who founded the kingdom of heaven upon earth, and dies to give his work its final consecration, never existed" (QHJ 478). Schweitzer's Jesus is only a deeply thoughtful and ethical thinker who has seen clearly where the path of love must lead: he must allow himself to be broken on "the wheel of history" to fulfill what he thought was required by Jewish eschatological belief to bring about the Messianic Kingdom and to serve as the very atonement for the rest of the humankind to save them from the tribulation (PSJ 52).[40] As mistaken as the historical Jesus was about his ability to usher in the Kingdom of God on earth, his actions reveal a complete surrender of personal will to live out an ethic of love born of the same pre-rational compassion as the one at the heart of Reverence for Life.

What Schweitzer says this means for Christianity today is this: "The truth is that he [Jesus] cannot be an authority for us at the level of understanding, but only at the level of the *will*. His role can only be that of a powerful influence which elicits hopes and longings inherent in us and inspires us to heights and to a clarity we would not achieve if dependent on our own devices and without the influence of his personality" (QHJ 482 [emphasis added]). It is important to note that there are no supernatural metaphysics in this statement, only something akin to Schopenhauer's understanding of grace (POC 290). This is Schweitzer's prescription for liberalizing religion. But his understanding of Christianity is not the grounding for his Reverence for Life ethic: it is the other way around.

As mentioned in chapter 1, elemental morality was his solution for uniting the Reverence for Life philosophy with an actively engaged ethic. The key passage from *The Philosophy of Civilization* is as follows: "Nor does [Schopenhauer] need ... to sever all connection with Jesus and religious ethics. He can appeal as often as he likes to the fact that his philosophy only establishes what has always been accepted by the piety of Christianity and of the [Hindu] Indians as the essential element of the moral ... Elemental morality now once more obtains its right place in a thinking connection to the universe" (POC 240).

For Schweitzer, the elemental morality of both philosophy and religion is a self-sacrificial love aimed at promoting other life through compassion. Here one must keep in mind a very unusual aspect of the German language and the German way of looking at the world. The word for "intellectual" and for "spiritual" is the same: *Geistig*. In English these are very different and sometimes even diametrically opposed concepts. Yet in German the rational mind is synonymous with a person's very soul. This fact explains much of German intellectual history, including, for example,

Hegel's philosophy of *Geist*. For this reason, great care is required when trying to determine whether, in *The Philosophy of Civilization*, Schweitzer is referring to the academic intellectual (*Geistig*) or the religious spiritual (*Geistig*).

Take, for example, a famous sentence from the English translation of this book: "There must come about a spiritualizing [*Vergeistigung*] of the masses" (POC 336). And this sentence: "The only thing that can help us is that we renounce the power which is given us over one another. But that is an act of spirituality [*Geistigkeit*]" (337). In both cases the italicized terms contain the same root: *Geist*. Because of this, the English translation is very misleading. A better turn of phrase would be "an intellectual awakening" because of the specific contexts in which he uses the terms. Schweitzer is calling for people to begin thinking about the elemental questions of life and about the state of civilization in which they find themselves. He says as much in the sentence that immediately follows the first example: "The mass of individuals must begin to reflect about their lives, about what they want to secure for their lives in the struggle for existence, about what makes their circumstances difficult, and what they deny themselves" (336). The context is the same in the other example as well.

And so, to put it in its most simple and clearest terms, a religion without any divinity is merely an intellectualized form of mysticism – and for Schweitzer, specifically, an Ethical Mysticism. He describes it this way: "The way to true mysticism leads up through *rational thought* to [a] deep experience of the world and our will-to-live" (POC 81 [emphasis added]). By rational thought Schweitzer means philosophy. He is not preaching Christianity in *The Philosophy of Civilization*, only a mystical appreciation of the natural world that comes by way of his unique synthesis of the philosophical systems of Schopenhauer and Nietzsche. Jesus was an ethical teacher, yes. But for Schweitzer he was no God, and this is why some Christians ungraciously call him an "Antichrist" (Melamed and Melamed 2003, 181).

Schweitzer's metaphysics do not look past empirical reality. Schweitzer was a natural scientist. For him, the elemental nature philosophy of the will-to-live and the cosmological causality of the universal Will are truths in harmony with science and, at the same time, are revealed intuitively within rational consciousness. The "I + will-to-live" nexus is a type of naturalism that yields an ethical worldview that upholds human dignity and moral agency. The hermeneutics that appears at the conclusion of *The Quest of the Historical Jesus* is, therefore, not aimed at illuminating ancient texts but, rather, at revealing the essence of humanity. It is one part of his larger Reverence for Life project – a project that also includes a virtue ethic.

Virtue Ethic

For Schweitzer, the sublime of suffering – the cringe at seeing someone in terrible pain, the profound angst of a parent's worry, the inconsolable loss in grieving – reveals that there truly is a pre-rational bond uniting the self and the other. Pain diminishes the essence of existence and love nurtures its development. But not only that, Schweitzer also sees here a principle of rational pleasure (*eudaimonia*) not based in self-sought desires but on promoting the physical, emotional, and spiritual development of the ones we love. Moreover, because this concept of pain and pleasure has a greater range and is not limited to the Kantian intellect, Schweitzer's virtue ethic can be inclusive of the well-being for all life – not just family and friends but extended to all of humanity and even the natural world.

Schweitzer describes this virtue ethic in the last written piece about the philosophical grounding of Reverence for Life, the same one that outlines the New Rationalism. The virtue ethic was integral to that project. And as previously mentioned, he began with a meditation that leads to the discovery that "we find the simple fact of consciousness is this, *I will to live*" (*E-RFL* 227 [emphasis in original]). We value our own existence and want to further our own desires. Schweitzer calls this recognition "the first spiritual act" (229). But he says we must embrace the nihilistic fact that, as mortal beings, we will die someday. A truly rational being must come to accept that his or her life is dependent upon cosmological circumstances and biological facts beyond his or her control. This leads to the "second spiritual act" of resignation (229).

The person now stands in a precarious place. An antagonistic tension exists between the self-aware person and the positivistic material cosmos that will cause that person to age and die. This is the dualism of Reverence for Life. Only two choices are presented to such a person: to retreat into an unthinking life of self-seeking egotism or to meditate further and discover that, during the time we possess, people have a unique spiritual freedom that arises from being recursively aware of our motivations and actions. The pre-rational will-to-live can then overcome the intellect that has become resigned to the fact that immortality is denied to us. At this moment we discover that "there is within each of us a modulation, an inner exaltation, which lifts [us] above the buffetings with which [cosmological] events assail us" (*E-RFL* 229). The will-to-live thereby allows us to "triumph ... over whatever happens to us" despite naturalistic necessity (229).

The exact inner ontological alchemy here is not spelled out by Schweitzer. He only says that such a person has "passed beyond" mere resignation and now discovers a new state of being wherein "resignation to the will-to-live leads directly to this first virtue: sincerity" (E-RFL 230). A new disposition has arisen. The person now becomes resolved to live *sincerely* and to honour his or her own will-to-live through the only avenue left open. That person must devote his or her elective freedoms to cherishing other lives because: "if I am [a] thinking [and sincere] being, I must regard this other life than my own with equal reverence. For I shall know that it longs for fullness and development as deeply as I do myself" (230). The dualism has now given way to a monism of the universal will-to-live to become an Ethical Mysticism. Schweitzer's words recall those of Schopenhauer, which identify compassion as a love extending to the other when the reality of "I and not-I" disappears. This is Schweitzer's opening to a reverence for *all* life. But Schweitzer cannot use Buddhist metaphysics or theology to establish his case. It instead comes through the New Rationalism that engages Descartes' first principle from a hermeneutical perspective – and it all depends upon a claim of a common essence to all life, a subject to which this chapter will return in a moment. But there is another issue here too that must be dealt with first.

What has been outlined above, despite its sophistication, would still have to be considered a bare-bones virtue ethic. Throughout his life Schweitzer was torn between many different concerns and responsibilities, and, because of this, his academic works never received the priority and attention he would have been able to provide otherwise. For example, as one editor observes, his "manuscripts contain such [marginal] notes as: 'rough draft produced in the waiting room in Paris en route to Le Havre, February 7, 5:00–8:00 A.M.'" (RFL 145). These rough drafts, however, were often what would become the final published manuscript because he never had the time to revisit and expand them. The unfinished nature of his publications is perhaps most noticeable with respect to the Reverence for Life virtue ethic. There are only fragments of his vision for the virtue ethic, and these are scattered through his many disparate works. In one, he writes: "Sincerity is the first ethical principle which appears. However lacking one may be in other respects, sincerity is the one thing he must possess" (E-RFL 230). In another, he writes that the virtue ethics of Aristotle are advantageous to Reverence for Life and that his chapters on moral excellence and friendship in *Nicomachean Ethics* are "deep and true" (POC 125). And in his sermons he speaks of gratitude, kindness, and compassion both as personal virtues and as mystical laws of existence integral to the very fulfillment of our destiny as human beings (*RFL* 125–6, also 141). While bare-bones, as I have said, his works I still feel are substantial enough for any person to *flesh-out* a full and living ethic as a personal and lived experience modelled on his life example.

The Devotional Reality of Reverence for Life

Schweitzer's virtue ethic sets up a strong dichotomous tension between boundless compassion and an ethical response that is generally proportional to the relative sentience of the non-human life. One consequence of this attracts particular criticism in the literature: How does a person deal with the intense feelings of guilt that arise from not being able to prevent the suffering of all the life we are suppose to pity? We cannot, after all, stop to save every dying worm when walking down the street, the effort would be endless and futile. And having fresh flowers for a holiday table centrepiece shouldn't be a grievous moral sin, should it?

Mike Martin, a professor of philosophy at Chapman University, California, identifies certain flaws in Schweitzer's philosophy but still provides an overall favourable assessment of Reverence for Life as an environmental ethic. Criticisms include an expanded discussion of points made in his earlier works such as that the worldview of Reverence for Life is overly "guilt mongering" about the necessary death of non-human life to provide for human well-being (Martin 2007, 26–7; see also Martin 2002, 166). According to him, "Schweitzer says his ethics makes absolute demands that render us guilty each time we kill" (Martin 2007, 40). This, Martin concludes, is entirely unrealistic because, put simply, it is not possible for people to live without participating in the destruction of other lives in some way. Take dietary decisions, for example. People cannot survive nutritionally on lettuce alone, and even if they restrict themselves to a strict vegetarian diet that allows only for the consumption of nuts and seeds for protein, the incipient life within these foodstuffs will be destroyed. The natural teleology of the will-to-live is to germinate, sprout, reach maturity, and reproduce, and so, potential future life has been prevented from coming into existence even with a fruitarian lifestyle. No one can possibly escape the trap of guilt Schweitzer sets with the absolute demands of Reverence for Life.

Martin (2007, 40–1) remarks: "Most of us, however, would be crushed by the comparable feelings of guilt, assuming we could take seriously Schweitzer's extreme beliefs about guilt." He therefore offers the reader a modified view. According to him, we should look at Reverence for Life as a call "to stop killing thoughtlessly, to think before we kill ... [Schweitzer actually] intends that we should think *well* by exercising good moral judgment" (41 [emphasis in original]) before making those necessary and practical decisions about the basic necessities of life. He is certainly right on the mark with this last comment. But, even so, there is yet another problem here. Schweitzer would appear to have impeached himself over his own ethic. As a medical doctor, Schweitzer routinely killed pathogens and parasites by the countless millions in order to save human life. He also killed lower life forms, such as river fish, to nourish sick animals back to health. Even more suspect is an incident in which Schweitzer once shot hawks to save fledgling weaverbirds because he was so moved by the cries of distress from the adult birds who were unable to protect their young (40). Apparently, Schweitzer had anthropomorphized the suffering of the defenseless birds being attacked by the hawks and decided to defend them to honour *his own* psychological need to help the helpless. This would seem to contradict his claim about the intrinsic value of all life. Hawks, after all, are birds of prey that need to eat flesh in order to survive, just like the weaverbirds need to eat seeds, which is itself a type of predation on plant germination. Which life is more deserving of its existence? And how did Schweitzer finally decide? Not only is there at least the aura of hypocrisy here, but Schweitzer's life example sometimes seems to reveal an extremely relative and subjective measure for the value of that life.

To live one must destroy. Even vegetarianism takes life, albeit plant life – it is still life nonetheless. All life shares equally in will-to-live. This is why Schweitzer declares: "the ethics of reverence for life [can] know nothing of a relative ethic" (*POC* 317). The duty to preserve all life is absolute and always remains absolute. Schweitzer remained steadfast and refused to lay down rules for every possible situation where life-taking and life-saving conflicts arise; he feared this would externalize the morality in a codified object for rational cross-examination, leaving it vulnerable to egotistical rationalization, depreciating negotiations, and ultimately superficiality of conviction. Reverence for Life is a moral compass, not a systematized guidebook. There is instead another rubric and a different means of creating a realistic, living ethic for society.

Schweitzer declares that every life taken incurs guilt (*Schuld*) requiring atonement (*POC* 317–18). The problem here is with the English translation of the German words *Schuld* and *schuldig*, which appear throughout his book. The text prepared by C.T. Campion for the English publication of *The Philosophy of Civilization* translates these particular words as "guilt" and "guilty," respectively, which is very misleading. In English, they connote a disempowering disgrace. To be guilty is to have been judged by someone to have done something wrong: a guilty person is a morally bad person. Once internalized, guilt can become a crippling shame that damages a person's self-worth and self-esteem. When his words are translated in this way, Schweitzer's philosophy becomes coloured with a very heavy-handed and oppressive judgmentalism that rubs many people the wrong way.

But the German words *Schuld* and *schuldig* actually have a different set of meanings and associations.[41] They can mean "guilt" or "guilty," as in the common expressions: *Der Mann is schuldig!* (The man is guilty!) or *Es ist meine Schuld* (It is my fault). Yet they can also mean simply that a debt is owed: *Ich stehe in deiner Schuld* (I am in your debt) or *Ich schulde dir drei Euro* (I owe you three Euros). It is in this sense of owing a personal debt that Schweitzer uses the words *Schuld* and *schuldig*. He is not saying that people are morally wrong or at fault for destroying a will-to-live by eating food, only that the taking of any life incurs a "life-debt" that must be repaid through ethical service. This is the reality of his absolutism. Not guilt but a reverential sense of obligation he is seeking to instill in the moral fabric of a person. *Schuld* is a call to greater consciousness about how one's decisions impact the non-human world and to live one's life with a contemplative awareness to give back *more* than a person takes for him- or herself. It functions like a secularized version of "saying grace" before each meal. This is how Schweitzer envisions people becoming conscientious moral beings in relation to the daily food and commodities taken from nature. The life-debt consciousness is an integral part of his virtue ethic, both as an expression of gratitude and as a reminder of one's commitment to Reverence for Life principles.

What Schweitzer describes is perhaps best encapsulated by Henry David Thoreau's aphorism from *Walden*, paraphrased here, that "the cost of a thing is the amount of life that is required to be exchanged for it." Thoreau is specifically referring to one's own life spent in debt or in service to another person in order to gain the means of purchasing the necessities of life. David Orr (1994, 172), however, widens the meaning to include the plant and animal life that has to be destroyed to provide humans with the economic commodities they consume. This idea is further developed by Peter G. Brown (2001, 61), who opens Schweitzer's philosophy to a whole new level of consideration, that of the quantifiable economic analysis of humankind's ever-growing and uncompensated debt to the natural world. This is a subject that is explored in my final chapter.

With all this in mind, we can now look at the question of whether Schweitzer lived up to his own ethic. Schweitzer was neither naïve nor a hypocrite. As a medical doctor, he knew that "the necessity to destroy and to injure life [was] imposed upon [him]" (*POC* 316). Therefore, he wrote that he often had to "choose between the ethical and the necessary, and, if I choose the latter, must take it upon myself to incur guilt [*schuldig*] by an act of injury to life" (324). Likewise, he said that each person in life must similarly "decide for himself in each case how far he can remain ethical and how far he must submit himself to the necessity for destruction of and injury to life, and therewith incur guilt [*Schuld*]" (317). These unavoidable life-debts require a recompense for each ethical trade-off, and the atonement must take the form of devotional service to others such that each act of altruism "attempt[s] to cancel part of man's ever new debt [*Schuld*] to the animal world" (318). Accordingly, Schweitzer cautions: "we must perceive every act of destruction always as something terrible and ask ourselves, in every case, whether we can bear the responsibility as to whether it is necessary or not" (*APR* 27). It has been rightly said that Ethical Mysticism is a lived philosophy "with calluses on its hands" (Meyer 2002, 35n49). It makes people directly and fully responsible for the decisions they make – not only in the immediate sense but also with respect to larger ethical, social, and ecological repercussions. Unthinking egotism is not a valid lifestyle. Schweitzer is simply saying that people must roll up their sleeves and get to work to make the world a better place for the entire "commonwealth of life" in the biosphere (to use Peter Brown's expression).

Schweitzer practised what he preached. He made real world decisions about the necessary destruction of life for a greater good, such as saving the lives of his patients – human and non-human alike. He also knew he would fall short of his own absolute ethic. But by rising again to atone with even greater conviction by helping another life, Schweitzer sought to repay that ever-increasing debt and thereby to inspire others to help him in the greater cause of establishing a new philosophy of civilization. The life-debt (*Schuld*) mindset begets renewed determination, deepened sensitivity, and humility. It builds true character. In this way Reverence for Life allows for larger social and ecological visions to become manifested through its "microscopic" and individualized focus. It aims to change hearts and minds.

Using this criterion and Schweitzer's life and works, an informal scale of responsibility and prioritization can be discerned. Nevertheless, the taking of life is never justifiable in the sense that consequentialism presents its logic, for the same action may serve or act against the actualization of the Reverence for Life ethic at different times or in different challenges to human conscience and rationalized egotism. Moreover, all decisions that take life incur a debt – always. Only those actions that serve to redress suffering or to promote the Reverence for Life ethic itself can serve as partial payment in a never-ending atonement consisting of lifelong devotion. Schweitzer himself stopped eating meat in the last few years of his life because he felt that he was no longer giving back enough to justify the death of a sentient animal merely to satisfy his palate. He ate lentil soup instead (Brabazon 2000, 495).

Nevertheless, Schweitzer could still be accused of a "debt mongering" that is not at all that far removed from those uncomfortable associations with guilt and shame mentioned earlier. True enough. It could even be said that Schweitzer indulges a certain sermonizing in his philosophy that is not likely to convert those who are not already among his readership. But none of this should be seen as a flaw in his work. Particularly in environmental literature, many great and respected thinkers have proposed "new cosmologies," all of which serve to conjure in the mind a sense of greater connection and responsibility to the world of nature. Thomas Berry, Brian Swimme, and Peter G. Brown are just a few of the names in this emergent field. While some are more mystical than others, they all tend to draw equally on insights from ecology, as they do from theoretical physics, philosophy, and religion. They all also engage in an implicit (although not heavy-handed) "should-type" moralizing that implores their readers to change their economic lifestyles to help safeguard the environment. Schweitzer's own views on life-debt and Reverence for Life should be considered in that same light. It, too, is a new cosmology, and similarly voluntarist. Schweitzer never berated his reader to drop everything and join him in Africa. He knew few people would be willing or able to devote themselves selflessly to others. Instead, his virtue ethic came with an unspoken scale of actualization: Reverence for Life was an exhortation, a call to ever greater conscientious moral action – whatever that may be for any particular person. Schweitzer merely wants his reader to have an attitude of openness towards ethical progress. He believes that, with this beginning and through the influence of moral exemplars like himself, the course of civilization can be changed for the better. But there is yet another, more fundamental, problem with his philosophy that must now be examined.

A New Problem?

The basis for Schweitzer's essentialist understanding of human nature originates in Schopenhauer, who had turned to the study of causality in time (etiology) as a way of mitigating subjectivity and to demonstrate that causality exists outside the perceiving self. But when it came to the study of living beings, Schopenhauer first had to establish the will-to-live in the subjective self and then to infer its existence in outer phenomena, "the direct knowledge of which lies nearest to us ... [and] leads to the indirect knowledge of all the others" (*WWR-2* §22, 111). This is perhaps the weakest point of Schopenhauer's philosophy. He can only argue as follows: "Knowledge of the identical in different phenomena and of the different in similar phenomena is, as Plato so often remarks, the condition of philosophy. But hitherto the identity of the inner essence of any striving and operating force in nature with the will [in the inner self] has not been recognized" (111). He thus concludes that the phenomenal other is *essentially* the same as the experiencing self. But this is not proof, only uncritical inference.

Understandably, Nietzsche attacks Schopenhauer on this very point. Nietzsche makes his Will to Power not a unitary force but, rather, myriad and competing forces both outside and inside the experiencing self. And so, "to every soul there belongs another world; for every soul, every other soul is an afterworld" (*PN-TSZ III* "The Convalescent" §2, 329). Michel Foucault (1984), taking his cue from Nietzsche, declares that nothing at all exists that can serve as the basis for an essentialist ontology, for "nothing in man – not even his body – is sufficiently stable to serve as the basis for self-recognition or for understanding other men."[42] Much of Nietzsche's philosophy of the Will to Power is an outgrowth of and reaction to Schopenhauer's philosophy of the Will: where Schopenhauer has Platonic Idealism underlying phenomena, a unitary cosmological Will, an ethic of compassion, and bodily asceticism, Nietzsche upheld the Heraclitean chaos of the sense world, manifold naturalistic wills, Darwinian competition, and a Dionysian life-embrace. His work changed philosophy forever.

Nietzsche unfroze the river of becoming, and humanity has been washed into a postmodern sea. Interpersonal disclosure proceeds through the medium of language signs. Each body is like a text written in memory and enclosed in words: the "essence" of humanity and community is generated through and accorded with ever-changing and evolving cultural narratives. Belonging and identification within a group involves the process of self-inscribing into these cultural stories. The self is thereby read *into* these texts, erasing and transcribing elements of the particular for a sense of the new essence created interpersonally with the other-worldly other. There is no other essence to humanity than this. Arguably, this anti-essentialist turn in philosophy can be traced to Nietzsche – but was he right to reject essentialism entirely? This last question is addressed in the next chapter, where I turn to specific criticisms of Schweitzer's philosophy.

Conclusions

I have outlined Schweitzer's New Rationalism project, showing how it presents a new description of consciousness that is different than the one established by Descartes. It was also shown to support a type of virtue ethics. This new beginning was needed to rid European philosophy of its biases against non-human life and to substantiate the claim that the sublime of compassion creates a real connection to another life. But this creates a particular problem for philosophy: essentialism. Nietzsche had undermined the postulate established by Kant that all humans shared a similar inner essence (a priori time), which he called the soul. Schweitzer not only brings this old idea back, but he actually extends it to become a common essence for all life, plants and animals included!

More than anything else, this is perhaps the single most objectionable aspect of Schweitzer's work for academics today. Before such a bold new postulate can ever be taken seriously, it will have to be proven by painstaking philosophical argumentation how it overcomes Nietzsche's challenge to Kant since this is now the prevailing truth in academia. The next chapter will take an in-depth look at all the related questions involved here, from essentialism to the metaphysics of compassion. This will also be an opportunity to further explore the subject of apophatic hermeneutics and how Schweitzer's works resonate with those of Jean-Luc Marion. In turn, the discussion will lead to another question that all the previous chapters have only partially addressed. This is the subject of Schweitzer's own religious worldview and how that does, or does not, inform his Reverence for Life ethic. All these topics will be looked at next as the discussion now turns to metaphysics and mysticism.

Chapter 5

Metaphysics and Mysticism

The New Rationalism project arose from Schweitzer's scholarly work on the New Testament, and this raises several important questions. First and foremost are the philosophical problems associated with essentialism, a theory that has fallen out of favour in contemporary academic circles. Frankly, the New Rationalism may come across as outmoded and unsupportable because of certain basic assumptions that anchor mainstream hermeneutical and phenomenological theory. One of my aims in this chapter is to show that Schweitzer's work should not be seen as conflicting with these modern theories and that he deserves continued academic consideration. Next is the question of whether the New Rationalism project is inherently religious. My position, repeated throughout these opening chapters, is that Reverence for Life (the elemental nature philosophy) is secular, while only Ethical Mysticism, which emerges from the New Rationalism, can become a religious worldview even though it is itself not necessarily religious.

But my answers to these questions need to be carefully nuanced because certain metaphysical principles can be referred to as "theological" in one very specific sense, an Aristotelian sense. Another complicating factor is that it is notoriously difficult to distinguish between what is a religious belief and what is a secular belief. It all depends on how the terms are defined, and this quickly moves the question into a technical mire about words themselves. As this chapter turns to that more in-depth investigation of the New Rationalism, I will try to approach these issues without becoming overly bogged down in legalistic nuance. In brief, I conclude that the essentialism of the New Rationalism project is not something that should be dismissed by hermeneutical and phenomenological philosophers, even though it is "onto-theological," to use Heidegger's term to describe Aristotelian-inspired metaphysics. And while the New Rationalism supports a kind of mysticism that is not inherently Christian or religious in any traditional sense, admittedly this conclusion may strike some readers as perplexing. I therefore offer how it *could* be called a "religion of nature," to use a phrase now popular in academia, even though I do not believe this description is particularly helpful.

The Philosophy of the Pre-Rational

To begin with, it must be kept in mind that Schweitzer's Reverence for Life ethic is grounded in pre-rational intuitions. This is a subject virtually (but not entirely) ignored in Western philosophy. Schopenhauer discovered something in Kant's epistemology that permitted him to develop his ethics of compassion from an intuitive basis. This is also what allowed Schweitzer to secure a type of mysticism that could inform a person's conscience and give him or her ethical guidance. In brief, and before I turn to a more detailed analysis, it should be kept in mind that the pre-rational describes a range of psychological phenomena that has its origin in certain limitations and common predispositions of the human brain.

Kant once declared that "intuitions [from the senses] without [accompanying rational] concepts are blind" (Kant 2007, 93; B75/A51). It is a curious statement and quite noteworthy. What he is saying is that much more comes to the rational mind than the intellect can fully comprehend. Stated another way, Kant is conceding that people are actually blind to the full experience of the natural world because of the brain's limited perceptual capacities. But those sensory intuitions still exist: we feel them. They just do not correspond to an isolatable and discrete rational concept fully available to the analytical mind.

Nevertheless, Kant did try to examine one of these unconceptualized intuitions: the sublime. Schopenhauer made special note of this in section 39 of *The World as Will and Representation*: "The impression of the sublime can arise ... whose immensity reduces the [sense of self for an] individual to nought" (*WWR* 205). Put simply, there can arise in consciousness a peculiar feeling in response to certain sensory experiences that overwhelm the intellect's faculties. For example, the vast and terrible impression that comes over a person when witnessing an approaching tornado. It is an experience in which rational consciousness is obliterated before the inhuman and incomprehensible power of nature. Kant refers to this as the "dynamical" sublime. A similar feeling of raw selfless perception can also arise when confronted with the enormity of a phenomenon – for example, a breathtaking vista overlooking a ravine framed by sheer cliffs. This is the "mathematical" sublime. The sense of self can momentarily evanesce in sheer wonderment and awe in such settings; in effect, the intellect steps aside (as it were) and the sensory experiences are intuited pre-rationally. Only later do we come up with words and descriptions that attempt to convey to others what we experienced. But whereas Kant's sublime points to a super-sensuous substratum of Nature that is "beyond all measure" of the senses (*EF* 323), Schopenhauer's sublime includes a *sub-intelligible* aspect revealed to the pre-rational part of our consciousness.

Schweitzer's Ethical Mysticism is based, in part, on Schopenhauer's description of the pre-rational sublime. Specifically, for Schweitzer it is the sublime that arises in us when we perceive suffering in another sentient being: the initial horror at seeing someone in deep pain can affect us in a very peculiar way. This feeling becomes the doorway to a kind of mysticism that conveys a sense that all life shares a common essence, such that as one suffers so does the other. A profound ethical disposition can then emerge from that awareness, and this, in turn, can inform a person's conscience and guide him ethically. But in order to establish this, Schweitzer needs Schopenhauer's groundbreaking work, which had made certain important advancements on Kant's philosophy, including this one (*WWR* §39, 206–7):

> The sublime can indeed be extended to cover the ethical, namely
> what is described as the sublime character ... Such a character
> will accordingly consider men in a purely objective way, and
> not according to the relations they might have to his will [and
> intentions]. For example, he will observe their faults, and even their
> hatred and injustice to himself, without being thereby stirred to
> hatred on his own part ... For, in the course of his own life and in its
> misfortunes, he will look less at his own individual lot than at the
> lot of mankind as a whole, and accordingly will conduct himself in
> this respect rather as a knower [of sublime ethical truth] than as a
> [self-centred, egotistical] sufferer.

It is noteworthy that, for Schopenhauer, the sublime can also be found in the ordinary experience of the natural world, for example, during peaceful nature walks. The sublime becomes a catharsis for the mind, a therapeutic encounter needed to restore the normal and healthy operation of the brain – to cleanse it of the noise and clutter associated with the unnatural urban creations of so-called civilized life (*WWR* II, §33, 403). An appreciation of Schopenhauer's work renders intelligible much of what Schweitzer writes about in *The Philosophy of Civilization*. Yet Schweitzer's reliance on Schopenhauer also made him a magnet for criticism by some academics today.

The Charge of Philosophical Shortcomings

One of the most penetrating and perceptive criticisms of Schweitzer's Reverence for Life ethic is set forth by Ara Paul Barsam (2008). He questioned how a person can bring forth his or her own inner self as an object of representation for the knowing mind. This revisits the "new problem" of essentialism identified at the end of the last chapter and strikes at the very heart of Reverence for Life because, as Barsam writes, "following Schopenhauer, Schweitzer sees this [will-to-live theory] as the basis on which the knowing subject understands itself as identical with the [universal] will [and] as thing-in-itself" (10). The underlying difficulty here, according to Barsam, is the idea of "direct cognitive contact with the [Kantian] thing-in-itself inside us" (10).

The exact basis for his criticism is not revealed. Barsam appears to be relying on the commentaries by the hermeneutic philosopher Martin Heidegger who had argued that the there-beingness (*Dasein*) of rational consciousness is a psychological projection unable to fathom its own origins. According to this line of thought, what is actually being contemplated cannot be the Kantian thing itself but only a rational concept invented by the mind. As such, Barsam appears to conclude that Schweitzer fails to identify a true *pre-rational* essence for life. We are thus pushed back to the original Cartesian claim that only species with rational minds and who are capable of conceptual knowledge can be the subjects for philosophy and ethics. Barsam (2008, 10) thus concludes that, "as an exercise in metaphysics, Schweitzer's doctrine of the will as thing-in-itself is flawed ... [and] collapses under analytical probing."

Barsam (2008, 10) argues that the real issue here resides with Schopenhauer, upon whom Schweitzer relied (see also Barsam 2002, 218). Curiously though, he does not identify this as a critical structural flaw that sinks Reverence for Life before it can set sail; rather, he takes Schweitzer as presenting the universal Will and the will-to-live as being "theological concepts and not solely philosophical ones" (Barsam 2008, 6). With this revisionist twist, Barsam proceeds to recast the will-to-live as merely a spiritual "analogy" used to transfer the sense of self to another life though sympathy and compassion (14). With this change in place, he says the whole world can then be seen as a manifestation of the will-to-live, where every other being is now *imagined* as another "self" since, "although this may sound like radical subjectivity, Schweitzer believed (and needed to believe) everyone *would* recognize this feeling" (14 [emphasis in original]) of altruistic sympathy for other life as if it were affecting one's own self. Barsam describes the analogy as a psychological trick based in ecstatic religion to create an emotional attachment, and he argues that this is precisely how Schweitzer intended to draw persons into an ethical relationship with the rest of the world.

To summarize Barsam's argument, he criticizes the philosophical will-to-live theory for being, simultaneously, the ultimate object of inner subjectivity and an ascription of objects in the phenomenal world. Put simply, just as the tongue cannot taste itself, so too it is claimed that the mind does not have access to its pre-cognitive origins. But, as outlined in the previous chapter, Schweitzer's hermeneutical understanding of consciousness accounts for the historical and cultural factors that shape personal identity, and it does so in a way that allows for cognitive contact with the Kantian thing in itself at the heart of consciousness. Schweitzer is able to do this, as well as to extend recognition of the will-to-live for other life, through Schopenhauer's philosophy. This is something he specifically indicates in the following passage: "The world, [Schopenhauer] says, I can understand only by *analogy* with myself. Myself, when looked at from outside, I conceive as a physical phenomenon in space and time, but looked at from within, as will-to-live. Everything, accordingly, which meets me in the world of phenomena is a manifestation of the will-to-live" (*POC* 237 [emphasis added]).

The criticisms of Barsam take on a new light in terms of these findings. He is certainly right in saying it is by way of an "analogy" that the experiences of the other are perceived as affecting the will-to-live in one's inner self. But this is not a psychological trick, nor is it romanticism run amok or any kind of theological postulate; rather, Schweitzer is relying upon Schopenhauer's ground-breaking work, which established the will-to-live as the essence of both the self and the other.

To state this another way, the analogy mentioned above concerns how Schopenhauer escaped "the lair of the skull,"[43] which is to say, how he dispelled the Cartesian doubt about the reality of the natural world as it appears to human perception. Philosophy has always struggled with the problem of solipsism (i.e., the possible unreality of the outer world), and Schopenhauer acknowledges the weak non-definitive nature of his argumentation. But he contends that "theoretical egoism" (solipsism) is merely rhetorical deceit and that, "as a serious conviction ... it could only be found in a madhouse" (*WWR*-2 §19, 104). The reality of the external world must be conceded if philosophy is to be taken seriously, and this holds true even if its existence can only be established by way of Schopenhauer's analogy to the experiencing self.

Empirical science supports and confirms the cosmological claim that the will-to-live exists externally to the experiencing self. All species are given an orientation to life through the biological will-to-live, and there is an identifiable will-to-live for each and every life form in nature – what we today call DNA. Scientific findings also support the view that there is/are an evolutionary force(s), which Schweitzer poetically interprets as a Creative Force. Schweitzer follows Nietzsche in interpreting science through an "artistic lens" to create a life-affirming cultural truth. He feels he can do this because of the mystery of life as it appears from the perspective of a person's life-view. For Schweitzer, the questions of why anything exists at all, of why life should strive to perpetuate itself against all the natural forces set against it, and of why people should seek deeper meaning in an apparently meaningless cosmos are scientifically unanswerable. All we can know for certain is what is contained within our will-to-live – that life itself is good and that "evil is what annihilates, hampers, or hinders life" (*E-RFL*, 230). This is all the direction we need in life in order to become ethical beings.

The analogy employed by Schopenhauer allowed him to conduct an analysis of causality in the natural world from a philosophical perspective and thereby establish the existence of a cosmological Will. The analogy also allows him to argue that this unitary Will is a common essence for all phenomenal reality. For Schopenhauer, the cosmological Will is the Kantian thing in itself, which Heidegger insists does not exist. This brings us to the key issue with respect to Barsam's criticism of Schweitzer: essentialism.

Nietzsche would attack the idea of a common essence to humanity, and Schweitzer was not ignorant of this. He was also acutely aware that the natural evolutionary forces are myriad, not a single thing called causality. This is why he considered the hermeneutical analysis of being to be so crucial. He needed a defensible first principle for ontological consciousness, and he established it by having the first fact of consciousness the

"I + will-to-live" nexus. Schweitzer's essentialism is therefore not based on the Kantian soul as a common and simple essence of humanity but, rather, on Schopenhauer's Will. Schweitzer's ontology also reflects the complexity of biological and cultural factors that makes each person a unique phenomenon, just as Nietzsche argues. Yet he also believed that no life is entirely alien to another. This then is his true reason for adopting Schopenhauer's epistemological analogy. It is what allows him to keep the door open to the essentialism that applies to all life and that may be experienced through the sublime of compassion.

Nevertheless, it could still be said that Schweitzer stands on no firmer ground than does Schopenhauer. Schweitzer begins with the "I + will-to-live" first fact of consciousness. He then uses an analogy of what is experienced within a person's consciousness and extrapolates it to confirm the existence of other wills-to-live externally. Ethical Mysticism then provides a path for a particularized being to experience unity with that Being that is established through epagoge and that is confirmed through the pre-rational intuition of the sublime. Schweitzer thereby unifies the head (through epagoge) and the heart (through the sublime). The resultant essentialism then sets the stage for Reverence for Life to become a virtue ethic that can support a culturally determined a priori value system synthetically united under the New Rationalism. Even so, we still have to ask, are Schweitzer's arguments about essentialism *necessarily* true?

An elemental nature philosophy is one claim, and one that can be defended as being coherent, self-consistent, and grounded in a first principle of cosmological causality. But an "apophatic hermeneutics" founding a New Rationalism that supports an essentialist ontology for all life, that is another matter altogether. In the end, all we can say is that essentialism is a life-affirming possibility arising from the "I + will-to-live" nexus in rational consciousness. For Nietzsche, the validity of any truth claim is found in life-affirmation. And, to use his words, "who could venture to denigrate those means?" By this measure, the essentialism of Reverence for Life cannot be dismissed as a mere analogy romanticising the imagined experiences of other life but, rather, must be regarded as a true and real foundation for ethics. Against the seas of nihilism, and in the chaotic waters of postmodernity, Schweitzer offers humanity a trustworthy and secure ground for a new philosophy of civilization.

This is my assessment. But, as mentioned at the beginning of this chapter, since Schweitzer's time academia has moved on to other theories — theories that, in some very significant ways, are quite different from his. This brings us to our next question: How does Schweitzer's work compare to that of these other thinkers? It is my belief that the New Rationalism project is a valuable complement to modern phenomenological and hermeneutical research because it offers certain advantages that the latter do not. With this in mind, I now provide a brief overview of modern hermeneutics and phenomenology as they relate to Schweitzer's elemental New Rationalism.

The Untimely Rebirth of First Philosophy

The epistemological project begun by Descartes became greatly complicated by Nietzsche. The seemingly modest claim of a common ontological self-awareness for every human being in Descartes' famous first principle ("I think therefore I am") was no longer credible. The Cartesian ego had been assumed to be something shared by all people, or at least by those adults with normal and healthy brains capable of recursive self-reflection. This later became the basis for the Kantian conception of the soul, the ultimate object of inner sense. Because of Descartes, Kant considered that point of conscious self-awareness, that "perpetual now" that opens up in the mind for rational reflection (*topos noētos*), to be a simple essence whose form was a priori time. But Nietzsche had revealed just how much biological factors, cultural influences, and historicity come to bear on even that first moment of ontological self-awareness. Put simply, due to the great diversity of these influences taking place in each person's mind, it could no longer be claimed that everyone's experience of consciousness was identical. The Transcendental *I* suddenly became an unsuitable starting point for philosophy. Nietzsche had, in effect, thrown the entirety of Western philosophical tradition right back to the proverbial drawing board. The search had to begin anew for a new ontological first principle.

Out of this maelstrom of re-evaluation two figures in particular would emerge to offer possible solutions. The first is the phenomenology of Edmund Husserl (1859–1938) and the second is the hermeneutics of Martin Heidegger (1889–1976), Husserl's erstwhile student. Husserl and Heidegger each developed a new understanding of recursive self-awareness that more fully reflected the true complexity of that experience, while, at the same time, isolating a particular state of consciousness that could serve as a universal starting point for a comprehensive study of the human condition. Their different but complementary systems offered theoretical frameworks that could support entirely new investigations and reveal fascinating new insights never attempted before. It was like academics had found an undiscovered frontier in which each professor could stake out his or her own unexplored area. Philosophy had been reborn. There even emerged the possibility of establishing a new "first philosophy" over and against the empirical sciences.

But before I turn to that last point, where the work of Schweitzer fits into all this needs to be discussed a little further. His description of the first fact of consciousness, as has already been outlined, reflected the complexity of our biological and cultural life, yet he also showed how people all share the will-to-live as common essence. He likewise emphasizes our embodied experience: we are mortal beings who possess a unique ontological freedom born both of our rationality and our pre-rationality. This places his work in comparative relation to the two figures just mentioned. But Husserl's system is phenomenological – meaning that the key problem for him is how the phenomenal world appears to an experiencing subject. It is the Cartesian project taken up anew. And, like Descartes, Husserl assumes that the external non-self world simply could not be definitively proven to exist. And so, while Buffon and Schopenhauer use physics to mitigate subjectivity, the phenomenologists either would not do this or failed to consider this approach at all. Rather, their Cartesian scepticism necessitates that all the world be considered as merely phenomena. Husserl advances from this meagre starting point by considering the psychosomatic unity of the embodied subject who experiences the world through his or her own flesh, the very instrument by which sensory information is intuited by the mind. Stated another way, for Husserl, the body of the self is already implicated in perception: "First of all, it is flesh that is the *means* [*Mittel*] *of all perception* ... It is the means that everything that appears [to the mind] has *eo ipso* [by itself] a relationship to [the] flesh [of the self]" (Marion 2002, 89 [emphasis in original]). He anticipates the existentialists, who also begin with the experience of existence rather than searching for a metaphysical first principle. It was an improvement on Descartes. But for Heidegger, his former mentor did not go far enough in bringing the external world into the domain of philosophy.

Nevertheless, in seeking to advance Husserl's work, Heidegger could not break free of his phenomenological spell. Like Husserl, he regards the empirical world as epistemologically dubious. He instead asserts that certain aspects of external reality become entwined with consciousness as experiencing subjects regard the non-self objects and daily circumstances of their lives. Stated another way, the there-beingness of life already has a social world incorporated into that first moment of self-awareness – or, as he himself writes with regard to the constitution of *Dasein*: "Ahead of itself Being already in the world [is] as Being alongside entities encountered within the world" (Gelven 1989, 121). Behind his characteristically peculiar manner of expression is a simple premise: to be human is to be concerned with many things external to the self. For example, the inner life of a person may be informed by such seemingly random concerns as the condition of his or her backyard garden or how to pay next month's bills. In this subtle way, Heidegger brings the non-self world more fully into that first moment of self-awareness. Yet, and despite the great diversity of factors that influence a person's state of consciousness, he could still claim that the particular mode of awareness that opens up rational reflection within each and every experiencing subject is the a priori existential of *Dasein* and that, consequently, this mode of being would be universal for all people. *Dasein* as *Dasein* thereby became a new first principle for a post-Nietzschean hermeneutical philosophy. This is (arguably) an improvement on Husserl's work, and at its heart is the claim that ontology is prior to epistemology. As such, Heidegger further subsumes (or so he believed) the natural sciences to hermeneutical philosophy. The stage was now set for the ascendance of a new "first philosophy" in academia.

Notably, both Husserl and Heidegger draw upon certain insights of, and claims made by, ancient Greek philosophers. Particularly important is Aristotle, for whom all the regional sciences, everything from medicine to astronomy, were linked together and subsumed under one theory. Metaphysics for Aristotle was a first philosophy that governed the "second philosophies" of science, politics, poetics, and so on. The place of metaphysics was of such cosmological importance that he even referred to it as a theology. And thanks to him all philosophers henceforth had a position of unique authority as the world's intellectuals par excellence – that is, until the emergence of empirical science in the modern era. For the public at large today, when it comes to answering questions pertaining to the basic facts about the world, scientists are seen as the only qualified judges of truth. It is certainly no longer the philosophers to whom most people turn, and it is most definitely not the theologians! The suggestion that the scientist of today is *merely* a natural philosopher would only bring a condescending smile to his or her face. The sciences are wholly autonomous and, for the most part, not at all interested in metaphysics. This has been a disconcerting turn of events for many philosophers. Jean-Luc Marion (2002, 1), for example, openly worries:

[Because] each of the sciences has gained, at different moments, but always according to an irrepressible forward motion, an apparently definitive autonomy from philosophy, in such a way that not only no single one acknowledges toward philosophy any other debt than a historical one ... [With] all the positive areas [for scientific investigation] having found a taker [by a respective scientific discipline], the question would rather be to see if there remains a proper area for philosophy anymore.

These are demoralizing words. Besides ethics, what is left for the philosopher today? Even then, evolutionary sociobiology and other such sciences are attempting to situate ethics entirely within naturalism. The implication is that, since at least the time of Nietzsche, philosophy has been slowly dying off, that an inexorable decline has increasingly marginalized its role in academia. Against this emergent reality some suspect that a sort of coup has taken place. Science itself is now positioned as the first philosophy, with hermeneutics being relegated to a secondary and dependent status within the historical sciences and with phenomenology having no place at all anymore. Not surprisingly, there are those who would like to turn the tables and reassert philosophy to its former priority over such "regional affairs" as biology and physics – which is to say, they would like philosophy to once again have sole authority for establishing the epistemological preconditions for all scientific knowledge and, moreover, to "have at its disposal a domain and operations ... [that would] impose themselves as the condition of possibility of all other knowledge" (3). For Husserl and Heidegger this was an explicit aim of their work.[44] Now it is the strict "social constructionists" who are championing this exclusive status over the domain of truth.[45] Still, it should be remarked that not all philosophers are threatened by science. Schweitzer, for one, was most definitely not. And, simply put, this is where I believe his hermeneutics are especially helpful today.

Schweitzer's New Rationalism advances hermeneutical philosophy by keeping it elemental. This may seem an ironic statement, but it strikes to the heart of the serious problems I detect in the various "first philosophy" undertakings described earlier. Schweitzer is not interested in fanciful metaphysics or elaborate articulations of theory, not that he sees such projects as illegitimate (quite the opposite in fact), only that they are all incapable of becoming a living philosophy of the people. But there is another and more fundamental reason: Schweitzer wants to maintain a vital connection between philosophy and the natural sciences. As mentioned in chapter 1, when considering how facts are established in the sciences as opposed to how they are established in the humanities, Schweitzer concludes that both sets of facts have to coexist side by side – and he further insists that academics must not be dismissive of the opposing side's viewpoint. By keeping his hermeneutic elemental, he could do this without subsuming one to the other.

Schweitzer's elemental thinking is revealed in his transformation of Schopenhauer's will-to-live theory and Darwin's social instincts. Darwin had shown how social instincts were both evolutionarily based yet also dependent upon rational reflection to actualize within society. Schweitzer describes these natural instincts as being contained within the will-to-live, and they, in turn, influence the first fact of consciousness through the "I + will-to-live" nexus. Here it is important to note that Schweitzer does not claim a transcendental ego that would, in turn, make experience possible; rather, the first fact of consciousness arrives whole, singular, and uniquely specific to each person as *I will to live*. Only the will-to-live can be parsed out of that ontological state of being through Schopenhauer's etiology and analogy to the experiencing self. The will-to-live is only metaphysical in the strict Aristotelian sense, meaning that Schopenhauer uses the cosmological Will to describe the causes of things.[46] But it is not metaphysical in the more common usage of the term, which is to say something far-fetched and unprovable.

Schweitzer draws on the works of Schopenhauer and Nietzsche in order to establish the actual existence of the empirical world. For him it is simply not acceptable to regard external reality as merely insubstantial phenomena appearing in rational consciousness or as just hermeneutically meaningful aspects of the social world caught up in the initial constitution of *Dasein*. Natural science exists for Schweitzer as fully legitimate with no caveats whatsoever – only the ethical nihilism that emerges from its reductionist methodologies was considered by him as wrongheaded and dangerous. His elemental New Rationalism seeks only to create linkages between philosophy and natural science (see figure 1). Then, through the synthetic a priori and an apophatically informed analogy to the experiencing self, Ethical Mysticism emerges as a secondary and more expansive metaphysic that promotes life-affirmation and Reverence for Life cultural values. It always remains informed by science but is not limited to its unspoken nihilism. The New Rationalism is therefore no threat to declare itself as a first philosophy.

This, in my opinion, is Schweitzer's true genius.[47] His work is a keystone for empiricism and philosophical rationality, allowing each its own proper legitimacy without subsuming one within the other by means of an insurgent first philosophy. Phenomenology and hermeneutics can remain, and rightfully so, as the unquestioned theoretical models par excellence

Figure 1

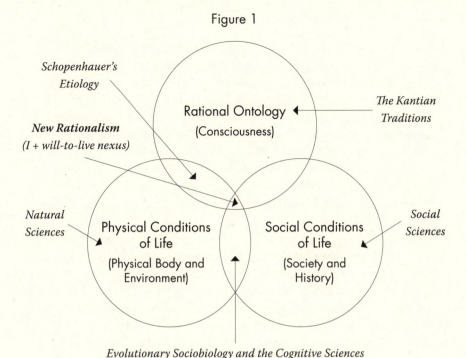

Evolutionary Sociobiology and the Cognitive Sciences

Notes

1 This figure is adapted from my earlier publication, *On First Principles* (Goodin 2010a).

2 The aim of this figure is to show the areas of overlap and exclusion in the scientific and philosophical investigations of life. The range and scale of these overlaps are not meant to be representatively depicted. For example, postmodern analysis can make (and has made) substantial contributions to our understandings of the natural body and the physical conditions of life from a cultural perspective. Graphically, however, it would be exceedingly problematic to try to give a relative and scaled representation of each field and subfield in relation to every other one.

3 Schweitzer's "I + will-to-live" nexus, as the linkage between all the disparate academic domains investigating internal and external reality, provides a means to begin reconciling the competing truth claims of these different fields. His work starts as an elemental nature philosophy in agreement with natural science. He then builds a secondary metaphysic from that basis. Ethical mysticism however never subsumes the facts of natural science to phenomenology or hermeneutics, but interprets scientific truths the way an artist finds meaning in the world, just as Nietzsche had once done. It is a hermeneutic therefore both in the original Greek meaning of the word as "to interpret," and also as philosophical discipline that examines how language and culture affect ontology.

for examining the social world of human subjective experience, while, in turn, each of the sciences rightfully partitions the natural world for its particularized studies. In our uniquely recursive self-awareness, there is enough distinction between the biological brain and the human mind for philosophy and science to each have its own proper domain. Schweitzer shows how they can come together at one critical point of intersection in the "I + will-to-live" first fact of rational consciousness.

But all this points to a more interesting question. Heidegger refers to metaphysics as "onto-theology" in homage to Aristotle's metaphysical theology. Schweitzer's ontology is indeed metaphysical in this limited Aristotelian sense.[48] So can it be said that there is a hidden theology present here too? My position, repeated throughout these opening chapters, is that Reverence for Life is not theological, that it is in fact a secular philosophy. However, it is not possible to always clearly demarcate between the two in any given situation, let alone in Schweitzer. As I now turn to the question of religion and theology as it relates to Schweitzer's philosophy, it will quickly be observed that it all comes down to what exactly is meant by such terms as "theology," "religion," and "mysticism." Depending on how those words are defined, Reverence for Life is (or is not) all of those things. In what follows I seek to establish why I believe that Reverence for Life is best and properly understood as secular philosophy, while Ethical Mysticism may be considered a kind of mysticism that is not itself necessarily religious.

On the Subject of Religion

As any student of religious studies knows, the word "religion" is very hard to define. The problem is that, in an attempt to be inclusive of all those elements of religious expression found in historical and contemporary cultures, the definition becomes hopelessly vague. The simple word "religion" encompasses the atheistic Theravāda Buddhism at one end of the spectrum, and at the other end it describes the very cultural cohesiveness of a traditional society with an animistic worldview in which every part of daily life is informed with religious significance in some way or another. Only in modern industrialized societies does the idea of religion become separated from such daily activities as working, eating, recreation, and even hygiene. For this reason scholars have had to distinguish between what at first were presumed to be the original animistic religions of hunter-gatherer societies and what was assumed to be their cultural evolution into formal, textual-based and institutionalized religion such as found in the Judeo-Christian traditions. This understanding was later abandoned since it presuppose animism to be a primitive form of later ecclesial developments in those cultures that produced the same scholars studying these "traditional" societies. And so it is now fairly accepted practice to just speak of religions geographically and historically – the religions originating in the Middle East, for example.

Now with respect to the question: Is Reverence for Life religious? It all depends on what is meant. This investigation holds the definition of religion to mean that Reverence for Life is inseparable from an established world religion such as Christianity, or, as some have suggested, to Hinduism or Buddhism via Schopenhauer. My conclusion is that Reverence for Life is not dependent upon such religious underpinnings. Could it then be claimed that Reverence for Life is something akin to the animism of a traditional society wherein everything in one's life is informed by that worldview? My conclusion is that only Ethical Mysticism fits that category, but even then not necessarily so. A parent's devotion to his or her children is not animistic mysticism but something emerging from biology first. Likewise, Schweitzer's Ethical Mysticism emerges from Darwin's social instincts before it can be extrapolated into a religious worldview – or not, as the case may be. So again it is concluded that even the Ethical Mysticism of Reverence for Life is not religion. It is only something that may be brought into religion as a personal lived experience or left secular entirely, if the person so wishes.

All that being said, Schweitzer was a Lutheran minister and his hermeneutics did first emerge from his study of the historical Jesus. This makes the line of demarcation between religion and philosophy in Schweitzer's works very problematic. For this reason, many previous commentators have come to the conclusion that Reverence for Life is either a Christian ethic or some kind of universalist religion arising from Schweitzer's perspective on the historical Jesus and the apostle Paul. Yet, as I show in chapter 1, such language does not appear in Schweitzer's primary work on Reverence for Life, *The Philosophy of Civilization*.

How "Christian" is Reverence for Life is an important question to consider. As both a biblical scholar of historical criticism and a theologian, Schweitzer had a quite complex relationship to Christianity, and this is reflected in his writings. Another problem is that Christianity is itself a rather nebulous label, inclusive of many divergent forms of this religion. For example, if Christianity is defined traditionally, which is to say by those denominations that uphold the Nicene confessions of faith concerning the Trinitarian personhood of God, then Reverence for Life is most certainly neither Catholic nor Orthodox. But since Schweitzer was Lutheran, the real question is whether Reverence for Life is inherently Lutheran, or perhaps more narrowly definable as an expression of early twentieth-century Protestant religious thought.

Protestantism and Reverence for Life

At this point it is useful to compare Schweitzer to someone who is perhaps his closest contemporary in terms of both religion and worldview. Karl Barth (1886–1968) is also without a doubt the most important historical figure to have ever examined Schweitzer's work, yet, for the most part, his criticisms and commentary have been overlooked in subsequent scholarship. While the aim of the following discussion is to examine whether Reverence for Life is a form of Protestant Christianity, it also allows me to remedy this huge oversight in scholarship. The following discussion on the difference between theological ethics and Reverence for Life, while fascinating in its own right, also helps redress the lingering historical criticism that Schweitzer's work is merely errant sentimentality.

Barth (1961) takes up the question of Schweitzer's Reverence for Life ethic in his *Church Dogmatics*. From the outset, Barth indicates an irreconcilable problem with his fellow Protestant. He declares that the starting place for religious ethics cannot be what Schweitzer sets forth because "where Schweitzer places life we see the command of God" (324). Not only are Schweitzer's theological liberalism and views on the historical Jesus opposed to Barth's own Christology (which upholds more traditional perspectives on divine revelation), but Schweitzer's Reverence for Life project develops from philosophical meditations on the mystery of life – not the Gospels. Nevertheless, Barth is willing to consider Schweitzer's Reverence for Life ethic seriously. His comments and criticisms are revealing.

Barth (1961, 333) begins by indicating: "we shall have to remember that with human life as our real problem, we must take seriously the problem of animals (and a certain sense even of plants) as a marginal problem for ethics." Barth writes that people can indeed seriously err before the eyes of God with respect to the improper treatment of non-human life. He even recognizes that humankind could ruin the global environment by perpetrating "so much senseless waste and destruction from which a reverent humanity should refrain in this sphere and of which it has obviously been guilty to its own destruction" (351). So too, of ethics, Barth writes that it is possible to "murder an animal" if the killing is not performed with a reverential attitude towards God (355). He further warns that killing an animal "is at least very similar to homicide" and that, because of this, humankind's dominion over nature comes with the terrible knowledge that each and every killing is the "annihilation ... of a single being, a unique creature existing in an individuality which we cannot fathom but also cannot deny" (352). This special relationship between humankind and animal life is underscored in exceptionally stark language: "Whenever man exercises his lordship over the animal, and especially across every hunting lodge, abattoir and vivisection chamber, there should be written in letters of fire the words of St. Paul in [Romans 8:18] ... concerning the 'earnest expectation' [apokaradokia] of the creature – for what? – for the 'manifestation of the children of God,' and therefore for the liberation of those who now keep them imprisoned and even dispatch them from life to death" (355).

These are quite amazing declarations, and at first glance would seem to put Barth on the same page as Schweitzer. But the argumentation substantiating these points comes from a very different set of premises, and this is where Barth's criticisms of Schweitzer come into play. They all come down to a simple problem: Barth is a theologian, and he attacks Schweitzer for not establishing his ethics as would be expected of one. In Barth's (1961, 326) opinion, Schweitzer and all those who advocate a naturalistic ethic are "tyrannically" elevating life as it is revealed in creation to become "the actual ethical lord, teacher and master of man." This is not acceptable to Barth for several reasons. For one thing, "the Word of God is addressed to man ... [and] man is not addressed concerning animal and vegetable life, nor life in general, but concerning his own human life" (323–4). Nevertheless, the human being does not exist independently from other people; rather, "man's creaturely existence as such is not his [own] property; it is a loan ... in the broadest sense it is meant for the service of God" (327). And this service is to be expressed in light of the fact that "man is determined for fellowship" with others (332). This is because, "as God addresses man, He also speaks to him through the solidarity which exists between him and other men" (331). It is in this sense, and in this sense only, that human actions towards non-human life become a subject for theological ethics. People are charged with duties to the plant and animal world because of humankind's overall communitarian responsibility to other persons and their greater service to God. While plants and animals are morally considerable beings because of this circumstantial relationship, religious reverence must only be directed towards the Creator and never towards His creations (Romans 1:25).

Schweitzer, in contrast, does consider each and every life to be intrinsically morally considerable, and not because it is circumstantially related to human affairs. And he actually reverences this life, not the Creator. This is a direct contravention of the scriptural prohibition in Romans 1:25. Plainly enough, this is not a Christian theological argument as is the one set forth by Barth – not even close. And, while Barth agrees with Schweitzer that non-human life is indeed a serious ethical consideration, he cannot join with him in "reverencing" life as such. Rather, Barth says the proper disposition is a "respect for life," and he subtitles this section (§55) of *Church Dogmatics* thusly to both honour Schweitzer and to critique his central thought with this turn of his phrase.

Nevertheless, Barth's deep respect for Schweitzer leads him to defend him against the charge of sentimentality and the alleged impracticability of his Reverence for Life ethic. The key passage reads as follows: "We certainly cannot dismiss it [Reverence for Life] as 'sentimental.' Nor may we take the easy course of questioning the practicability of the instructions given, let alone the wider consequences and applications. The directness of the insight and feeling revealed (not unlike those of Francis of Assisi), and the constraint expressed, are stronger than such criticism. Those who can only smile at this point are themselves subjects for tears" (Barth 1961, 349).

Barth goes on to recount a story about a German theologian, who, during the First World War, felt compelled to travel whenever he could to a certain weir near Bamberg to rescue snails that would be caught in it and perish. Barth writes that even in this "bizarre action" there was sublime nobility (350). As for the central question of what demands non-human life can place on humanity to redress its suffering, Barth concludes, "it may well be insolvable and barely tangible, but it is genuine and cannot be ignored" (350). Barth insists that Reverence for Life cannot be discredited as errant sentimentality, even though its highest ideals may seem overly romantic and impracticable. While Schweitzer's moral compass may not point in a direction that many willingly concede is a necessity of thought, it does indeed point truly.

Is Reverence for Life at All Biblical?

At this point it is fairly obvious that Schweitzer's Christianity is rather unorthodox. His letters to his future wife, Hélène Bresslau, confirm this in very personal confession. While undoubtedly meant playfully, he wrote to Hélène that an eternity in heaven with saints Loyola and Jerome would be unbearable: "No, I decline. Rather to hell. The crowd will be much more congenial. With Julian the Apostate, Caesar, Socrates, Plato, and Heraclitus one can have a decent conversation" (*Letter* 54). Even more noteworthy is a letter from 1902. After reading Ignatius of Antioch in Greek and becoming quite frustrated with his hatred of the visible world, Schweitzer responds: "The saint would not be pleased with me if he knew how much nature distracted me. Is it strength or weakness to live in such a mystical union with nature, to feel the effects of its smile and tears deeply in one's soul?" (43). But perhaps the most sensational of all, in a letter from 1904 (53), Schweitzer ponders whether atheism should be considered a religion – after all, did not Jesus himself die an atheist when he asked on the cross why God had forsaken him?[49] His frustration with tradition and orthodox faith would seem at first glance to suggest Schweitzer was at heart an agnostic. But he still preached, and preached sincerely, about creating the Kingdom of God on earth. In a letter from October of 1905 he passionately writes: "I know what revival is, for I feel that Jesus revived me when I was immersed in my scholarly research and He said to me, 'Go where I need you.' And I *will* follow him" (*Letters* 5 [emphasis in original]).[50] Schweitzer truly felt that his medical work in Africa was very much "serving at the outpost of the Kingdom of God" (28).

In light of all this, could a case be made that Reverence for Life is still biblical (however loosely defined) even if it falls short of being considered a full and true Protestant theology? At first glance there would seem to be a case for this. Timothy Dansdill (2007, 71) makes special note of a passage in *The Philosophy of Civilization* in which Schweitzer appears to endorse a Christian understanding of dominion over nature. In this passage Schweitzer discusses his vision of a new rationalist ethic emerging from the elemental nature philosophy Reverence for Life: "This leads to a lordship of the spirit over the powers of Nature, to the perfecting of the religious, social, economic, and practical association of men, and the spiritual perfecting of individuals and of the community" (*POC* 98). Dansdill takes the idiomatic language of lordship to mean that Schweitzer had given an "unwitting endorsement of the ethos of divine dominion," which is incompatible with the spirit of modern environmental ethics (75). He further notes how this apparent claim by Schweitzer hinders its popular acceptance in today's increasingly secularized society. Not only that, deference to scriptural authority would greatly undermine Schweitzer's assertion that Reverence for Life is somehow a necessity of logical thought (78).

Dansdill is certainly correct in saying that Schweitzer often promotes an anthropocentric vision with respect to non-human nature and that he gives the human species special and elevated standing in relation to the rest of the natural world. But this cannot be the "dominion" from the Genesis creation narratives. For one thing, as the Orthodox priest Igor Cvetkov charges: "Albert Schweitzer is not a theologian, because in his study of Christ he was not interested in Christianity but [only] in the person of Christ" (Kizima 2007, 97). While to say that Schweitzer was not interested in Christianity is an overstatement, the point remains that Schweitzer's scientifically minded understanding of religion allowed for no supreme deity and no special revelation to humanity through Holy Scriptures. For him, Jesus was an ordinary human being who possessed an unfathomably profound moral character.

So, what do we make of this? A key conclusion of this investigation concerns the interface between philosophy and religion, which is something that remains constant throughout Schweitzer's entire body of work. This is the idea of elemental morality, which he took from the works of Schopenhauer. Not only would this become the lens through which he would see his own Christian faith, but it was also the answer he needed to redress certain philosophical questions concerning the Reverence for Life ethic. Put simply, the common thread here is Schopenhauer, not Christ. This is because, in his critical analysis of Schopenhauer's philosophy, Schweitzer found a way to establish the interface between religion and philosophical ethics (POC 240). And, as discussed in chapter 4 in relation to *The Quest of the Historical Jesus*, this elemental thinking would become the philosophical lens through which Schweitzer saw his own faith (see also CRW 76–7). Schopenhauer also provided him with an ethical framework that enabled him to establish compassion as an elemental morality in harmony with both Jesus and evolutionary science. Schweitzer's Reverence for Life philosophy is therefore not secretly declaring that Christianity encompasses all other faiths, or that Schweitzer sees his brand of liberal Lutheranism as being inclusive of other scriptures and religions – quite the opposite in fact.[51] Rather, the claim is that the rootstock of Reverence for Life's elemental nature philosophy can be explicated as a worldview that is compatible with any world religion or with none at all. The common ground is established through secular philosophy before it becomes diversified and particularized for any given world culture. This is how Reverence for Life can become a philosophy for *all* civilizations, not just the Christian ones.

This fact is highlighted in one of the most important studies of the life and legacy of Schweitzer, which was prepared by Jackson Lee Ice. His nearly completed manuscript was edited and published posthumously in

1994 by his family and professional associates. The book represents three decades of Ice's research into several controversies that came to surround Schweitzer, including whether he believed in God at all. Ice concludes that Schweitzer held to no conception of the metaphysical divine, whether defined traditionally, as any kind of *Weltgeist* (pantheistic world spirit), or even as a sociological construct used "for the purpose of arousing religious emotions and ethical sentiments" (10). This last point, however, is not exactly correct since Schweitzer does use idiomatic references to religious themes throughout his works. But Ice is right that, even here, there is no sense that Schweitzer is drawing upon theistic authority; rather, he is merely illustrating a point through the use of widely known religious imagery and terms.

Schweitzer's metaphysics do not look past empirical reality. It is an elemental nature philosophy of the will-to-live as it becomes synthesized within ontological consciousness (the New Rationalism) that grounds a type of devotion he called a "mysticism of reality" (Ethical Mysticism). Ice (1994, 11 [emphasis added]) similarly concludes that "the knowledge of the will-to-live [is arrived at] through reason and *not* by revelation or faith." He supports his claim by pointing to Schweitzer's own comments in a personal letter written in response to a question regarding whether he believed that religion was necessary for Reverence for Life: "Hence there arises the question whether the religious ethic of Love is possible without the belief in an ethical God and World Sovereign, or knowledge of this God, which can be replaced by a belief in Him. Here I dare say that the ethical religion of love can exist without the belief in a world-ruling divine personality which corresponds to such an ethical religion" (9).

Put simply, the philosophical grounding of the elemental nature philosophy precedes its theological applications and not the other way around. Curiously, however, this is not Ice's final assessment. Even though he notes that the will-to-live concept emerges from philosophical reflection and not theology, because of what seems to him to be the apparent inconsistency of Schweitzer's arguments, Ice decides that the phrase "Reverence for Life" is holophrastic in that "it means and represents many things for Schweitzer" (12). Ice contextualized his conclusion this way because of certain of Schweitzer's comments that have been misunderstood by his contemporaries.

Take, for example, Schweitzer's famous declaration: "The ethic of Reverence for Life is the ethic of love widened into universality. It is the ethic of Jesus, now recognized as a logical consequence of thought" (*OLT* 232). Such talk, however, was saved for his autobiography. In his instructions to the publisher, dated 5 June 1931, Schweitzer indicates that the auto-biography is merely his own reflections and not a follow-up to his philo-sophical work. He therefore asks: "In advertising the work, please avoid anything noisy since this would not be in keeping with either the spirit of the book or me" (*Letters* 120). Rather, he says of the book: "Its mean-ing lies in the way it takes a position on the spiritual issues of our time by focusing on *one man's experiences*. It has turned into a kind of confession" (210 [emphasis added]). Caution is therefore required in trying to discern hidden meaning in *The Philosophy of Civilization* through the lens of his autobiography, especially with respect to any suspected Christian aims in his philosophical works. For Schweitzer, Reverence for Life harmon-izes with his Christian faith as *one man's experience*. He is certainly not saying that everyone had to become Christian before they could become ethical.

Reading Christianity into Schweitzer's philosophical works on Rever-ence for Life is like a botanist trying to establish the taxonomy of a species based on the characteristics of its flowers and fruit. What this fails to take into account is that the visible floral structures are supported by a differ-ent species of rootstock, upon which the Christian elements have been grafted. The interface of the philosophical with the religious in Schweit-zer's thought is one of the most distinctive aspects of his work, and it is also what is most perplexing to his readers.

Universalist Religion

Now we turn to the next possibility. If Reverence for Life is not Christian-ity, or is not even based in biblical authority, another possibility is that it is religious in some other way. This is Mike Martin's conclusion. Martin (2007, 32) finds that Reverence for Life becomes, in effect, a kind of bio-theism emerging from its metaphysics: "Although Schweitzer's spiritual beliefs are not pellucid, they veer toward biotheism: the view that all life in its creative aspects constitutes a sacred force – a universal, infinite Will to Live, of which each organism is a part." This is potentially problematic because the divine would be situated within the person and, at the same time, metaphysically connected to all other life. Nature, then, is as much God as the self is divine. This would make Reverence for Life not Chris-tianity but its own religion, potentially an elaboration of Schopenhauer's own distinctive interpretation of Buddhism.

Barsam (2002) reaches a similar conclusion, writing that Schweitzer's early exposure to Indian thought had a formative and lasting influence on him. In particular, Barsam detects a strong presence of the Jain doctrine of *ahimsa*, which upholds the ethical principle of non-violence for all sentient beings: "Schweitzer reacts to a great range of intellectual stimuli, assimilating, modifying, picking and choosing, and then gradually constructing his own ethics ... Among the significant influences of Jesus, St. Paul, and others, Schweitzer's rapport with Jainism and *ahimsa* helped him articulate and discern the meaning of 'reverence' [for all life]" (245).[52] The implication here is that Reverence for Life is, in effect, an eclectic mishmash of many religious doctrines that Schweitzer uniquely synthesizes into a new universalist religion in its own right. Moreover, this alleged "new religion" includes a strong bio-theistic character that arises from its secret Indian heritage. If correct, such devotional bio-theism would stand in considerable tension with traditional Western perspectives within Christianity and the other Abrahamic faiths. While philosophically inclined persons of any faith may not have a problem with any of this, Schweitzer's project to find ecumenical common ground through elemental morality would be greatly compromised if it *also* required people everywhere to convert to a brand new pantheistic religion of his own invention.

Thankfully, Schweitzer had something else in mind rather than any of these unappealing alternatives. It was not religious conversion he was after, but something that falls short of being considered a full religion: mysticism. He knew that a philosophical truth could not become a living ethic within society if it remained an academic formulation. Something else was needed to complement any academic expression of ethics: "Our great mistake ... is thinking that without mysticism we can reach an ethical world- and life-view, which shall satisfy [rational] thought" (*POC* 303). This is why his philosophy required a second step in the form of Ethical Mysticism.

It is this particular aspect of his work that has sown so much confusion about Reverence for Life. Ethical Mysticism, however, is not necessarily dependent on *religious* expression. As will be recalled from the previous chapter, what he wants for his reader is an "intellectual awakening." Likewise, he believes that the head and the heart must come together if one is to have a complete ethic. This is why he follows Schopenhauer in presenting mysticism as emerging from the pre-rational sublime, where it produces, to use Schopenhauer's expression, "an exaltation beyond our own individuality" (*WWR* §39, 206). This is where it begins. Where it ends depends entirely on the individual whose intellectual awakening, in turn, depends on his or her particular culture, history, and educational background. In the personal synthesis of Schweitzer's philosophy and the sublime, any number of religious or non-religious conceptions is possible, including pantheistic bio-theism. This is because a life-view is particular to each person and his or her cultural background. Schweitzer's claim to universality, however, only arises from its philosophical grounding, not from any of the possible expanded religious life-views.

Philosophical Theism

Now, if the focus moves away from Ethical Mysticism and back to the elemental nature philosophy from which it emerges, can we make the case that it is *itself* a philosophically oriented bio-theism, such as the kind that asks for devotion to an Absolute Being knowable through higher rationality – like, for example, the divine *Nous* of Plotinus? The answer here is less clear. As I briefly mention at the end of chapter 2, Schweitzer has no interest in reifying the conceptual abstractions of rational thought. Here are his comments on this issue (*POC* 304–5):

> The Essence of Being, the Absolute, the Spirit of the Universe, and all such similar expressions denote nothing actual, but something conceived in abstractions which for that reason is also absolutely unimaginable. The only reality is the Being which manifests itself in phenomena ... There is no Essence of Being, but only infinite Being in infinite manifestations. It is only through the manifestations of Being, and only with those which I enter into relations, that my being has intercourse with infinite Being.

Reverence for Life is indeed devotional, and it does seek to enter into a kind of communion with the essence of Being as it is revealed in individual life. But there is no ultimate "Being of beings" that could become a surrogate for an idea of God, however defined. Schweitzer's epagoge does not progress further than confirming a universal will-to-live: he does not reify this to then become the guarantor who bequeaths a soul to each new particularized being born into the world. There is no room here for Plato's Demiurge, Aristotle's unmoved mover, or Plotinus's One as an object of devotion. Schweitzer keeps his metaphysics and mysticism very elemental, very immediate to sensory intuition, and thus very trustworthy.

In addition, his elemental nature philosophy cannot itself be bio-theism because there is no actual "theism" here. Even when Schweitzer spoke of his own Christian faith, it was not really a theistic vision he promoted.

For him, "God" (I explain what he means by this in a moment) could only be known as a direct and personal experience, and this differs from how "God" is encountered impersonally in the external world of nature: "In the world He appears to me as the mysterious, marvellous creative Force; within me He reveals Himself as ethical Will" (CRW 76). From this quote it is evident that this so-called "God" is merely Schopenhauer's cosmological Will and nothing more. In nature it is an evolutionary creative force, but when this naturalistic Will becomes expressed in the "I + will-to-live" first fact of consciousness, it is then capable of becoming an ethical force.

Schweitzer describes the difference this way: "the God who is known through philosophy and the God whom I experience as ethical Will do not coincide. They are one; but how they are one, I do not understand" (CRW 77). While this indescribable mystery is an opening to the pre-rational intuitive ways of knowing mentioned in chapter 4, there is a very serious disconnect here between Schweitzer's elemental nature philosophy and the Christian God of revelation. They are not the same. Schweitzer can only present to his Christian audience a simile to try to show how they could possibly relate. He likens the idea of divinity to the warm Gulf Stream moving invisibly in the cold Atlantic Ocean. The waters move differently and with different qualities, yet they remain integrally together and singular: "Similarly, there is the God of love within the God of the forces of the universe – one with Him, and yet so totally different" (78; see also POC 79). This theistic language suggests, at least at a cursory glance, that his Christianity is a kind of pantheism with dualistic and monistic aspects. But in fact there is no God here at all, only the Heraclitean flux of naturalistic causality as it is uniquely manifested in rational consciousness. It is Schopenhauer's cosmological Will, which can become an ethical Will in persons. That is all.

It is only Christian in that Schweitzer identified the ethical Will as being the same as the one once experienced by the historical Jesus, who was for Schweitzer an ordinary human being and the most profound exemplar of compassionate love. Jesus could then become the focus of his own religious devotion. This is one possible extrapolation of the elemental nature philosophy, here in terms of a Christian cultural worldview. But even then it is quite noteworthy that not everything within traditional Christianity could be reconciled with his own Ethical Mysticism. No room remains for a personal God, a world Sovereign, an eschatological Judge, or even a miracle-working Messiah. There is only the inner voice of conscience that emerges within ontological consciousness due to the

Darwinian social instincts contained within our biological will-to-live. This is the same Ethical Force heeded by the historical Jesus, and it is the same for each person. It only becomes "divine" as one possible cultural life-view. For this reason, it cannot be claimed that Reverence for Life is necessarily bio-theistic or pantheistic. Ethical Mysticism can remain entirely atheistic and naturalistic.

A Religion of Nature

One last possibility still needs to be explored. Is the elemental nature philosophy – which is to say, the belief in a universal will-to-live and cosmological Will – something that would be called a "religion of nature" in its own right? This is an expression now popular in academia. It is used to describe, in a very generic manner, any nature spirituality that develops from an ideological way of seeing the world. An example of this would be a personal sense of belongingness that originates from meditations on Henry David Thoreau's book *Walden*. But is this religion? Not really. It is only religion in a very literal sense of the word itself – that is, "to reconnect" a person with something more meaningful in some sense. A religion of nature is no more formal than that: there are no churches, no doctrines, and no other expressions of what it is or what it is not, other than what each person feels to be true. The word "religion," used in this very non-specific way, could even be used to describe other cultural phenomena, such as heart-felt patriotism or a deep conviction to a political ideology (e.g., the aptly named "free market" fundamentalism of the libertarian party). Under this rubric, the Reverence for Life elemental nature philosophy *could* be considered a religion of nature. However, I do not feel this be a particularly useful or helpful description. Schweitzer's philosophy is best considered as just that: a philosophy. Instead, and to the extent the phrase is actually clarifying, it is only proper to consider Ethical Mysticism as a religion of nature.

"To relate oneself in the spirit of reverence for life to the multiform manifestations of the will-to-live which together constitute the world is ethical mysticism" (*POC* 79). This is an important sentence from Schweitzer's book. It points out one key difference between Ethical Mysticism and elemental nature philosophy. The phrase "to relate oneself in the spirit of reverence for life" indicates the agency and cultural distinctiveness Schweitzer recognized in each person. He does not prescribe a specific mystical interpretation of the world, other than the recognition of the universal will-to-live and cosmological Will. He leaves up to the individual how to elaborate a complete worldview from this starting point. So long as it remains in the same spirit as his overall project, they can develop any harmonization at all with their own religion, or retain a secular and strictly intellectual understanding of the universe based in, for example, theoretical physics and quantum string theory.

This is why, even when Schweitzer does use the word "religious" while speaking about Ethical Mysticism, it is only to describe its devotional character: "We must all wander in the field of knowledge to the point where knowledge passes over into [a personal] experience of the world. We must all, through [rational] thought, become religious [*religiös*]" (*poc* 81). The German word *religiös* can be translated as "devotional." At its highest manifestation, any mysticism begins to take on a devotional character – that is, the experience of deep contemplative thought is felt in the same way as a person feels the experience of religious devotion. This is a subtle point, but there is a difference between something that has a devotional character and actual religion. Take, for example, spending an afternoon marvelling at wildflowers, lost in a peaceful sublime of sunlight and the play of summer zephyrs across the landscape, all the while meditating on the universal will-to-live manifested in each individual plant and every crawling insect. This is the kind of devotional mysticism Schweitzer describes with the German word *religiös*: this is the spirit of Reverence for Life. While it may be similar to the kind of devotional inner life of a person who is praying or reverencing an icon of a Saint, Schweitzer does not have any particular religion in mind for his reader. His only aim is to promote his or her ethical development and moral conviction. He sees mysticism as the means to do this.

The religious character of Ethical Mysticism therefore comes from the nature of devotion itself. Whether directed at a god or at a philosophical ideal, devotion causes a person to forego self-seeking ends for some greater good. Parental sacrifice for the sake of children falls into this latter category. Similarly, Reverence for Life asks for a devotion to a deepened world- and life-affirmation. It begins with a natural inclination towards sympathy and calls upon people to bring themselves, the other, and the non-human world to the greatest personal and/or natural development possible (*poc* 278). The personal experience of this devotion can become, a least for some, a mysticism much like that which is experienced within religion.

But there is one last point to take from this discussion. As mentioned in the Introduction, Schweitzer refers to mysticism as *das Irrationale* because it develops from and exceeds rational thought. The non-rational is, in one sense, merely the point at which rational thought becomes lost in the profundity of its contemplation, thereby becoming its own sublime.

But *das Irrationale* can also become exceedingly religious in one very extraordinary way. I speak of this next, as I turn to Schweitzer's own devotional life. This is a subject he never wrote much about, so my comments are constrained and limited. However, in the epilogue I extrapolate from the available evidence and offer my own personal thoughts on what *das Irrationale* may mean for understanding Schweitzer and his ethic.

Schweitzer's Own Religious Worldview

Now with respect to Schweitzer himself and his own practice of Ethical Mysticism, Martin is certainly correct when he says that Schweitzer's religious outlook is not pellucid. An excerpt from a letter Schweitzer wrote in 1925 reveals how complex and unorthodox his views are in relation to traditional religion. Evidently written in that very moment, the letter tells of a meditation on Palm Sunday in which nature itself performs the liturgy – one in which humanity becomes the interloper (*Letters* 82):

> I am sitting alone on a tree root, celebrating Palm Sunday, peering through palms at the blue sky, with insects humming all around me ... Once there were villages here; now nature has become everything. I am thinking of the procession into Jerusalem. In the trees, the birds are singing alien melodies. Huge ants are wandering over my body. Oh, how silent everything is, how overwhelmingly silent. That powerful and tragic hosanna, utterly unrestrained by human din, is penetrating this hush, from time into timelessness. For this is timelessness. There will never be history here because this lake belongs exclusively to the sunshine, the trees, the insects, the birds, the clouds reflected in the water.

While the interplay of images and themes is rich beyond description, one thing is obvious. The meditation is permeated with the feeling of the sublime. Schweitzer writes that "every philosophy has its mystical aspects, and every profound thought is mystical" (*E-RFL* 234). There is a point of crossover at which one becomes the other, and this is exactly what Reverence for Life attempts to achieve. But how Reverence for Life becomes extrapolated into a personal life-view depends entirely upon the person, place, and historic time. There is no prescribed interpretation of the world within Reverence for Life, except that the will-to-live is to be understood to exist universally as a consequence of evolutionary forces. Beyond that common thread, Ethical Mysticism can be anything at all. That said, however, it does seem the Palm Sunday meditation shows convincingly the lived experience of Ethical Mysticism for Schweitzer personally was devotionally intermeshed with Lutheran Christianity in a very unique and unorthodox way.

Further insight is found in a letter dated 27 July 1950. Schweitzer had written to the Mother Superior of a community of nuns to explain the kind of synergy he was attempting to achieve: "When I came to formulate the idea of reverence for life as the fundamental idea of ethics, I felt I was enunciating, as a philosophical and religious idea, something intrinsic to St. Francis [of Assisi] but in a new revelation of his thinking" (*Letters* 212). The Catholic saint was evidently a profound influence on this particular Lutheran minister, and in 1955 he writes of him again (262 [emphasis in original]):

Around 1894, during my student days, I was absolutely shaken when I got to know St. Francis. Since childhood I had taken the same road and reached the same spirit, but I have never been able to speak or write about him and me together. I never refer to him. I am very reluctant to do so. He is a famous saint, I am an ordinary man. He possessed an intimacy of speech that is his alone. None of us should try to imitate his speech; no one should adopt it for himself. It was *granted only to him. The rest of us speak in ordinary words.*

The letter is a testament to Schweitzer's humility, and, academic assessments aside for the moment, the scholar of today is left wishing he had given to the world more such deeply spiritual works as the Palm Sunday mediation. Perhaps the fact that he did not reflects his own conviction that Reverence for Life must be regarded first and foremost as an elemental nature philosophy. So he confines himself to ordinary words in two volumes devoted to the history of philosophical thought from ancient Greece to his present day. He leaves the profounder expression of Ethical Mysticism for each reader to develop on his or her own, in ways that would be personally meaningful. It is a sensible conclusion, but not one that satisfies an appetite whetted by that 1925 letter that only hints at just how profound a mystic he really was at heart.

Conclusions: Mysticism and Reverence for Life

It was Nietzsche who preoccupied Schweitzer's mind and kept him focused on the problem of ethics for that day in 1915 when Reverence for Life suddenly dawned on him. The personal letter discussed at the beginning of chapter 3 reveals just how important Nietzsche was for Schweitzer. But why, we may ask, was this the case? It is very revealing that Schweitzer would write that Nietzsche had "a religious [*heilige*] reverence for life" (*POC* 247n8). At first glance, this is an astounding claim. The German word here, *heilige*, literally means "sacred" or "holy." But Nietzsche despised all religion, and especially Christianity! He was also never one to hide his venomous hatred for all things coming from the Church: "The Christian resolve to find the world ugly and bad *has made* the world ugly and bad" (*GS* §130, 185 [emphasis added]). His deep unquenchable hatred of Christianity even led him to give what he felt to be a long overdue and much needed obituary *for the very idea of God*. He felt he had to rid the world of its darkening shadow under which an oppressed humanity cowered in powerlessness (*GS* §108, 167).

So why in the world does Schweitzer say that Nietzsche has a *religious* reverence for life? The answer is mysticism. Put simply, what Nietzsche calls an artistic and aesthetic interpretation of reality, Schweitzer makes into an Ethical Mysticism aimed at the natural world. They are describing the same thing. Like Nietzsche, Schweitzer believed the ultimate test of a culturally defined truth was whether it was life-affirming, correlated to the best available science, and (for Schweitzer) if it was also based in the permanent unchanging elemental truths of Reverence for Life. This is also exactly how Schweitzer makes the natural world no longer "ugly and bad" through Reverence for Life. The sacred (*heilige*) Reverence for Life he sees in Nietzsche comes from the fact that Nietzsche values the celebration of natural life to its fullest potential as the highest of all possible virtues. Nietzsche had found a path through "the thicket" to create culturally determined truth in his critique of Schopenhauer's philosophy. Through him, Schweitzer embraces this same reverence and extends it to all life – human and non-human alike.

Ethical Mysticism is no more inherently religious than what Schweitzer's own words say about the holy (*heilige*) atheist Nietzsche. This is where it begins. Where it ends is up to the person for whom a mystical worldview becomes meaningful – and Schweitzer takes his own experience of mysticism far beyond the modest expression of Reverence for Life he detects in Nietzsche (a subject to be revisited in the epilogue). And, while the secondary metaphysic that emerges from elemental nature philosophy through the synthetic a priori to become cultural values associated with the life-affirming Reverence for Life is indeed onto-theological, it is not a theistic theology in any real sense. True, this comes down to being a matter of debate about academic terms, and admittedly it can equally be claimed that Schweitzer's work constitutes a religion of nature. However, such a position would not be in keeping with the spirit and intention of his work. It was meant to be a philosophy of civilization, and as such it would be most helpful and constructive to consider it as an exciting and provocative offshoot of Continental philosophy – and one that continues to have applications and avenues for development within contemporary hermeneutical and phenomenological theory.

Chapter 6

Practical Governance

The previous chapter examines the related subjects of metaphysics and mysticism. Reverence for Life is metaphysical only in the Aristotelian sense, not in the more fanciful associations that the common usage of the term might suggest. It is also onto-theological according to Heidegger's definition, but it is not theological in the sense of being inseparable from Christianity or philosophical theism. Reverence for Life begins as an elemental nature philosophy, not a theology, and only Ethical Mysticism can become a religious worldview. Reverence for Life is mystical, yes. But it is not something limited to Christians. As Schweitzer declares: "My appeal is to thinking men and women whom I wish to provoke to elemental thought about these questions of existence which occur to the mind of every human being" (*OLT* 199). This is a philosophy for everyone. Yet there is another important issue that I have not yet addressed. Historically, the foremost criticism of Schweitzer's philosophy concerns its apparent impracticability in terms of what he himself purported it to be – a philosophy of civilization. I now turn to a discussion of this topic and reveal for the reader what Schweitzer has to say about civil society and ethical governance.

Contra Schopenhauer and Nietzsche

What emerges from the writings of Schweitzer on the subject of governmental authority stands in sharp opposition to the writings of the two figures with whom he otherwise agrees when it comes to questions of philosophical cosmology, Schopenhauer and Nietzsche. Unlike them, Schweitzer is in no way pessimistic about his hopes for the emergence of a civilization that could respect and even promote the intrinsic dignity of each person. This is surprising, considering his affinity for the ideas of these two philosophers. Even more surprising is the fact that Schweitzer firmly believed in democracy, universal human rights, and that our civilization is actually capable of creating laws and institutions that would emerge through a spirit of reciprocity shared by all in society. This may sound like uncontroversial, even hackneyed banalities by today's standards. Who, after all, would seriously argue against the ideas of democracy and human rights? Such a question reveals a much welcomed (and greatly needed) expectation that has emerged only in recent times, having had its genesis in the collective soul-searching and the re-evaluation of civilization that occurred in the aftermath of the Second World War. To appreciate the distinctiveness of Schweitzer, it is necessary to show how extraordinary his writings really are when compared against the expectations of his times.

Schopenhauer had created a very pessimistic outlook on the human condition and prospects for civilization. Nietzsche would in turn deepen this pessimism, twisting it into a cruel and fascist-tinged shadow that hung over the world with the political repercussions of his Will to Power theory. This became all too clear in Nietzsche's heralding of an ascendant *Übermenschen*, an idea that was greedily co-opted by the Nazis to support their perverse racial ideology (thanks, in part, to redacted texts prepared by Nietzsche's sister after his death). This historical background is important for appreciating certain aspects of Schweitzer's own counter-narrative to Schopenhauer and Nietzsche. I will therefore provide a brief overview of Schopenhauer's and Nietzsche's views of the human condition and the civil state before attempting to explain how Schweitzer broke from them.

Schopenhauer's views on civil society are remarkable for several reasons, one of which is that he created an important conceptual framework for later developments on the part of Nietzsche. Schopenhauer begins his great pessimistic portrayal of civilization by reminding his reader that human history, across all cultures and times, has manifested monarchies as the most common and stable form of government (*PP-OLP* §7, 153). An ascendant king typically seizes power as a military commander who needs to consider the endemic population as a necessary logistical resource for his military campaigns, which are aimed at even greater regional control. The king regards the human "herd" simply as a means to provide his army with provisions, while the local people, in turn, look to their king to protect them from outside forces seeking to seize their lands for the same militaristic reasons (*PP-OLP* §6, 151). The people follow willingly, betraying an inborn "monarchical instinct" to be ruled over by another; more rarely, this natural instinct allows an individual to rise up to become such a leader himself (*PP-OLP* §7, 153).

Schopenhauer writes that republics are "anti-natural" and exceedingly uncommon in human history. He points out that in the so-called democratic republics of ancient Greece, Rome, Carthage, and even in the United States of America (during this point of history), the majority of the population always consisted of slaves (*PP-OLP* §7, 153). Democracy, in his opinion, is little more than the pretence and hypocrisy of a ruling elite: it could never offer the people, *all* the people, true and lasting justice. Schopenhauer therefore tells his reader that the only possible utopia for the modern world would have to arise from a "despotism of the wise" (154). This would take the form of an aristocracy of the most gifted and noble philosophers together with "the cleverest and most gifted women," who would have monarchical and hereditary rule over their nation-states. Schopenhauer, always the champion of Plato, would have society ruled over by Philosopher-Kings. Nietzsche's Will to Power theory and slave/master morality was directly inspired by these writings.[53]

On the subject of ethics, Schopenhauer proclaims that, on the one hand, all people are equal with regard to their inherent human rights because they are all incarnations of the will-to-live equally. Nevertheless, people differ in their natural gifts at birth (e.g., intelligence, strength, ambition, etc.), and this results in corresponding social inequality (*PP-OLP* §2, 148). As such, the only natural right in a civic context is the freedom to exercise one's will-to-live-based instincts, provided that they do not impinge upon another's right to the same freedom (148). The force of law may therefore be legitimately made to "stand on the side of justice" by protecting a right to personal liberty (*PP-OLP* §6, 151). But justice here is a negative concept: it represents the negation of an injustice committed against another's rights (*PP-OLP* §1, 148). The law only seeks to protect citizens from each other – a fact that hints at another significant aspect of Schopenhauer's views on the human condition.

Despite the potential for most individuals to be given, at birth, the natural gifts to become successful and respectable in society, Schopenhauer describes the typical human being as "a dreadful wild animal" (*PP-OE* §5, 138). He remarks: "We know this wild animal only in the tamed state called civilization and we are therefore shocked by the occasional out-

breaks of its true nature" (138). But wild animals only show their vicious-
ness in pursuit of prey. The human species is the only one to "cause pain to
others with no other object than causing pain" in another sentient being
(139). Schopenhauer presents human slavery and animal vivisection as
unimpeachable testimony concerning this irredeemable human instinct
for wanton cruelty that lurks in the hearts of many (*OBM* §19, 171, 175–7).
Worst of all, he says, is the sin of *Schadenfreude*, which resonates as "the
laughter of Hell" in this world of injustices we create for ourselves (*PP-OE*
§5, 140). But there is no Satan here – there is no need, for we alone are evil.
Only a very few people are born (or otherwise become) truly compassionate and ethical beings. As a consequence, for Schopenhauer there is no
possibility of improving the human race through society. There is only the
king, who, through laws and vigilant enforcement, can save us from the
worst aspects of our own nature.

The story of civilization is much the same for Nietzsche. For him, democracy is simply an ill-advised form of mob rule that can only lead to the
hollow and joyless world of the Last Man – a world government for a homogenized society consisting of "no shepherd and one herd" controlled by
economic forces alone (*PN-TSZ*, Prologue §5, 130; *CW* §2, 321).[54] Instead,
Nietzsche upholds for his readers the daring hero of the French Revolution, Napoleon (*GS* §23, 98; *WTP* §104, 66). Nietzsche values only those
true warriors who overthrow what he considers to be an aberrant social
trend towards democracy (*WTP* §747, 396).[55] Gone is the romanticism of
Schopenhauer's noble republic of Philosopher-Kings: the *Übermensch*
will forcibly impose his *Will* upon society. I will not further outline Nietzsche's political views because what attracted the Nazis to them should
now be more than apparent. This much has been said only to highlight
the true distinctiveness of Schweitzer, who would stand against both
Schopenhauer and Nietzsche – and do so publicly.

We are now in a place to appreciate a very powerful event in Schweitzer's life. He would give a speech against Nazism in Frankfurt, Germany,
on 22 March 1932, less than a year before Hitler would be sworn into
power as Chancellor. The occasion for Schweitzer's speech was the cen-
tennial anniversary of the death of the great German hero, Johann Wolfgang von Goethe. His speech was used to critique Nazism, and it reveals,
perhaps more compellingly than anything else, his very different perspective on the human person (Brabazon 1976, 354):

What is it that [Goethe] says to our era? He tells it, that the frightful
drama which is now being played through can only come to an

end, if it removes from its path the economic and social magic [i.e., Nazi propaganda] to which it has surrendered itself, unlearns the incantations with which it has been befooled, and is determined, whatever the cost, to get back to a natural relationship with reality. To individuals he says: "Do not abandon the ideal of personal, individual manhood, even if it runs contrary to circumstances such have developed. Do not believe that this ideal is lost, even when it no longer seems tenable along with the opportunistic theories which endeavour simply to adjust the spiritual to the materials. Remain human with your own souls! Do not become mere human things which allow to have stuffed into them souls which are adjusted to the mass-will and pulse in measure with it!" ... There arises a question which even half a lifetime ago we should have regarded as impossible: Is there any longer any sense in holding on to the ideal of personal human individuality, when circumstances are developing in just the opposite direction, or is it not on the contrary our duty to adjust ourselves to a new ideal of human existence, in accordance with which man is destined to attain a differently constituted perfection of his being in unreserved absorption into organized society?"

In this daring and courageous address to the people, Schweitzer warned that Germany was about to make a deal with the Devil – and he meant this quite literally: "After all, what is now taking place in this terrible epoch of ours except a gigantic repetition of the drama of Faust upon the stage of the world? ... In deeds of violence and murders a thousandfold, a brutalized humanity plays its cruel game! Mephistopheles leers at us with a thousand grimaces!" (*Goethe* 56–7). This proved to be horrifyingly prophetic – only the scale of the coming holocaust escaped the awful precision of his words that day. Schweitzer was all but powerless to stop it. His reputation and the power of his words were insufficient. And so he left Germany for Africa, buying up all the medical supplies he could in anticipation of a new war and the shortages for his hospital that would result, and he vowed never to return while Hitler was in power (Brabazon 2000, 382). The animosity was mutual. Schweitzer's African hospital was an extreme embarrassment to the Nazis: he was an affront to everything Nazism stood for, and they actively worked to destroy his academic reputation (382).[56] This is part of the reason that Schweitzer remains marginalized as a scholar even today.

Up to this point I have only outlined what Schweitzer stood against in relation to his philosophical predecessors. Now the question must be asked: What exactly does Reverence for Life propose with respect to civil authority, social responsibility, and human potential? Here the story becomes more sketchy and speculative because Schweitzer never completed the final volumes of *The Philosophy of Civilization*, which were to deal with these issues. Nevertheless, there are other writings of his that do provide important details about his vision for the civil state within the Reverence for Life worldview. While these greatly clarify much of what hitherto has been presumed to be his greatest shortcoming as a philosopher, my investigation will also reveal new and potentially serious problems. My findings perhaps provide an answer to why he never completed those final volumes. It may be he too realized that there were underlying problems with his political philosophy and that this is what kept him from finishing the remaining volumes. But let's start with what he was able to work out first.

The Sermons on Property

Schweitzer seeds important elements of his thought throughout his many disparate works. Some of his most direct engagements with questions of civil authority, social responsibility, and the practical expressions of his ethic appear in a series of sermons he prepared in 1919 – manuscripts that remained hidden away in archives before being published for the first time in 1974. The content of these sermons are not the typical Sunday-morning homilies that one would expect.

Schweitzer had just been released from a French POW camp. During the long recovery from the dysentery he had contracted while there, he served as a vicar at Saint Nicolai Church in Strasbourg (*APR* xii). The sermons he gave aimed at the postwar circumstances affecting his congregation. They were also an integral part of his formative reflections on Reverence for Life, which would later become *The Philosophy of Civilization*. Nonetheless, the content of the sermons are qualitatively different from what appears in his subsequent books. This is because, in works meant for publication, he preferred to be much more conservative and reserved (Brabazon 1975, 106). Here, however, Schweitzer had a very specific audience in mind and the sermons were not intended for publication: his arguments are much more focused, concise, and particularized for this very reason. Schweitzer provides specifics about his ethic that are not found anywhere else. From a scholarly perspective, this is a much needed specificity. Most notable of the subjects he would address were those that concerned his views on civil authority and personal property.

"What I say to you concerning property is necessarily unfinished and contradictory" (APR 74). This statement, taken here out of context, highlights an aspect of Schweitzer's work that needs to be commented upon first. As previously mentioned, his political thought, much like certain other aspects of his ethic, was left incomplete. Yet for Schweitzer this is not a flaw in his system but, rather, the acknowledgment of an irreconcilable problem at the heart of society itself. It is simply not possible to maximize individual liberty and, at the same time, to guarantee political stability and lawful coexistence. These two principles, liberty and security, are antinomic: they stand against each other. Schweitzer recognizes this and uses the seeming impasse as a creative tension to generate the possibility for true progress in civilization. With this in mind, let's now turn to his argument.

Schweitzer begins, somewhat uncharacteristically for him, with a series of definitions. The first concerns the "essence" of property itself. He says it is formed by the investment of human labour over time, whether in terms of physical work to obtain land resources (such as with agricultural activity) or in terms of the mental creativity and effort expended in business ventures to accumulate profit: "possessions or property are thus *accumulated work* and are *justified as such*" (APR 62 [emphasis in original]). This understanding of property, reminiscent of both Aristotle and John Locke,[57] is used by Schweitzer to support the right of people to claim ownership of the products of their labour even if those possessions and land rights represent, directly or indirectly, a deprivation of others of a right of access to that private wealth. This is a principle of ownership. But as one of the two antinomic principles at the heart of society, it cannot be exclusive or absolute. Furthermore, because "*society* creates the ordered conditions that made it possible for the individual to retain what he has earned," he also asserts that, "in the final analysis, society is the master of property" and can therefore make certain claims on that personal wealth (62–3 [emphasis in original]). But the right of society as "master of property" is neither exclusive nor absolute because an equal claim for an individual right to private wealth counters it.

There is a strong tension here between the antinomic poles of ownership. On the one hand, there is the individual owner with his or her private property, made through personal labour; on the other, there are all the other people in society who indirectly enabled such persons to attain their wealth and positions of entitlement. This would not be a problem except for the great inequalities that emerge in modern capitalist societies. Not everyone can become rich in such economies: there are always some unfortunates who, often through no fault of their own, become unemployed, impoverished, or even destitute. What, if anything, should individual owners and society to do for them? This is the problem Schweitzer tries to solve in his sermons on Reverence for Life.

Schweitzer begins by highlighting the problem at the heart of the antinomy. The right to personal wealth is "guaranteed by society without consideration of the needs of the needy" within that society (APR 63). Yet because property and wealth are only possible because of the conditions created in collective society, this becomes a basis for making certain impositions upon private wealth. This is where the second principle – society as final owner – allows for the antinomy to partially give way to possible solutions that are defined by their circumstantial contexts. In terms of the postwar reconstruction happening in Europe, Schweitzer justifies the practical necessities for the collective good from that basis:

> When required for the well-being of the general community, the community has the right to reduce individuals' property and draw on it for itself. In the time of great misery that we face, it can do nothing else than proceed to do so. It will tax property in unprecedented ways. Exploitation of the mined treasures of the land as well as many other things will be snatched from private control and saved for the state ... It will come with terrible injustice to those who own property ... As to how they are to be carried out, religion has nothing to say. It is a matter of choosing outward means that are appropriate to the goals, and this is something about which the members of a people must make up their minds. (64)

First off, it needs to be noted that there is a principle here regarding the separation of church and state. But the dividing line is not all that clear, seeing how these comments were, after all, made in a sermon. Second, and more to the point, Schweitzer clearly asserts the right of state authorities to impose on individuals for the greater good. However, it must be underscored that Schweitzer's sympathies are clearly with the property owners. They attained what they have through hard work or were lucky enough to inherit wealth from the work of their parents. The very *essence* of that property comes from the individuals and those individuals alone. They created it. Society as such only manifested the conditions for the intangible essence of work and mental effort to take its subsequent phenomenal form as wealth. This is the antinomy, only partially resolved. It can never be fully resolved. The answers to all such problems of practical necessity must also remain incomplete, imperfect, and, to a certain extent, even contradictory – just as Schweitzer announced at the beginning of this discussion.

This, then, is the true reality of society. People exchange their free exercise of personal liberty for those benefits that only come out of collective interdependent communities. For us today this may mean, for example, obeying speed limits, serving jury duty, and paying our taxes. There is no universal truth to be found in philosophy regarding how these social arrangements must be constituted. These laws are socially constructed from a great variety of criteria and are changeable for this very reason. No philosopher can invariably say, as an a priori given fact, at what age driver's licences should be granted, how a legal system should be constituted, or what an appropriate level of taxation should be. These are merely social realities emerging out of social contracts and political compromise – a subject Schweitzer also addresses, and which I will address momentarily.

But the next question that arises from what has just been discussed concerns how we would situate Schweitzer's sensibilities on the economic spectrum of free market capitalism, socialism, or communism. It must be recalled that in 1919, the time of these sermons, the Bolshevik Revolution of 1917 was very much on people's minds. Some in Europe looked upon that revolution favourably and enviously. Schweitzer was certainly not one of them. Against these popular ideas that were then gaining wider influence, Schweitzer preaches: "It appears as if one wanted to solve all the material and social problems through a power struggle between capital and labor, on the one hand, and through the functioning of organizations, on the other. Where we find this conviction spread around in [the] common 'wisdom' and in the press, we must be frightened" (APR 90).

Schweitzer had no interest in such revolutionary struggles; moreover, he believed they were entirely wrong-headed. He makes it clear that society should not "nationalize everything" (APR 64); rather, he firmly believes that "the boundaries of the economic, social capacity of the state [must be made] much narrower" because socialism or communism would lead to "the ruin of society" (64–5). Schweitzer is a capitalist through and through. But he is not what would be called a libertarian – someone who believes that government is best only when it governs the least. He would never, for example, endorse the extreme free market ideology of Ayn Rand and those who call themselves libertarians today.

Property ownership is individual – yes. Yet societal governance must be democratic, which means collectively determined and aimed at collective public goods. Governments have the right to tax and otherwise impose upon property owners for these societal interests and other national goals chosen through democratic procedures. Individual property ownership is never absolute. Owners, Schweitzer says, are in a sense "stewards" of their property who gain certain rights through their labour; but this ownership comes with the idea of having a "responsibility" to greater society (*APR* 64–6). It is even the case that "all property belongs to society" when it is required for the public good (65). The pendulum of law thus alternates between the antinomic poles of the individual and the societal, favouring one or the other according to time and circumstance. There can be no predefined ethical point of perfect balance set between them.

On Public Institutions

As for the actual form of government and which is best in terms of social justice, Schweitzer says that the separation of powers in a system of checks and balances is both valid and wise (*APR* 90; see also *POC* 16). Such an oppositional arrangement, he indicates, will facilitate political agreements arising from compromise, and this is a good thing. Nevertheless, he also says that political compromises cannot produce real social progress, which "will never originate out of that [process]" (*APR* 90). Schweitzer takes pains to stress this point: governments cannot produce the types of agreements that will allow society to work together "for a better future" (ibid.). Rather, this has to come through "the creation of a reciprocity of trust that can only come out of the encounter of both minds" between individual persons (ibid.).

We have arrived at yet another antinomy within Schweitzer's system: political compromises needed for practical governance versus the interpersonal reciprocity that allows for true social progress. The positive repercussion of this is that political compromises serve to check governmental excess. They thereby help to preserve personal liberty and to safeguard the balance of the first antinomy between the individual and the societal. Furthermore, in a representational form of democracy, such as in a parliamentary system, the people themselves elect those who will negotiate the political compromises needed for the practical administration of society and for deciding on the types of social goods to be promoted for the betterment of all. But the tension between individual rights and societal laws is not fully addressed through compromise. This is merely a citizen safeguard and a concession to practical necessity.

Schweitzer's political framework can be said to be elegant and consistent in balancing these antinomies. But now, moving on to the next series of questions: How does Schweitzer hope to achieve a philosophy of civilization that will *promote* a moral society out of this framework? So far it appears that he only aims at preserving a balance between opposing social forces. However, true social progress, as he says, can only arise from mutual trust and reciprocity, and that can only come from the encounter of "both minds" across the political divide (*APR* 90). This is rarely achieved even in a parliament. It is for this reason that he says that political and non-governmental "organizations *cannot* accomplish the great and decisive improvement of which our time has need" (90–1 [emphasis added]).

Instead, Schweitzer declares "that improvement, that great service which we need, can only be set in motion when more and more individual people, each according to the gifts that are peculiarly [theirs], enter into [society] and become active in it" (*APR* 91). What he is saying is this: the balance of the original antinomy between individual freedom and societal security must be weighted in favour of the former, and this is consistent throughout his Reverence for Life ethic. Personal freedom refers not merely to amassing wealth but, rather, to becoming a fully actualized person who, besides excelling in a career of one's choosing, will also act as an ethical agent within society. Schweitzer sees the creation of ethical personalities who will *want* to engage in such activism as the very foundation of his ethic. They are to be the cornerstone of a moral society. The people themselves, all of them, must become the guardians and defenders of social justice. We cannot delegate this responsibility to Philosopher-Kings or hope for an ascendant Napoleon to do it for us. Schweitzer insists that the answer, despite the scepticism of Schopenhauer and Nietzsche, must be found in democracy.

Governmental and non-governmental institutions will always be needed. They can be employed to act for the public good, such as in the case of those agencies devoted to the elimination of poverty and homelessness. But Schweitzer indicates that they will always be imperfect instruments born out of practical necessity. He likens the formation of these institutions to a group of people coming together to clear land for a public park, which, when that function outlives its usefulness, is later abandoned and allowed to regrow naturally (*POC* 16). The problem is that governmental and non-governmental institutions will do their best work only while "still under the influence of their working founders" (APR 83). This is because, due to their very nature, they are "too *impersonal*, too little human" (82 [emphasis in original]). They are incapable of acting quickly, and, due to their chartered responsibilities, they often cannot take the same risks with finances as could an individual. But their greatest flaw, he indicates, is that they "*cannot individualize* [their attention]" (81 [emphasis in original]). Institutions must obey their own regulations and policies, which are aimed at those generalized cases they were created to address, because "an organization cannot accomplish more than [what] lies in its nature" (ibid.). Yet, and despite these limitations, "they manage to do what an individual or many individuals working individually could not accomplish" (ibid.).

Utilitarianism and Practical Governance

Schweitzer was no utopian daydreamer. He realized tough decisions have to be made to make civil society possible. Just as a shopkeeper must fire an irresponsible employee "in spite of any sympathy he has for him and his family" (POC 232), there are times when an elected official has to make decisions that "sacrifice[] men and human happiness" for a greater good, such as by sending the military off to war to defend the nation (326). Utilitarian logic does come into play at the level of practical governance. Schweitzer even says that the basic ethical principle of compassion sometimes requires "an *ordering* and deepening, [and] also a widening of the current views of good and evil" if we are to have a viable society (310 [emphasis added]). Priorities for public policy must be made, and ethical trade-offs for which public goods are to be achieved must be decided upon.

It is for this reason that Schweitzer speaks favourably of utilitarianism in *The Philosophy of Civilization*. Specifically, the utilitarian credo of the greatest good for the greatest number is said to be a principle of governance that "guides us safely and accurately in questions of good and evil" (POC 156). He further writes that Bentham is one of the most powerful moralists who ever lived but that he made the mistake of thinking that morality was a kind of "enthusiasm" expected by an individual for the prevailing political wisdom in that society (157). The problem with his type of utilitarianism is that it takes on the vantage point of societal expectations, and because of this it is easily co-opted by other agendas. When this happens, the person and his or her "ethical conscience … [becomes]

fatally stunted by a biologic-sociological ethics [i.e., economic determinism] and this, moreover, [can become] finally corrupted by nationalism" (293). Here Schweitzer is referring to certain economic theories that are based on crude naturalistic Darwinian assumptions about human society and how these can be imposed upon individuals by "economic measures" (230–1).[58] When this happens, utilitarianism "loses its ethical character" entirely (234). Another danger of supra-personal utilitarianism is that it can quash the inner voice of conscience and cause the person to lose his or her sense of individuality to group-think. Schweitzer was also deeply worried that a political philosophy of utilitarian sacrifice can mutate into a "doctrine of being sacrificed *by* others [i.e., conscienceless leaders]" for a claimed greater good (230 [emphasis added]).

True utilitarianism, Schweitzer writes, has to become reconciled with his elemental nature philosophy and draw its strength from a person's moral conscience (*POC* 234). This is why Schweitzer's own utilitarian vision is rooted in a cosmological worldview that promotes an individualized ethic of self-fulfilment actualized through social altruism. This was to be the guiding vision for how the greatest good for the greatest number could be achieved. One could only hope that one's political leaders would be motivated by such concerns. But, failing that, practical necessity is still the rule of the day. This is why the people must always look for ways to engage in civil affairs on behalf of social justice and, in the process, become the moral conscience of society. The political concessions to practical necessity are therefore very much an undercurrent of and counterbalance to the driving force of ethical individualism. And so, while those in authority seek to maintain law and order, the individualism of Reverence for Life aims to keep the danger of excessive government power curbed and restrained. It is a check-and-balance system that is weighted in favour of the individual as the ultimate ethical authority: "Thus we serve society without abandoning ourselves to it" (327).

Even so, we have now arrived at a third antinomy: the deontological demands of Reverence for Life for individuals versus the consequentialist logic used by civil authorities. Schweitzer can be clear with respect to an absolute ethic for the individual. He can also explain how civil governance operates through a different necessity and why elected officials must sometimes set aside the rights of individuals for the good of the community – such as with the post-First World War taxation plans and the confiscation of certain property rights. There are times when actions like these must be taken for the common good. And because of this, he says: "We are not permitted to concur in every condemnation of men in leading positions of which we hear. We must take into consideration the responsibility they bear and the necessity in which they find themselves to set the material interests above … [individual] human [rights]" (*APR* 54). Nevertheless, how to determine the exact ethical balance between the antinomic poles is anything but clear, and obviously, at different times, this relationship is subject to great circumstantial tilting in favour either of the state or of the individual.

But there is also a more fundamental problem here. Schweitzer establishes two different ethics under Reverence for Life: a deontological one for the individual (which is governed by universal compassion and a *Schuld* consciousness) and a consequentialist one for state authorities (which is governed by practical necessity). We must now ask how this curious bifurcation of ethical systems came about and how, in turn, Schweitzer envisioned these two disparate systems working together under Reverence for Life. The answers are found in his critique of Kant's philosophy of religion, upon which Schweitzer modelled these antinomic dynamics.

Contra Kant

Kant attempts to conjoin his epistemology of critical idealism with the belief in a higher moral world complete with God as the "ethical common being" for our own ontology (*EF* 335). The perfection of civil society, he believes, could then be brought about by bringing it into harmony with the dictates of reason, and this, in turn, would have the cosmological consequence of having "moral [hu]mankind as the final end of the world" (334). The two worlds (the higher moral world and the present phenomenal one) were to be linked through an "attempted union between practical and theoretical reason" (337). But, according to Schweitzer, there are several underlying problems here.

Kant's ethic is built on three parallel claims: (1) personal free will (i.e., personal agency not determined by the empirical character of the phenomenal world), (2) a higher moral law accessible to the rational mind, and (3) a belief in immortality – all of which "do not lie within the realm of critical idealism" (*EF* 287). Kant wants to bridge his epistemology with the imagined higher moral world by defending these three ideas with logical antinomies. These antinomies are meant to free them from phenomenality, so that they can cross over to the pure a priori world of the divine. They are thus transported from "the conditioned [expression as an antinomy] to the unconditioned" use in pure theoretical reason (237). But the "ideas" are not identical in the two different worlds, and, divorced from the limited context of their antinomies, they are also subjected to "the unaccustomed atmosphere of the practical use of reason ... [whereupon each] collapses" (240). Schweitzer determines that, in effect, Kant uses philosophical sleight of hand to smuggle the ideas back and forth. He therefore concludes that a "philosophy of religion tailored and oriented to the presuppositions of critical idealism is a product which is self-disintegrating" (336) because either "the critical idealistic presuppositions neutralize their ethical determination, or the latter cancels the former" (340).

The true value of Kant's philosophy, according to Schweitzer, is not his philosophy of religion but his vision of a "self-perfecting ethical personality" (*EF* 341). It falls to every individual to help bring about the full realization of his or her innate potential and also to contribute to the same for greater society. Each person was thereby given a unique dignity by Kant. The phenomenal world before them remains open to moral influence through personal initiative and their ethical agency. But, as Schweitzer writes, Kant strays from this wonderful beginning because his philosophy aims at the "subordination" of personal motivations in preference to moral laws known only through disinterested, calculated logic (270). His ethic is entirely cold and impersonal, other than allowing for a sense of happiness that is said to result when morality becomes "its own reward" (247). According to Schweitzer, it is precisely for this reason that Schopenhauer is superior to Kant, if not as a moral person himself,[59] certainly as an ethical philosopher. This is because he "does away with the moral law [from a claimed higher world] in Kant's formulation, carries to completion the identification of the knowing subject with the moral person, defines the relationship between the intelligible and phenomenal world by rejecting every attempt at bringing it home in analogy to the relationship of reason and consequence, and makes no attempt to distinguish between human action and the area of general appearance" (339).

Behind this philosophical language is a straightforward conclusion. Schweitzer admires Schopenhauer for starting from Kant's critical idealism but regrounding his ethic "solely [in] the knowing subject" (339). There is no supposed higher world infringing upon the phenomenal here, at least not with respect to ethical commands. There is also no deference of the personal will to the inhuman calculated logic that tries to relate pure theoretical reason to phenomenal consequences. Schopenhauer's theory of the Will locates morality fully and completely within the individual alone, specifically in his or her will-to-live. The inner voice of compassion can thereby directly inform personal behaviour on an intuitive level. For Schweitzer, this allows morality to remain human, clear, and uncompromised.

But, as we have seen, an exclusive focus on the "knowing subject" drives a wedge between personal morality and societal ethics. Schweitzer faults Kant for trying to bring the phenomenal world into union with a higher world of pure a priori reason. Yet, by isolating personal morality from practical governance, Schweitzer arrives at the similar problem of trying to bring two separate worlds together. For Kant, it is the higher world and the phenomenal one; for Schweitzer, it is the personal and the societal. The *Schuld* mentality does not fully address this particular problem. So we arrive back at a recurring question that, up to this point, has only been partially addressed: How does Schweitzer attempt to bridge these two worlds?

The answer, I believe, is found in a comment he made about new laws holding true only if "they gain general approbation" within a society (*APR* 75). This observation is noteworthy because the process of forming a public consensus is not limited to the meeting of minds in a parliamentarian system governed by a general spirit of reciprocity. There is another way this consensus can arise. Schweitzer believes that a moral individual can move and affect others in society through the silent command of his or her personality: in this incremental way, such people can actually create a new ethical disposition in the general population. He reveals how this dynamic works in the following passage from his *Philosophy of Religion* (330):

> If it is the religious or ethical nature of the person which seizes
> the world of appearances and its events in a corresponding unique
> unity, one calls it moral or religious genius. Therefore, the nature
> of every religious genius is shown in that he constructs a unity by
> working over the wreckage of a religion destroyed either deliberately
> or unconsciously as the exigencies of his religious personality
> dictate it without concern as to whether, for the average person, the
> broken pieces fit into a structure or not. The genius seizes only what
> he needs for his new, unified image, lit by his own light – and the
> rest becomes blurred in the shade.

This passage specifically relates to the formation of a new cultural movement wherein such a "genius" constructs a new social unity out of the current cultural environment through the power of his or her charisma and force of personal will. This is how Schweitzer envisions the ordinary citizen engaging the political world, which is otherwise governed by utilitarian logic and practical necessity. In a democracy, that political world is still subjected to the will of the people, and those persons in Schweitzer's vision of the civil state are, in turn, governed by the deontological mandates of Reverence for Life. Moreover, because the laws created by a legislature under a spirit of compromise must be accepted by the people, and not simply imposed upon them, the public can actively resist them and/or insist on legislative changes of their own. In such a political atmosphere, an "ethical genius" personality can become a powerful force through grassroots organizations and other such popular movements that force elected officials to yield to the public will.

Schweitzer's political framework comes together at this one point of reconciliation. It is the power of moral exemplars that ensures that the proper balance is maintained between all these antinomic tensions. Under Reverence for Life, moral agents have the additional responsibility of engaging in civic affairs to create and to promote a new ethical disposition in society. This is to arise through the creation of a new social "unity" brought about by the power of their personality, each according to his or her abilities. Every person could thereby help to collectively create a new ethical *archē* that brings about true social progress. This is Schweitzer's hope.

The Ethical Personality

Not surprisingly, an example of the aforementioned social dynamic can be found in Schweitzer himself. In his fight against atomic weapons, he produced the first comprehensive environmental report on the bio-accumulation and bio-magnification of radionuclide contamination in nature associated with their development and testing. This report was delivered during his landmark 1958 "Declaration of Conscience" radio broadcast. Schweitzer used his acclaim to solidify public opinion, and his landmark research proved instrumental in the United Nations' subsequent passage of the worldwide 1963 limited test ban treaty (Cousins 1985, 175–7).[60]

Through the force of his reputation and the power of his argument, one man actually made a real difference in the world. Schweitzer had become the very kind of "ethical genius" he had written about in his 1899 dissertation on Kant's philosophy of religion. This was a stunning historical counterpoint to his failure in Frankfurt. If not the Second World War, he did what he could to help to prevent a third. This is, in fact, why he took on this new fight so late in his life.[61] An ethical personality can indeed become a powerful social force that shapes public opinion, drawing it away from reactionary fear and militaristic aggression and moving society towards trust, reciprocity, and the reachable dream of a better humanity.

Schweitzer inspired Rachel Carson (1962) to produce a similar study on bio-accumulation and bio-magnification of organochlorine pesticides – a book that she entitled *Silent Spring* and dedicated to Schweitzer. *Silent Spring* awakened the general public and inspired the modern environmental movement. Schweitzer and Carson were certainly extraordinary people. Each can be considered an ethical genius capable of rousing and establishing a new ethical disposition in others. The world certainly needs more such inspiring leaders. But we can't just sit around and wait for them to appear. So what would Schweitzer say to us about role of the average person and individual citizen?

This is where he distinguishes himself from Schopenhauer and Nietzsche. Schweitzer's views on the ethical genius mirror, at least in certain ways, the belief in an embedded monarchical instinct within the will-to-live for the ascendant king, on the one hand, and the *Übermensch* who breaks free of the mob mentality to rule over the human herd, on the other. But, and this is the key difference and why he turns to Kant instead of to them, Schweitzer believes *each and every human being* is capable of independent moral personhood – a stunning assertion considering his intellectual mentors and the brutal time in which he lived.

Everyone would be given a special dignity and role in the actualization of his philosophy of civilization. Schweitzer knew that the power of example manifested in individual acts of compassion under a deontological ethic have a chance to inspire others. As he said: "Do something wonderful, people may imitate it" (Cordero 2007, 131).[62] The Reverence for Life ethic is intended to be actualized precisely in this way: the power of an ethical genius exists in some measure within every person. At almost any time an opportunity can occur for someone to influence the moral character of another through exemplary behaviour. In a sense, each person allows something latent to emerge in the witness and this gives them permission to behave likewise. A person can thereby recruit additional agents to his or her cause. But this is not always for the best.

Schweitzer learned a terrible lesson about this during a life-changing event in his childhood. The incident in question was re-enacted for the Academy Award-winning 1957 documentary directed by Jerome Hill and Erica Anderson and entitled *Albert Schweitzer*. In the scene, Schweitzer recalls that, as a seven- or eight-year-old child, an older boy had recruited him to shoot stones at birds from slingshots. Despite his conscience, and "in obedience to his nod of command," he took aim with him (*MCY* 40). But just then church bells rang out. The young Schweitzer suddenly regained his conviction and chased the birds away to save them from the other boy.

An echo of this event later appears in a passage from his autobiography. When considering the future of humankind, he writes: "If men can be found who revolt against the spirit of thoughtlessness, and who are personalities sound enough and profound enough to let the ideals of ethical progress *radiate from them as a force*, there will start an activity of the spirit which will be strong enough to evoke a new mental and spiritual disposition in [hu]mankind" (*OLT* 241 [emphasis added]). Schweitzer was far too humble to present himself as such a figure: "I would fain prove myself worthy. How much of the work which I planned and have in mind shall I be able to complete?" (242). Yet perhaps history may show that his life and works were indeed profound and that he did in fact help to evoke a new mental and spiritual disposition in humankind that, albeit still burgeoning, may yet come to greater fruition.

Today we would call the social phenomenon of an ethical genius inspiring others a dynamic within evolutionary psychology, a carryover, as Nietzsche would say, from humankind's "herd" mentality. Simply stated, leaders attract followers. This dynamic exists beneficently in the social movements inspired by Gandhi and Martin Luther King Jr, both of whom led by example in the face of active persecution. This dynamic also exists in the bandwagon effect of politics as well as in contagious crowd violence that leads to riots. As a child, Schweitzer saw the power of this himself, and this may have played a role in his impulsive decision to rise and defend the weaverbird hatchlings from hungry hawks (see chapter 5). People can act impulsively, and for this reason sober-minded governmental institutions will always be needed for the common good. Here again is the wisdom of Schweitzer's antinomy, which balances the virtues (and flaws) of both ethical forces against each other in a system of checks and balances.

Nevertheless, the antinomy is not evenly balanced but, rather, is weighted in favour of the individual. Schweitzer sees institutions as blunt, inhuman instruments. Their peculiar logic of pragmatic necessity is seen as too dangerous, and he feels that the fate of society cannot be left to them alone. According to him: "*All problems* that need to be solved, the large like the small, *can only be solved through persuasive interchange* between individuals and between groups [of people]" (*APR* 90 [emphasis in original]). His position then changed, and the reasons for this change become apparent in the following section.

The Individual and the Necessary

Schweitzer is convinced, at least in his early sermons, that the real hope for civilization resides with the person and in the very human experience that occurs in the encounter between two people. When political ideology is set aside, the commonality between different worldviews can be found. A spirit of compromise can then emerge to allow for real and meaningful social progress. This happens because humanity shares a common essence: it can be revealed within each "I + will-to-live" nexus through interpersonal discourse, arising in the silent apophatic spaces behind the words. It is also felt in the shared aspirations of people's hopes, dreams, and fears, even though this essential humanity is most pronounced through the innate pre-rational response to another's suffering. Nevertheless, this intuition can be blocked by the cognitive veils of ideology, bigotry, resentment, and other psychological defence mechanisms. Schopenhauer writes of this same problem. Yet where Schopenhauer believes that some people are born with insufficient potential for developing real compassion, Schweitzer believes that each and every one of us can become a fully moral being.

But there is something else that stands in the way of this development. Just as government officials must sometimes ignore their dictates of conscience for the greater good, so too the ordinary citizen must sometimes do the same thing in her or his personal affairs. This sets up a very peculiar problem for Schweitzer. People must become more compassionate and, at the same time, be able to harden themselves against the dictates of their conscience to do what it necessary. Schweitzer gives an example of this when speaking about a person who takes it upon him- or herself to shun someone in the community as a form of public censure to correct that person's behaviour (*APR* 54):

In the very fight for the good we come to the point where we
interfere damagingly in the lives of people. I know that the influence
of this or of that person is bad, and I recognize it with others as
a duty – without my having anything personal against him – to
be cold toward him and to cooperate in that which is undertaken
against him. The purpose gives me the right. But I injure a person,

and perhaps with the best of intentions I do him an injustice in many respects. To be active beyond the borders of my own interests therefore means to become guilty. Whoever has not yet felt that has never sacrificed himself for something.

This is the reality of living in a society that is caught between the antinomies of freedom and security. For the greater public good, people must sometimes act against the dictates of conscience, as in this example of shunning. They must block their personal sympathies and proceed with calculated logic instead. The obvious problem here is that they must adopt a justifying rationale not all that different from that used by an unethical person who causes harm to others due to his or her own self-aggrandizing excuses.

This would also seem to be a very uncharacteristic prescription for an ethic based in boundless compassion. In part, this is where the *Schuld* mentality comes into the picture to remedy the impasse between sympathy and doing what is necessary, albeit after the damage to another has been done. But how can people *in all good conscience* do such hurtful things in the first place? And wouldn't this allowance for such necessarily hurtful actions become susceptible to rampant abuses and self-serving rationalizations?

Schweitzer is well aware of the dangers here, and he warns that people must never become callous. He gives an example of a business owner who must make a harsh decision that will affect the lives of his employees. He counsels: "When, however, you do experience the conflict between the material and the human considerations, you may not simply say, 'I serve a business. My action is impersonal. Therefore I only allow the business responsibility to speak and [therefore I] am exempted from ... human responsibility'" (APR 55). While all such people may be "on legally unimpeachable grounds," he declares that, "in order to be able to do what they do, they have killed personal morality, the truly human in themselves, and therewith the best in them is condemned to ruin" (ibid.). People must still sometimes do what they know is hurtful – for example, engaging in the aptly named "tough love" displayed by friends and family for another person's good. But they cannot become cold-hearted. A *Schuld* mentality becomes the atonement needed to reclaim their humanity. However, this is never calculable in such a way that the harm they have done is automatically absolved by some set number of good deeds.

An example of this kind of thinking is found in a revealing incident from Schweitzer's own life. He once had to physically confront, aggressively manhandle, and forcibly evict a "fetisher" from his hospital ward.[63] The trespasser was attempting to surgically implant magic fetishes made of animal bone and flesh into the bodies of Schweitzer's recovering patients in order to protect them from evil spirits. Schweitzer considered the man to be nothing less than a murderer. Several people had died from serious infections resulting from this man's private practice, and many of his patients had been taken to Schweitzer for last minute life-saving medical care. He was a menace to society and a direct threat to people in the hospital ward. He would also not be deterred by harsh words alone, so Schweitzer assaulted the man – but just enough to make him leave.

So, we must now ask, was what Schweitzer did justifiable? I think most of us would agree that he did the right thing. But was another human being mistreated and deprived of some of his rights? Yes, we would have to admit that Schweitzer wronged that man by assaulting him and thereby becoming guilty (*Schuldig*) under the deontological mandate of Reverence for Life. Still, the action was necessary to protect the lives of his recovering patients, and so Schweitzer willingly took both the responsibility and the guilt associated with that greater good.

This may all sound hopelessly convoluted. But there was a greater danger that Schweitzer feared. No system of ethics should ever be devised to use consequentialist justifications to absolve people from feeling responsible for what they need to do. This would distort a person's conscience and forever bury his or her heart beneath the mind's cold and inhuman logic. As Schweitzer puts it: "Man *may never* stop being human" (*APR* 55 [emphasis added]). He counsels: "wrest from humanity the impossible, never be quiet, never allow yourself to have what one calls a good conscience. For the ethical person there is no such thing as a good conscience, but always only battle with oneself, doubting and questioning" (ibid).

Reverence for Life is a virtue ethic of personal responsibility and unforgiving accountability. It strives to remain elemental in even its social expression, always returning to the antinomic tension between the head and the heart – between what we feel is wrong and what we know we have to do anyway. Redemption is never found by holding on to justifications that silence the inner voice of conscience; rather, it is found by doubting and questioning ourselves, and through the atonement of ethical service to others for mistakes made and regrets accumulated. This is a tough prescription for a philosophy of civilization, and it is none too clear when it comes to giving people guidance on *exactly* what they need to do to live moral lives. There is only the *Schuld* consciousness, which keeps a cumulative tab on the life debts that are amassed through the practical necessities and political trade-offs of which every person, directly or indirectly, is culpable.

Discussion

Now we arrive at the key problems towards which this chapter has been working. Schweitzer's antinomies accurately reflect the irreconcilable conflicts at the heart of society. Rather than collapsing them to favour one over the other (e.g., personal freedom or state security; political compromises or full public consensus), he preserves them in a check-and-balance system in order to enable to creative possibilities. The convoluted and contrary nature of his ethical discourses is therefore not revealing a fundamental flaw of his ethic. It is all by design.

The trend in philosophy is to advocate for a utopian vision born out of pure theory. Such positions have certain advantages and often appear, to varying degrees, plausible or even authoritative on account of their philosophical backing. They also have the advantage of being hard to disprove or dismiss. After all, can we say that Schopenhauer is really wrong in his advocacy of Philosopher-Kings? Truly, wouldn't such enlightened monarchies be better for social justice and world peace than what we see happening around the planet today? Hard to say: possibly, possibly not. There is simply no way to prove him right or wrong. We can only admire the elegance of his sophistry and enter into endless debates over the merits of his proposal. That is the key advantage of utopian political philosophies. But they also carry a danger, and Schweitzer knew this.

In commenting on the complex causes behind the First World War, Schweitzer identifies Kant's philosophy as a contributing factor. He concludes that, "at best, [rationalist ethics such as Kant's] can teach us a certain decency and justice ... [yet] when the time came for our ethic to be tested, it fell away from us" (APR 9–11). The horrors of the war revealed the ultimate superficiality of ethics born of practical reason alone. Over 9 million solders died and countless civilians as well, and Schweitzer concluded that the Kantian legacy was partially to blame. Kant had helped create an atmosphere of optimism regarding the progressive development of civilization through his utopian vision of reconciling the present world to a higher world through the categorical imperative. As a result, focused on the universalization of the desired end, "many a brave man set out for battle in the belief that he was fighting for a day when war would no longer exist ... [which] proved to be completely wrong. Slaughter and destruction continued year after year and were carried on in the most inhumane way" (PP).

Utopia is a chimerical word. It could just as easily be translated from the Greek as "no place" or as "good place." Perhaps this is why utopias only exist in the imagination and philosophical discourses. Schweitzer had no interest in utopia. Reverence for Life would not aim for a fantastical vision of society. He had no illusion that compassion could perfect society to the point at which wars would only exist in history books. His philosophy aims at the real world, a world filled with imperfections, immoral people, and corrupt governments. The political antinomies are necessary safeguards against these realities. Schweitzer's ethic had to be kept "contradictory and incomplete" because this is the reality of society itself.

The problem is not, then, with Schweitzer's antinomic framework. It is with the idea of ethics itself, or at least with what it has become. People *want* ethics to be a means to assuage guilt, to allow them to say "we had no choice," or "it was for the best." They demand a codified cultural super-ego that would allow them to defer to its authority and thereby to deflect blame – for example, to know if the torture of suspected criminals is ever justifiable or whether political assassinations of foreign despots are legal. But this is exactly where Schweitzer insists that the true evil of society resides: "Common sense wants to protest here that we are only responsible for that which current legal opinion claims we are. But the deeper, thinking conscience teaches us that the circle of our responsibility is not so staked out. Rather, we must live in a state of advanced uneasiness" (APR 88). This ethical uneasiness is the true cost of civilization.

The solution to the problem of creating an ethical society is not in finding a better rulebook but in making better people. For this reason Schweitzer seeks to create an *elemental* political philosophy. He sets the individual as a watchdog for social justice, a safeguard to keep inhuman institutions from excess and to become the moral conscience they cannot manifest. But this creates four problems he could not adequately resolve, and this is what I believe prevented him from completing his work. The first problem is this. For the actual human beings in power, it appears that they must often perform their jobs by becoming inhuman and immoral in their political decision making. A person in authority therefore pays a very dear price for his or her power. Schweitzer can only offer such people a few words of advice: "In all of your activity, you may *never be an impersonal energy, an organ of execution* of some sort of thing, *an agent of society*" (APR 55 [emphasis in original]). He goes on: "you must, rather, set your own personal morality over against that in all things, however embarrassing it is for you, and try, in everything you must do, to act according to humanity and according to your responsibility for the destiny that you are preparing for another person" (ibid.). This last part is in itself a most curious statement. In some undefined way, people in positions of power can help others find their own sense of personhood. How this is accomplished is not exactly clear.

The second problem involves the aforementioned issue of individual persons sometimes having to act in hurtful ways in order to be socially responsible. There is little guidance given about how or when this can be done. Such actions apparently emerge from an inner dialogue between a person's mind and heart, and thus they are an entirely subjective affair. There can be no way to objectively determine the rightness or wrongness of such actions beforehand. People can only do what they feel is right and suffer the consequences. A person must live in that state of ethical uneasiness and take action when circumstances require, such as when Schweitzer confronted the fetisher in his hospital ward. This is the reality of moral personhood, but still a dangerous principle around which to build an ethic.

Before introducing the third problem, it is necessary to briefly recap what has already been said. In 1919, when his sermons were written, Schweitzer held that institutions are imperfect instruments for the public good born out of practical necessity. The people in control of these public and private institutions faced a difficult moral dilemma. They often had to act impersonally and callously in order to ensure the efficient operation of their agency or business. Yet they also had to strive to remain human and compassionate – an impossible contradiction that nevertheless remained true. At the end of the day, a *Schuld* consciousness can only partially help such people remain good and moral. Ultimately, it is the power of the ethical genius who engages in civic and political affairs that would need to correct the institutional injustices of such a system.

But Schweitzer had also indicated that people must sometimes widen their views of good and evil in relation to greater social goods. This prescription could be greatly abused by those in power, and this is the third problem. I believe it is no coincidence that Schweitzer's last attempted draft for the final two volumes of *The Philosophy of Civilization* was written in 1945 (*KP III*, 16). Hitler had ascended to power in a surge of public enthusiasm, and he showed the world how terrible a charismatic "evil genius" can be if allowed to take control. It may well be that Schweitzer began to see his own concessions to necessary evil in his 1919 sermons (which were never meant to be published) as too dangerous to be put into writing.

But there is another complicating factor here that became apparent during Schweitzer's fight against atomic weapons, and this is the fourth problem. One nuclear industry critic, US atomic energy commissioner William Libby, claimed (falsely) that Schweitzer had failed to consider natural background radiation in his research (Brabazon 2000, 459). Schweitzer knew this was an attempt at subterfuge for he had carefully distinguished between naturally radioactive elements and unnatural isotopes resulting from nuclear testing. He decided not to respond to this critic so as to avoid dignifying the criticism. Two thousand American scientists subsequently embraced Schweitzer's report and signed a petition to the United Nations demanding the immediate stoppage of further testing (463). William Libby later resigned from the Atomic Energy Commission and conceded that Schweitzer was correct in indicating that radionuclide contamination of the environment was of "real concern" (Cousins 1985, 243).[64] This incident is noteworthy because in his 1958 "Declaration of Conscience" speech, Schweitzer spoke out against the power of public institutions. Apparently, he had lost faith in their efficacy:

Public opinion in all nations concerned must inspire and accept the agreement [against nuclear weapons]. When public opinion has been created in the countries concerned and among all nations – an opinion informed of the dangers involved in going on with the tests and led by the reason which this information imposes – then the statesmen may reach an agreement to stop the experiments. A public opinion of this kind stands in no need of plebiscites or of forming of committees to express itself. It works through just being there.

In this speech, Schweitzer places his faith entirely in the people alone, and in particular those ethical geniuses that could inspire the world's population to a conviction that could overcome the institutional *Will* set against them. His confrontation with the US Atomic Energy Commission showed him that public institutions could themselves become a great danger to the public welfare. They could not always be trusted. But only a little over a decade earlier it had been made abundantly clear that "geniuses" could also influence the public to malevolent ends. An ethic rooted in an antinomy that has the power of personalities to influence others at one end, and the inhuman logic of institutions to become agents of public welfare at the other, can sometimes become dominated by one or the other to undesirable ends, with no means to correct excesses.

In summary, the four problems Schweitzer could not fully resolve are: (1) people in business and other positions of authority must sometimes act against the dictates of their conscience; (2) ordinary people must often do the same in their personal affairs; (3) immoral and evil geniuses can influence society to malevolent ends; and (4) governmental institutions can become misdirected and begin working against the public good. Each threatens the antinomic balance that enables the possibility of the emergence of a truly moral society. In the end, Schweitzer could only assert the need for the development of true, self-determining personalities that could break free of the economic and institutional forces set against them. Reverence for Life is a virtue ethic. Its political expression would, in the final analysis, be entirely and necessarily dependent on such moral and visionary people to keep civilization on the right track. By this measure, Reverence for Life succeeds as a political philosophy.

Final Comments

The never completed volumes of Schweitzer's *The Philosophy of Civilization* were to detail exactly how a civil authority could be brought into agreement with his Reverence for Life philosophy. His thought on this subject is complex, sophisticated, and, at times, elegant. It is also contradictory and incomplete. This, however, is by design. It reflects Schweitzer's conviction that three antinomies exist at the heart of society: (1) freedom and security, (2) political compromise and public consensus, and (3) the utilitarianism of institutional necessity and the absolute deontological demands of personal morality.

People are given a unique dignity through their recursive self-awareness. They can become the author of their own lives. Personal freedom therefore desires to be maximized, to live as free as possible, to work and to earn personal wealth. But society functions through social contracts, whereby personal freedom is exchanged for law, order, and security. Society and the person are thereby drawn into conflict by an antinomic tension that can never be fully resolved. This basic antinomy expresses itself in different ways, depending on the context: liberty and security, private ownership and public responsibility, and so on. To mitigate these tensions, institutions are needed to employ depersonalized and, it is to be hoped, even-handed policies for the greater good and to keep the first antinomy in ethical relation. They must safeguard the public good. This means the greatest good for the greatest number – but not always for everyone. Institutions are too blunt and impersonal to do anything more. The governing institutions are therefore given their own antinomic principles: political compromise and public consensus. Public policies and laws, created through compromise, will only gain legitimacy if subsequently fully embraced by the people, who, in turn, are governed by the deontological demands of Reverence for Life. Individuals thereby check the power of the institutions and correct them when impersonal societal laws lose sight of justice. All three antinomies work together to prevent excess and to facilitate creative possibilities. Behind all this is the Reverence for Life virtue ethic, which promotes the development of ethical personhood for everyone. But Schweitzer's system only works if the antinomies remain in balance. If one gains dominance over the other, tyranny can result.

It is often claimed that the exception determines the rule. Schweitzer's political philosophy works well for general cases but not for the aberrant extremes. Charismatic but conscienceless geniuses can rise to sway the public opinion to their despicable ends. Powerful institutions like government agencies and multinational corporations can intentionally obfuscate and confuse the public to further their own self-serving ends, regardless of the public good. These realities are not even rare occurrences. Are we to then declare Schopenhauer and Nietzsche the true political philosophers and Schweitzer the daydreaming utopian? Is there no hope for democracy?

Maybe this is where faith enters Schweitzer's philosophy – not faith in divine intervention that will someday bring an evil world to justice, but faith in humanity itself. Like the essentialism of his New Rationalism, such faith cannot be validated by logical proofs but, rather, emerges as an apophatic possibility arising from our "I + will-to-live" ontological consciousness. The various synthetic a priori dreams of civilization have all come from that intangible foundation within human nature, being brought together into culturally cohesive wholes by the powerful personalities that define those eras.

It is a testament to Schweitzer's wisdom that he creates an antinomic framework for public governance and that he also acknowledges the role of charismatic ethical geniuses in moving civilization on the path towards true progress. This has always been the case in the past. This is the reason history remembers great figures such as the historical Jesus, Kant, Goethe, and maybe even Schweitzer himself. Reverence for Life is a moral compass, not a systematized rulebook. It could therefore be argued that Schweitzer actually presents a more realistic framework for practical governance than did his predecessors, but it is not one without imperfections. In the absence of a better system, his will have to do.

Schweitzer's entire system comes down to a single cornerstone – the ethical personality. Reverence for Life is an internal certainty, not an externalized and tabulated set of rules. This may seem an insubstantial foundation for an ethic, something that is far too subjective and far too problematic to try to use to secure a philosophy of civilization. But there is a deeper reality here and a truth more compelling than any system of logic could ever hope to produce. Schopenhauer, ethical genius that he is, encapsulates this in a simple thought experiment. He once asked his reader to imagine a man hopelessly enamoured with a particular woman, but she has fallen in love with another. The scorned suitor is then driven to a most appalling thought. He believes that if that other man is "out of the picture" his beloved will turn to him. A perfect and undetectable plan for murder then comes to his mind, one so cunning that nobody would ever be the wiser. Nothing stands between him and the object of his desire. It is only a matter of following through on his impassioned intent. Now, Schopenhauer asks his reader to come up with an ethical argument that could make him change his mind. It could be Kant's categorical imperative or some other philosopher's intellectualized argument. Alternately, he says the reader may want to consider that the prospect of God's judgment and eternal hellfire might restrain the scorned man – anything at all. Schopenhauer then provides his own answer to the thought experiment. He writes that when it comes to *actually* murdering someone, and *exactly* what it would take to physically kill, the rejected lover could not go through with it. A compassionate heart cannot betray itself, not for such a selfish reason, and so he desists from his plan. The inner voice of compassion thereby restrains the rage and allows for a more sublime character to take its place. Schopenhauer then drives home his point by comparing the two men – the one from the reader's thought experiment and the one from his own: "Now I ask any honest and unbiased reader: Which of the two is the better man? To which of them would he prefer to entrust his own destiny?" (*OBM* §19, 169). Schweitzer's virtue ethic aims at instilling this very same compassionate conscience in everyone. He trusts that people will make good and moral decisions in their personal, professional, and political lives. Schweitzer believed his reader would recognize the merits of a society in which their neighbours, employers, and politicians were guided by that same kind of compassion described by Schopenhauer when deciding on what is truly necessary. This is the cornerstone upon which his philosophy of civilization rests.

Chapter 7

Environmental Ethics

The last chapter shows the complexity of Schweitzer's thought on the subject of civil governance. While it is my contention that his political framework is realistic, solid, and profound, the final picture – to put it lightly – was rather ambiguous as to exactly what a Reverence for Life society would look like, besides having a parliamentarian or bicameral government that checks and balances political power. These are sound principles for a representative democracy, yes. But a distinguishing feature of Schweitzer's ethic, after all, is its valuation of non-human life. How can this be incorporated into such a system of governance? To answer this remaining question, in this final chapter I examine the subject of environmental ethics in a contemporary context.

I begin by taking note of the comments by the acclaimed biographer of Schweitzer's life, James Brabazon (2002). In reflecting on the state of the world in this new century, he writes that if Schweitzer were alive today, he would say: "Very sorry, but I told you so" (5). Schweitzer was deeply concerned about the development of ethical personhood in the face of "enormous industrial organizations" and other threats to individuality, such as nationalism, fascism, and fundamentalist religion (5–6). In Brabazon's opinion, economic institutions are now more dangerous to humanity than Hitler and Stalin ever were (11). A sensational claim to be sure. He supports it by pointing out that crushing and dehumanizing economic realities are now silently reducing countless millions to destitution and starvation, while wilderness is being erased from the face of the earth by corporations chasing after that last dollar as demoralized billions simply sigh resignedly and say: "that's just the way it is." This, Brabazon writes, is what Reverence for Life seeks to oppose. Its power lies in the fact that "it takes away our excuses" for doing nothing (15). Change can only arise from individuals of strong ethical character, and only when they appear will the institutions that collectively control our lives be reformed: "That is why reverence for life is just as important now as when Schweitzer first spoke it – and always will be. The difference is that now the soil is far more fertile" (21). At the turn of the twenty-first century, Brabazon believes that the world is finally ready to hear what Schweitzer has to say.

Brabazon's comments certainly appear to be well founded, especially if the economic commentary in chapter 1 is kept in mind. Even so, Schweitzer only provides a few direct references to environmental issues. He mostly writes about the dehumanizing and disempowering economic circumstances of modern life, and how these prevented the emergence of ethical personalities who would be guided by Reverence for Life to fight for social justice. While Schweitzer believes that such people would also be compassionate towards non-human life, Reverence for Life, as reflected in his writings, is not really an environmental ethic in the contemporary sense – which is to say, it does not adequately take into consideration ecological wholes, long-term sustainability, co-evolutionary dynamics, and other abstractions beyond immediate perception.

Nevertheless, despite such concerns not being directly addressed, at the heart of Reverence for Life is an *elemental* nature philosophy. Schweitzer always intended that it would be developed further by those "thinking men and women" of particular cultures, times, and circumstances he could not know. The universal truths in his philosophical framework were to become the seeds of thought for their own synthetic a priori projects. Schweitzer's New Rationalism would allow these other persons to give the specific contextual answers that he could not, trapped as he was in his own culturally and historically determined worldview. That is the beauty of an ethic built around universal truths contained within the "I + will-to-live" nexus. It allows a new cultural ethos to emerge as a historically conditioned reality anywhere and for any time.

It is therefore both possible and permissible to look for ways to expand Schweitzer's writings through other systems of ethics that are compatible with Reverence for Life. With this in mind, I begin this exploration on environmental ethics by looking at Aldo Leopold, whose Land Ethic mirrors

Schweitzer's work in many ways. Curiously, there is no evidence that they ever read each other's writings: they appear to have developed their ethical systems independently. This, in part, explains certain divergences in their otherwise remarkably similar ethical worldviews. For example, Leopold often takes a macroscopic view, focusing on the health of an entire biotic community. Schweitzer, on the other hand, tends to focus on the well-being of individual life. While many commentators allege that, for this reason, their systems are incompatible, my investigation reveals that this is not the case. There is a natural complementarity between Schweitzer's work and that of Leopold, such that they harmonize to produce a more complete environmental ethic than either could alone.

I then turn to Colin Duncan's economic commentary. His work explores the question of how to develop strong local economies that are in balance with their adjoining agricultural and ecological systems. The focus here is not the ethical dimensions of human activity in relation to non-human life; rather, it is the problem of redressing the damage to the very personhood of those trapped in dehumanizing economic relationships, such as those described by Brabazon. Duncan's commentary allows us to return to the central subject of chapter 1: ethical personhood in economic society. Brabazon is certainly correct in identifying the centrality of this idea in Schweitzer's philosophy, and Duncan reveals one way in which this can be achieved in terms of practical governance. His emphasis on ecologically sustainable agricultural communities united under a local currency reveals a potentially powerful solution to reconnecting human-to-human reciprocity in modern economic life, at least in certain circumstances. Duncan's work can add an important practical dimension to the largely theoretical work of Schweitzer and, to some extent, to Leopold's as well.

Finally, in response to global environmental crises and the great need to bring people together for concerted action, a number of prominent academics have sought to create new cosmologies that combine science, metaphysics, and religious themes. They are intended to be nondenominational and uncontroversial. In this way, they seek to serve as an effective intermediary for consensus building in a pluralistic society. In effect, they produce what Schweitzer calls a worldview – that is, a way of seeing the world through a common rubric of understanding. Schweitzer's ethic is meant to be exactly that, only under a different name. My investigation will therefore conclude with a discussion of Reverence for Life in relation to one of these new cosmologies: the commonwealth of life model developed by Peter G. Brown.

Schweitzer and Leopold

The great American wildlife ecologist Aldo Leopold is known as the author of a set of nature essays and conservation commentaries entitled *The Sand County Almanac*. His writings are hailed as being among the most beautiful American prose on the subject ever created, easily the equal to the works of Henry David Thoreau and John Muir. Those who have read his book know the purity and passion of his expression; those who have not read it should. His work is an unquestioned masterpiece of its genre. It begins with anecdotal stories from his own experience of working with the land over the course of a year, taking the reader from the cold snows of January, month by month, to the December winter once again. Each of the stories contains either a simple moral lesson about environmental history, or discusses the lives of animals, or simply portrays the breathtaking beauty and harmony of nature. His book appeals to age-old wisdom about living in ecological reciprocity with the local biotic community, and it extends to virtually every area in which humankind's relationship to the earth is manifested – from economics, to education, to religion, and even to the deeper spiritual appreciation of nature.

In its final edited form (it was published posthumously), *The Sand County Almanac* concludes with a series of philosophically minded essays. But Leopold would not be considered as a philosopher in the strict academic sense; rather, he was a man of uncommon wisdom and ethical vision who, through his scientific training and a lifetime of work in the applied ecological sciences, saw what type of changes needed to take place in order to achieve true environmental sustainability. However, and quite regrettably, many in the domain of philosophy look down on the field of applied ethics, and this is doubly true for an applied discipline based in scientific empiricism. Academic philosophers instead tend to prefer the pure theory of philosophical phenomenology, hermeneutics, existentialism, poststructuralism, social constructionism, or any of the other erudite theories in favour today. It is for this reason that Callicott (1987, 387) notes that some academics have considered Leopold's Land Ethic as being, at one extreme, merely incoherent and, at the other, "dangerous nonsense."

Nevertheless, others in academia consider Leopold's empirical sensibilities to be his foremost virtue since he is not so esoteric as to preclude wide appeal. Even so, some defenders concede that, as a philosophy, his work is "little more than a noble, but naive, moral plea, altogether lacking a supporting theoretical framework" (Callicott 1987, 387). The central problem remains that Leopold does not address those basic philosophical problems of ontological existence, Kantian sensory perception, and an accompanying theory of knowledge – all of which are subjects that Schweitzer does address. This is the first area in which a potential complementarity can be identified between the two thinkers. Since Schweitzer wanted his work to be developed further by other thinkers, it may be possible to use his writings to add that missing philosophical dimension needed by academia to recognize Leopold as more than merely someone writing about the practical wisdom of conservation.

But first, the allegation that Leopold is philosophically naïve should not be conceded so easily. Despite what uncharitable academics allege, Leopold's ethic is much more substantial than he is given credit for. Leopold borrows a key philosophical principle from the American pragmatist Arthur Twining Hadley (1856–1930) to ground his Land Ethic (Norton 2003, 15). In a 1923 essay, Leopold reveals his debt to Hadley: "How happy a definition is that one of Hadley's which states, 'Truth is that which prevails in the long run!'" (Leopold 1991, 96).[65] What Leopold does here is quite profound and not obvious at first glance. In a most innovative way he employs Hadley's principle as an empirical test for any ecological philosophy. He uses it as a kind of natural selection for testing the veracity of philosophical hypotheses. What he means is this: Traditional ecological knowledge can be seen as trustworthy because it survived throughout history; those cultural beliefs were shaped and adapted to the ecological limits of that geographic region. It is a process of natural selection for cultural values. Leopold adopts some of that ecological wisdom in his Land Ethic because it has been determined by that time-tested and empirical measure to be verifiable *Truth*.

This opening, derived from Hadley, allows Leopold to use the ecological wisdom of Isaiah and Ezekiel in his Land Ethic; further, it is why he wrote an entire essay entitled "The Forestry of the Prophets" about ecological awareness in the Hebrew Bible (71–7).[66] In Leopold's opinion, the ancient Hebrews had acquired empirically verifiable, culturally defined ecological *Truth* that helped them to survive as a viable community. This is noteworthy because Leopold combines science, religion, and philosophy in order to arrive at something remarkably similar to one aspect of Schweitzer's project. As is mentioned in chapter 4, Schweitzer takes Nietzsche's idea that a culturally defined truth must be evaluated on the basis of whether or not it is ultimately life-affirming and correlated to the best available empirical science. This is how its *Truth* is to be ascertained. For both writers, a cultural truth must be based on, but not limited to, scientific findings.

However, before this relationship of complementarity can be further investigated, the question of Schweitzer's own ecological awareness and sensitivity to conservation matters must be addressed. Up until this point, I have only shown Schweitzer to be an academic philosopher. But he is much more than that. Just like Leopold, he is very much focused on how his theories can be practically expressed in real-world ecological and social contexts. Even though this is not reflected in his written works, it is revealed in the construction and operation of his hospital. Therefore, as a necessary and useful aside, some of that history will now be recounted.

Schweitzer's Land Ethic

Mougin and Mougin (2007, 21) report that, when building his hospital, Schweitzer chose to use local building materials such as timber rather than the concrete and bricks available from the colonial authorities. One reason for this was his personal economic philosophy of self-sufficiency. He also considered the superior attributes of the local materials in terms of heat dissipation, and he wanted to give recovering patients a sense of familiarity during their time of stress by replicating aspects of local dwellings (21–2). Not only that, Schweitzer designed the facilities to make use of innovative passive solar architecture. He even created a natural filtration water treatment system because he did not want to become dependent on the expensive chemicals available from the colonial stores (22). In all this it must be recalled that Schweitzer was practising such green design techniques decades before environmentalism became a buzzword. For him it was merely Reverence for Life expressed in a real-world economic scenario. It was also a pedagogy aimed at moral lessons concerning his philosophy. This is perhaps most clear in the design of his hospital garden.

Local swidden agricultural practice was to "slash and burn" parts of the surrounding rainforest, to intensively harvest crops on the cleared land until the soil was exhausted, and then to move on to another section of jungle. With a low population and nearly endless jungle, there was no need for conservation. Yet Schweitzer decided against this practice. He only cleared and terraced a few hectares near the hospital grounds next to the river. Half the land would be cultivated each year, while the other half would be allowed to be inundated by the river during the rainy season. This replenished the soil with river sediments, just as in the Nile delta. Schweitzer also composted food wastes and animal manure to further improve soil productivity in the garden and the nearby orchards. One of his aims was to showcase his economic philosophy of self-sufficiency to the local people and "to set good examples for the community" by not destroying plants and trees unnecessarily (Mougin and Mougin 2007, 20).

Claudine and Damien Mougin are the current directors of Schweitzer's hospital, and they have brought back these facilities and practices. Twelve nursing stations have also been opened to extend service into the surrounding areas, each with "adjoining gardens to promote market gardening techniques" as part of their greater communitarian commitment to the well-being of the Gabonese (Mougin and Mougin 2007, 21). The directors are concerned, just as Schweitzer was, that local soil will become depleted by traditional agricultural techniques and that the people will become "more dependent on foreign food products" as a result. They worry about malnourishment caused by an improper diet from foreign junk foods since "undernourished children [are] arriving at the hospital in an area where water, land, and sunshine are plentiful" (21), just as was the case in Schweitzer's day. Schweitzer's desire to promote a sustainable subsistence economy for Gabon in harmony with regional ecological systems is continuing today at a local scale. Local sustainability is a subject that is attracting considerable attention in environmental ethics, and I return to it when I discuss the views of Colin Duncan.

Individual versus Collective Moral Consideration

Schweitzer, it could be said, foreshadows the environmental ethicist Aldo Leopold, whose own Land Ethic was developed in response to the wasteful land-use patterns he observed in North America. Like Leopold, Schweitzer is concerned with long-term ecological sustainability and with teaching these lessons to the communities living on the land. Schweitzer even went as far as to pay locals to bring in orphaned animals found in the jungle so that they could be raised under his veterinary care and returned to the wild. And he occasionally writes about this with unbridled joy (E-RFL 238–9). Teaching environmentalism is part of his greater ethical worldview. It therefore can be rightfully claimed that there *is* a common connection here with Leopold on the practical governance of environmental resources within a worldview that includes the local biotic community. But the correspondences run even deeper.

Aldo Leopold's (1966, 262) famous Land Ethic is presented in *The Sand County Almanac* clearly and simply: "A thing is right when it tends to preserve the integrity, stability, and beauty of the biotic community. It is wrong when it tends otherwise." A very similar axiomatic principle is presented in Schweitzer's own ethic: "evil is what annihilates, hampers, or hinders life ... goodness, by the same token, is the saving or helping of life, the enabling of whatever life I can to attain its highest development" (*E-RFL* 230). The difference between the two remarkably similar adages is that Leopold considers the collective biotic community while Schweitzer considers the actions that affect particular life. This reveals another possible problem that needs to be addressed.

Callicott (1987, 391 [emphasis in original]) claims that Reverence for Life "provides no possibility whatever for the moral consideration of wholes – of threatened *populations* of animals and plants, or of endemic, rare, or endangered *species*, or of biotic *communities*, or most expansively, of the *biosphere* in its totality" (see also Callicott 1986, 250). It is easy to see how he comes to that conclusion. The importance of biodiversity for ecological community resilience is not something of which Schweitzer would have been aware, given his time in history and academic background. The question of whether or not Schweitzer was at all sensitive to ecosystem dynamics in the modern sense is not clear, and there is at least some anecdotal evidence that would seem to suggest that he was not.

In a letter dated 12 August 1960, Schweitzer mentions that large numbers of weaverbirds had taken up residence at his hospital (*Letters* 303). The birds would join in when the hospital chickens were fed, and they built nests in the palm trees nearest the kitchen coops. The congregation of nests was unnaturally numerous because of the chicken feed, and the palms were slowing dying as a result of having their leaves continually stripped by the birds. Schweitzer writes: "The poor palms could be rescued if we shot the birds, but we can't get ourselves to do that. As a result, we have lost dozens of trees" (303). Perhaps it is revealing that the letter is to the director of the Association for the Prevention to the Cruelty to Animals. Nevertheless, even though he laments the life that is dying out in those trees, neither he nor his staff could kill weaverbirds to save them (unlike the hawks mentioned previously). His affection for the birds and their beautifully woven nests kept him, in this case, from taking life to save life.

This example certainly does not bode well for environmental ethics. Environmental managers must sometimes make seemingly harsh decisions in order to rebalance an ecological community adversely affected by human activity. On occasion, these decisions involve culling species that are overpopulated and are degrading the local environment. Leopold (1991, 342) himself became extremely frustrated with those sentimental but misguided persons who, out of a misplaced sense of "chivalry," protested the killing of does and fawns during the necessary culling of deer populations. To put it bluntly, kind-heartedness and compassion are not suitable bases for sound environmental planning. If, for the sake of argument, this one example of overpopulated weaverbirds is taken as indicative of his sensibilities on these matters, Schweitzer's ethic of individualized compassion would seem an ill-suited starting point for an environmental ethic, just as Callicott alleges.

But, in all fairness, it is not possible to conclude from this one letter that Schweitzer lacked an awareness of the need to balance relationships between species within ecosystems. The hospital was, after all, in the middle of a vast old-growth jungle, and a few lost palms and a few extra weaverbirds would not unbalance the co-evolutionary dynamics within the Gabonese rainforest community. It is also true that the weaverbirds would have greatly added to the aesthetic appeal of the hospital grounds to both hospital staff and recovering patients. Even Leopold (1991, 263) does not advocate trying to return nature to pre-settlement conditions; rather, he argues that any properly maintained landscape should become a "portrait" of its owner's aesthetic sensibilities. Such an imposition upon the land is therefore not only *not* improper but also the very purpose of Leopold's Land Ethic. Love for the beauty of the land and its biota is necessary for its caretaking because "husbandry of someone else's land [would be] a contraction in terms" (298). I therefore cannot fault Schweitzer for his decision here.

Despite Schweitzer's reluctance to sometimes make those tough decisions, his philosophy does combine an absolute ethic with a debt-based ethical consciousness. It is therefore permissible in Schweitzer's system to eat meat, shoot birds, chop down trees, kill harmful bacteria, or perform any of the other ethical trade-offs that people must make in order to live truly moral lives. He only asks that people bring a conscious awareness of the effect of their actions on each and every living being – and take that debt (*Schuld*) awareness and turn it into a deep and sincere intention to repay those trade-offs through good actions aimed at promoting life in others. Schweitzer's decisions with regard to the construction and operation of his hospital show that he could and did make ethical trade-offs in clearing the minimum amount of jungle in order to provide a greater good for the nearby human and biotic community through his medical and veterinary care. This shows his ethical *Schuld* repayment consciousness in action. For this reason, it can be legitimately claimed that Reverence for Life does expand from an individualist focus to include greater conscientious action directed at the betterment of the whole biotic community and, potentially, even at the biosphere in its entirety.

With this in mind, there is a precedent for a theoretical model in Schweitzer's writings that can be used to further support a Reverence for Life ecological framework. In the context of ethical personhood, Schweitzer emphasizes the relational aspects of human beings: no person exists independently of his or her fellows but, rather, must interact socially, economically, and ethically in order to create a viable community. Moreover, Schweitzer's focus on individualized moral consideration does not preclude his saying that some individuals may be *sacrificed* for a greater good. Considering that this comment was made in the context of political leaders and that it concerned events that affected human lives, such as a nation's decision to send soldiers off to war, it is a very small step indeed to extend this Reverence for Life principle to the practical governance of non-human life. In other words, Schweitzer's ethic for the human community readily expands to include necessary trade-offs of non-human life in lands needed for human economic subsistence and collective well-being – such as in the case of the hospital gardens and orchards he constructed for the benefit of the whole biotic community.

Anthropocentrism

It will quickly be noted that the basis for considering the biotic community in these arguments is ultimately self-serving. It is. Yet it is also in keeping with Leopold's own Land Ethic. He likewise believes that the "real end is a *universal symbiosis with land*, economic and [a]esthetic, public and private" (Leopold 1991, 188 [emphasis in original]). The Land Ethic, built as it is around time-tested ecological wisdom, seeks to create true sustainability for the human community through the biotic community. This brings us back to the concern regarding the anthropocentrism of both Schweitzer's and Leopold's ethics. Consider, for example, the following words from Leopold: "And if there be, indeed, a special nobility inherent in the human race – a special cosmic value, distinctive from and *superior* to all other life – by what token shall it be manifest? By a society decently respectful of its own *and all other life*, capable of inhabiting the earth without defiling it? ... [or as one that unthinkingly destroyed other species] and thereby exterminated itself?" (97 [emphases added]).

Leopold held that humans had a special status above other animals. Schweitzer felt the same way. This was because our species alone had the potential to become an ethical Force in the world. This set us apart among beings that are otherwise equal in their will-to-live. A short passage from an early sermon is illustrative (*APR* 16–7 [emphasis in original]):

Nature teaches cruel egotism, interrupted only for a short time
by the urge it has placed in its creatures to offer love and help to
their young for as long as needed. But that the animal loves its own
young with self-sacrifice even to death, and thus can empathize in
that instance, makes it more horrible that it is denied sympathy for
creatures unrelated to itself. The world, delivered up to ignorant
egoism, is like a valley shrouded in darkness. Only on the peaks
above there is light. All must live in darkness. One creature alone
may ascend to see the light: the highest creature, *man*. He may
achieve knowledge of reverence for life; he may aspire to knowledge
of sharing and of compassion; he may step out and transcend the
ignorance in which the rest of creation languishes ... here, in [this]
one existence, life as such comes to consciousness of itself.

Humans alone have the potential to harmonize their personal will
with the ethical force contained within the universal will-to-live as it is
uniquely revealed in our ontological consciousness. For Schweitzer, this
means that humankind can actually become the thinking aspect of the
evolutionary Will: "I become [an] imaginative force like that which works
mysteriously in nature, and thus I give my existence a meaning from
within [when directed] outwards" (*POC* 283). The anthropocentrism of
this statement is obvious. But it is not the exaltation of the human species, only the designation of a particular responsibility to those who are
to think for the unconscious and capricious Creative Will of nature. This
could be the cause of much mischief on our part, and indeed it has been.
Schweitzer does not specify what direction human thought should take
the evolving biosphere, but the anthropocentrism is bound by Reverence
for Life. Schweitzer indicates that our creative agency only finds its proper
actualization when directed selflessly towards the biosphere.

This is not the Dominion of domination that Dansdill fears (see chapter
5). This is because, as Schweitzer writes: "In us beings who can move about
freely and are capable of pre-considered, purposive working, the impulse
to perfection is given in such a way that we aim at raising to their highest material and spiritual value both ourselves and every existing thing
which is open to our influence" (*POC* 282). This is humility and altruism,
not aggrandizement and the privileging of the human species over and
above so-called lower life forms. And, for this reason, "ethics consist ...
in my experiencing the compulsion to show to all [other] will[s]-to-live
the same reverence as I do to my own" (309). This, then, is the true nature
of Schweitzer's mysticism: "Whenever my life devotes itself in any way

to life, my finite will-to-live experiences union with the infinite [W]ill in which all life is one" (313). Schweitzer's philosophy reverses the power relationships that would ordinarily be expected of anthropocentrism. As the ones who think for the unconscious Will of nature, it falls to humans to redress the sufferings and injustices in the world, both the natural one and human society.

But there are other ethical implications here as well. Because humans alone have the potential to act as moral agents, every potential moral agent saved creates an opportunity for further actualization of the Reverence for Life ethic. This is why, generally speaking, Schweitzer's ethics can be said to have the saving of human life as its highest calling. It can be inferred from his life example that Schweitzer also directs moral agents to favour those animals who can suffer, with the ethical prioritization being generally proportional to the sentience of the non-human life form – for example, higher primates and mammals over fish and insects. Notwithstanding, the call of ethical responsibility is boundless, and Schweitzer will not endorse any kind of relative ethic or altruistic prioritization. He admonishes his readers that even dying worms on a sun-baked sidewalk should elicit our intense pity (KP III 403) and that not one flower should be plucked for idle amusement (POC 318), for "is it not possible that they feel and are sensitive even if we cannot demonstrate it?" (APR 25). Like Leopold, Schweitzer presents humanity as the thinking aspect of the biosphere and as the one that must ensure the collective and best good for all. But for both ethicists it is an anthropocentrism consisting of humility and stewardship, not exclusionary exploitation and unthinking domination. It is not an entitlement but a responsibility.

Practical Environmental Management

Reverence for Life is unapologetically deontological – which is to say, it supports an absolute ethic that refuses to make concessions to mitigating circumstances or to allow for special exceptions. Regardless of the situation, Schweitzer points a finger at us and charges that *we are responsible for the lives around us.* This is why academics have found Reverence for Life unworkable and unrealistic. But the tension between a conclusion that demands moral agents to honour each and every life irrespective of species, and the seeming impossibility of this task, is not something Schweitzer overlooks. As he points out in his 1936 article "The Ethics of Reverence for Life," this is the whole aim of his philosophy: "An absolute ethic calls for the creating of perfection in this life. It cannot be achieved; but that fact does not really matter. In this sense reverence for life is an absolute ethic. It does not lay down specific rules for each possible situation. It simply tells us that we are responsible for the lives about us" (*E-RFL* 130).

Schweitzer believes that an absolute ethic is needed to keep people and society forever striving for new levels of justice and social progress. By the same logic, the practical considerations of life will always ensure that we fall short of that ideal, that we never reach that infinitely receding horizon of perfection. But rather than merely ensuring that we accumulate guilt, which leaves people powerless, the absolute ethic becomes the very engine that drives Ethical Mysticism. Let me explain. Schweitzer believes that the "microscopic" focus on individual and particular life must never be lost in an ethical calculus of larger goods and lesser evils. The tension here is preserved and accentuated by Schweitzer, intentionally so. On one hand, the role of *Schuld* (that is to say, life-debts) becomes a necessary safeguard against those looking to offhandedly justify or tolerate unethical choices. Schweitzer considered the greatest danger of all was an excuse for necessary evils. As he puts it, "the good conscience is the work of the devil" (*POC* 318). It is an easy matter to come up with some kind of convenient story to pretend that a self-serving decision is morally acceptable for "the greatest number" or "in the long run" when, in reality, it may simply be a means of justifying one's exclusionary and selfish behaviour. Consequentialist logic can be dangerous. Only an absolute ethic can defeat the incipient evil lurking in the human spirit.

Ethical conviction takes its strength from a deep subjectivity because compassion is psychological and the impulse to act comes from a pre-rational reaction to suffering. This is both a strength and a potential flaw in such an ethic. There is an obvious danger that impassioned altruism may miss the "big picture" and result in greater harm – let's say, for example, if the hawks that Schweitzer once killed had been an endangered species and the weaverbirds were in fact over-populated, depleting their resource base, and collectively facing starvation. He does, however, leave a door open to deal with these larger considerations.

Through Reverence for Life, Schweitzer promotes an elemental nature philosophy that intentionally leaves the overall vision of its manifestation to be interpreted in situation-specific cultural and historical contexts. It allows for a specific strategy towards which altruistic impulses may be directed, such as the one based on Leopold's Land Ethic. Even so, Schweitzer considered the microscopic focus on individual life necessary for keeping policy decisions from obscuring the consequences to individual lives from the necessary trade-offs. Yet he allowed for the necessary work to be done *regardless.*

So how does this come together into a workable ethic? It is true that Schweitzer refuses to lay down rules for indicating when ethical trade-offs can be made or to tabulate the exact type of repayment that must be made in each case. He is not a consequentialist in this sense. How a personal life-debt is to be repaid is quite subjective. But this is not a flaw in Reverence for Life. It is trust. Leopold's Land Ethic is similarly undefined and non-specific for the same reason (Leopold 1991, 337):

> If the individual has a warm personal understanding of land, he
> will perceive of his own accord that it is something more than a
> breadbasket. He will see the land as a community of which he is
> only a member, albeit the dominant one. He will see the beauty,
> as well as the utility, of the whole, and know the two cannot be
> separated. We love (and make intelligent use of) what we have
> learned to understand ... Once you learn to read the land, I have no
> fear of what you will do to it, or with it. And I know many pleasant
> things it will do to you.

Schweitzer similarly declares that "it is not by receiving instruction about the agreement between [the] ethical and necessary that a man makes progress in ethics, but only by coming to hear more and more plainly the voice of the ethical, by becoming ruled more and more by the longing to preserve and promote life, and by becoming more and more obstinate in resistance to the necessity for destroying or injuring life" (*POC* 317). Like Leopold, Schweitzer believes and *trusts* that each individual "alone has to judge this issue, by letting himself be guided by a feeling of the highest possible responsibility towards other life" (317–18). While this may seem an insubstantial and ambiguous foundation for an ethic, both writers aim for changing hearts and minds and then trust people to act with true moral character. Its wisdom depends entirely on whether most people are, at heart, naturally good and moral beings. But lest Schweitzer be accused of unfounded optimism, his views on civil authority should also be kept in mind (see chapter 6). It is trust within the democratic safeguards of communitarian vigilance and legal enforcement for the greater public welfare.

It is not possible to fully reveal the potential synergy between Schweitzer and Leopold. The task would take an entire book, if not several, to show the depth of their thought and how deep the correspondences go between them. The discussion provided above can only point the way for others to carry forward this exciting work. An academically rigorous philosophy that fully accounts for the natural world apart from Cartesian perception was the missing piece that would have given Aldo Leopold the standing he needed to be respected in this field. Likewise, it is possible to extend the Reverence for Life ethic beyond the individual to collective communitarian well-being. The way is now clear for scholars to look for other ways to combine the ethical systems of these two great figures. In what follows I offer some possibilities.

Colin Duncan and Local Economies

Schweitzer became deeply troubled about the damaging consequences for the development of moral character that were emerging in modern market economies. He found that these dehumanizing changes had taken place not only in Europe but also in one of its African colonies. People were increasingly becoming dependent on "soulless" industrialized institutions for subsistence when, previously, individual well-being had been provided through interdependent communitarianism. Another serious problem was that people everywhere were being overworked and driven to seek unthinking distraction. Little time and inclination was left for developing community relations or for seeking personal enrichment and strengthening ethical personhood. Schweitzer's prescription to remedy this situation is not fully specified. But he does point to the need for society to provide for a more equitable distribution of wealth and, wherever possible, to create a subsistence economy in order to enable these community-building relationships to take place.

Colin Duncan (1996) engages in a similar critique of political economy, but he does so with the aim of finding ways to re-embed human relationships in new ecologically sustainability communities. His research focuses on Kozo Uno (1897–1977), a Japanese economist who had come to the conclusion that modern economic relations denied people the opportunity to achieve full personhood (146–7). The problem is that, as Duncan explains, "workers have essentially no contact (except by the merest accident) with the eventual users of the goods they make … This system thus implies a separation of labour from life, and *that* is fundamentally what renders it inhuman" (148 [emphasis in original]). Schweitzer came to the same conclusion about modern economic life. Their views, arrived at independently, are remarkably similar. Consider, for example, the following words from Schweitzer: "The type of man who once cultivated his own bit of land becomes a worker who tends a machine in a factory; manual workers and independent trades-people become [institutionalized] employees. They lose the elementary freedom of the man who lives in his own house and finds himself in immediate connection with Mother Earth ... The conditions of their existence are therefore unnatural" (POC 87).

Duncan likewise identifies agricultural life as the fundamental unit of historical social organization. But neither he nor Schweitzer calls for the abandonment of modern life and a return to rural community origins; rather, both believe that the relationships typified by those more immediate settings can be recreated in new ways. Duncan (1996, 177) begins by widening definitions: "By the term 'agricultural' I mean here something broader than field-produced, more like 'life-produced,' so as to include wood, fish, wool, etc., not just vegetation edible by humans." The entirety of rural life and the economic exchanges that take place therein can then be brought within this concept. It refers not just to the farmer but the weaver, the village store owner, the baker, the artisan, and everyone else in the local town or village. Duncan then describes ways for "federating agricultural communities with urban areas" under special exchange and tax arrangements (176). The aim of this rural/urban federation would be to allow "the best of both worlds" and to collectively add to the quality of life for all. It produces a synergy of interests: "[the] farmers would have a much-expanded and steady market on which to base expanded production plans" (177). In exchange, "the farm communities would be happy to spend their credits with city-dwellers who were able to supply specialized services such as education, medicine, music, etc." (ibid.).

These local rural economic communities would operate and be federated with urban centres through a new concept of currency: the local exchange trading system (LETS). Prototypes of such a local currency system have already been established, including on Vancouver Island in Canada (Duncan 1996, 171). LETS is based on a generalized trading of services and goods; it is not limited to specific individuals and trade agreements but circulated throughout the entire community: "In contrast to barter, however, the two parties need not wait until they can do a reciprocal deal with each other. The vendor may spend the credit (or part of it) with any other person or firm willing to trade under the system. Likewise the purchase may pay off the debt by performing some service or selling some good to some other party. At all times the system is in a state of perfect monetary stability. The absolute value of the money supply necessarily remains zero" (171).

What are the advantages of such a system? For one thing, it is not based on a loan-debt concept of money under a private banking "federal reserve" institutional arrangement that obligates repayment at interest. This often leads to obligatory economic expansion into the natural world in the search for new sources of wealth to repay those loans (e.g., those activities Brabazon describes at the beginning of this chapter). Such a system of currency makes capitalism necessarily expansionist: it must grow or die just to repay the hidden debt in the money itself. LETS, on the other hand, can promote economic growth without this unnatural incentive. This would greatly help society to avoid "jobs versus owls" dilemmas, which result in so much destruction of the natural world. Second, LETS is *one* way in which to envision Leopold's Land Ethic's being translated into a functioning economic system in harmony with local agricultural means. But the greatest advantage, according to Duncan (1996, 179), is that such a system would honour "the cultural basis of personality." Capitalism, as it is manifested in the world today, cannot do this. And, moreover, it stands against the manifestation of "full personhood" for those people trapped on the treadmills of debt and consumerism (ibid.). LETS also has "a liberating effect on the self-esteem of many individuals who indeed have nothing of value to offer from the perspective of the conventional, 'outside' economy" (171). It makes the economy human again.

Restoring the capacity for self-chosen personhood in modern economic life is also Schweitzer's foremost concern. He saw this as a root cause of the crisis of civilization at the beginning of the twentieth century. However, he did not offer specific recommendations in terms of civil expression or practical governance. This is where the work of Colin Duncan can add to Reverence for Life. Duncan argues that the redress for economically disconnected human relations and for protecting bioregional cultural carrying capacity may be attained through "ecologically grounded, strong, local economies" (181). The key is to re-establish "contact with life" through those types of economic relations, including but not limited to agriculture, that facilitate interpersonal reciprocity within the community *and* the local ecology (177, 181). It is one way, but not the only way, to make both Schweitzer's and Leopold's visions an economic reality in the twenty-first century.

Duncan's work breaks down the false dichotomy that has the spectre of a stagnated state-planned economy as one alterative and the Nietzschean nightmare of socially atomized individuals surrendering the organization of society to inhuman market dynamics as the other. There are ways to democratically design an economy to have the best of both without the undesirable consequences of either – that is, to have the distributional efficiency of a market economy together with the social protection of legislation that provides for the public welfare (e.g., through pollution control laws, unemployment insurance, occupational safety standards, etc.). Stated another way, it is indeed possible to accomplish what the renowned economic historian Karl Polanyi calls the "rediscovery of society" for a modern industrialized world.[67]

Duncan's economic model could serve as one means of transcending the impasse of these undesirable alternatives, to achieve Polanyi's economic reforms, and to translate Schweitzer's commentary into practical governance. Schweitzer had similarly identified the transparent economic realities of agricultural life as the foundation of social personhood, and he believed that those no longer working in such agrarian settings could re-embed themselves in the greater human community through the Reverence for Life worldview. This was to be the necessary prescription to restore those social relations fragmented by the atomizing forces of modern market economies. But while Schweitzer had no interest in the collectivism of early twentieth-century counter-movements to capitalism, the locally administered "democratic federalism" described by Duncan, I believe, would be a proposal that Schweitzer could accept as a historically legitimate manifestation of cultural values in harmony with Reverence for Life.

Not only that, such an economic and ecological vision may be the answer, at least in part, to beginning to redress the horrifying problems of the modern world Brabazon describes at the start of this chapter. If anything, it could even be said that he did not go far enough. This is because Schweitzer had come to the conclusion that modern economic life had damaged the very *psyche* of people such that they "acquire thereby the mentality of unfree men, in which ideals of civilization can no longer be contemplated with the needful clarity, but become distorted to correspond with the surrounding atmosphere of struggle" (*POC* 88). This struggle, as he mentions earlier in the same passage, is "against Nature or the competition of his fellows" to the point at which it exceeds all normal social relations (ibid.). People were becoming hyper-competitive due to the "insecurity" of their economic livelihoods, having been deprived of direct self-sufficiency due to the new status of itinerant wage-earners in the modern labour market (10).[68] In such a competitive work environment people lose the "unbroken consciousness of responsibility" for the well-being of their neighbours (87). According to Schweitzer, in such unnatural social conditions a most curious and schizophrenic bifurcation of values emerges. People become ethically individualistic even while their other sensibilities and opinions become homogenized with the prevailing spirit of their peers (14, 17). Then, through the popular media, a spirit of superficiality takes over the mental life of susceptible people (12). Schweitzer was only speaking of the newspapers and magazines of his day. One can only wonder at what he would have thought of the popular entertainment programs now available through the internet and satellite television.

Schweitzer is describing the psychological dynamics that affect people as a result of their economic relations. This was the emerging *ethos* of modernity, and Schweitzer considered it a dangerous mixture of exclusionary self-seeking coupled with a collective group-think under the influence of corporate, social, and political organizations. Today there is an emerging social phenomenon that Schweitzer did not anticipate: a non-communitarian materialist culture that is unthinkingly perpetuating ecological degradation through competitive consumerism. If this is related to the same precipitating causes Schweitzer identifies for the social problems of his day, as I think it is, then perhaps his recommendations have particular relevance here as well. They are straightforward yet profound: "If society had so developed that *a continually widened circle of the population could enjoy a modest, but well-assured, condition of comfort*, civilization would have been more helped than it has been by all the material conquests which are lauded in its name" (*POC* 10 [emphasis added]). Schweitzer also insists: "Wealth must reach the community *in the most varied ways*, if it is to be of the greatest benefit of all" (320 [emphasis added]).

He is speaking here about a kind of libertarianism in which each person seeks her or his own self-chosen ends, some through business ventures that employ wage-earning workers and others through charitable service. Schweitzer is also in favour of progressive taxation arrived at through democratic processes, such as would be necessary to fund the various institutions needed for the maintenance and furtherance of public goods. He insists that the economy should be structured in such a way as to create a more equitable society – one with a better distribution of wealth among its citizens so that the fear of poverty and destitution would not influence their behaviour and more personal time would be allowed, thus enabling a true communitarian culture to emerge. This is a subject that is gaining attention in the field of environmental ethics today because economic inequality is correlated with ecological degradation (see, for example, Mikkelson, Gonzales, and Peterson [2007]). Since redressing social inequality is seen as a way of helping to safeguard the environment, Schweitzer's commentary can provide additional philosophical support for such research as well as a way of giving greater ethical context for considering the larger social and ethical issues of conservation.

New Cosmology and the Commonwealth of Life

A trend in recent environmental thought concerns the development of so-called new cosmologies. These are holistic worldviews that attempt to synthesize elements of modern science, physics, and religion into a coherent narrative that places the adherent of such visions into a psychological relationship with the natural world. It is believed that this is the way to facilitate popular action to protect, preserve, and restore the natural environment; it is seen as the catalyst for achieving a reciprocal relationship of interdependent communitarianism with everyone in society and with nature too. The cosmology may be either ideological or theological, sometimes exclusively so. Murray Bookchin (2007), for example, believes that the spiritual approach is wrongheaded. He refers to it as a "naive reductionism," arguing that it trivializes complex environmental problems as merely being psychological in origin (27). He contends that the real issues are social and economic, and he promotes a holistic worldview in which the human species is seen in strictly naturalistic and evolutionary terms. At the other end of the spectrum there is Thomas Berry (2009, 36), who detects a profound sense of alienation and spiritual anomie in the modern person resulting from "extreme anthropocentrism and dedication to consumerism." For him, it follows that the answer to the varied global ecological crises involves focusing on the development of a spiritual consciousness that embeds a person within a healthy spiritual and economic relationship with the biosphere. Schweitzer's Reverence for Life worldview resonates with both Bookchin and Berry. But Schweitzer is not overtly religious or theological, and he does not think that changes to economic society will be enough on their own: he places as much emphasis on the need to develop social personhood within economic society as he does on the need to promote a mystical worldview that provides a sense of connection to all life.

Such a balanced focus is perhaps best mirrored in the "commonwealth of life" cosmology developed by Peter G. Brown. His work was directly inspired by Schweitzer, among others. Brown emphasizes the need for economic reforms, yet, unlike Bookchin, he is not averse to religious mysticism. Instead, and in extending the spirit of Schweitzer's ethic, Brown and his co-author Geoffrey Garver describe their ecumenical approach this way: "Whatever traditions may inform individual practice, a basic framework of understanding can gather all people in the same 'communion' … within the commonwealth of life, to which is due the same respect and *reverence* that we value ourselves" (Brown and Garver 2009, 48 [see also 45] [emphasis added]). Religion is optional, not a prerequisite for environmental sustainability. That said, Brown's writings on the commonwealth of life cosmology are considerable, and the following discussion does not attempt to fully describe them. What the following seeks to do instead is to reveal how my findings can engage and advance certain aspects of Brown's ideas, carrying both his and Schweitzer's projects forward.

Peter Brown (2008, 168) begins with an understanding of Reverence for Life "as foundational but unfinished." He then turns to his own reading of Darwin and claims that evolutionary biology shows humanity is only separated from other species by degrees of genetic difference: "There are no clear, absolute distinctions between ourselves and other species" (8). This may seem a somewhat sensational claim, but what he is seeking to do here is to create an alternate scientific conception of Schweitzer's universal will-to-live. To this end, Brown describes all life as sharing an evolutionary unity divided by genetic differences that emerged in interdependent co-evolutionary descent – an argument that was first pioneered by Paul Taylor (1986).[69]

Brown (2008) then moves to develop another science-based conception of the universal will-to-live. The unique activity of life, all life, reveals an anti-entropic capacity realized in procreation, physiological development, and metabolic self-maintenance (172). This anti-entropic capacity can be scientifically estimated and measured as Net Primary Productivity in either a particular region or for the biosphere as a whole (Brown and Garver 2009, 120–1). Brown and Garver use this as a basis for creating an accounting system to determine the earth's total biotic potential. Since the biosphere's anti-entropic capacity is dependent primarily on sunlight for photosynthesis and subsequent herbivore metabolism, these are termed "flows" of annual revenue available from the biosphere's anti-entropic capacity. Stored biotic capital such as fossil fuels and standing woodlands are termed "stocks" of previously invested photosynthetic and metabolic activity (12; see also 57 and 64). From these science-based analogs to economic concepts, they then move to propose reforms to the failed economic institutions that have resulted in so much social strife and mismanagement of the biosphere's resources.

To this end, Brown (2008, 61) expands Thoreau's idea of "the cost of a thing is the amount of … life which is required to be exchanged for it, immediately or in the long run" to include non-human lives in part of his overall stewardship economics. This same quote was mentioned in chapter 4 in relation to how Schweitzer employs the German word *Schuld* to mean "life-debt." Schweitzer insists that humanity, individually and collectively, has a debt to the non-human world that needs to be repaid through conscientious ethical action (*POC* 318). It is therefore possible to take Schweitzer's ethics of debt and combine it with the ideas of "flows" and "stocks" that Brown and his colleague employ in relation to economic reforms. It could then be argued from this basis that the appropriations of flows and stocks from nature that previously supported biodiversity are a direct ethical problem that demands philosophical consideration as to whether or not such activities can be justified and, if necessary, how that life-debt must be repaid to restore the beauty, resilience, and integrity of those biotic communities.

What this means is that, instead of being merely a point of departure, Schweitzer's Reverence for Life ethic contributes direct philosophical support to Brown and Garver's proposals for redressing the loss of anti-entropic capacity in the biosphere resulting from human economic activity.[70] While Thoreau is an astute and powerful thinker, he is not an academically trained philosopher and ethicist. Schweitzer's concept of an ethical *Schuld* owed to the human and non-human world can integrate Reverence for Life more fully into Brown and Garver's project. This would securely root the following claim in Schweitzer's philosophy: "In a whole earth economy based on right relationship, with an expanded view of distributive justice, any use or disruption of resources that impairs the ability of life to flourish in its full diversity would be immoral" (Brown and Garver 2009, 94). Schweitzer offers them a new powerful avenue for relating economics with ethics.

There are also other exciting possibilities for such developments. For example, Brown and Garver propose a way to correlate the criteria of Leopold's Land Ethic (i.e., the integrity, resilience, and beauty of biotic communities) to ecological science. This is summarized by the formula $I = f(\text{PATE})$, which is a measure of the regional *I*mpacts that result from a function of total human *P*opulation, per capita *A*ffluence, *T*echnological factors, and their *E*thical attitudes on social and ecological justice. This famous formula was originally developed by Ehrlich and Holdren (76). However, the newly added element of that equation, Ethics (*E*), is tied to three basic human rights identified by Brown (2008, 20): a right to protection from bodily harm, a right to free association in religion and political affiliations, and a right to sustenance. These tripartite rights are the precursors of a "human capabilities" development paradigm (originally developed by Nobel Laureate Amartya Sen) that recognizes that real human personhood includes activities such as "doing, being, and relating," which are not adequately reflected in mainstream economic theory (16). In proposing this, Brown seeks to address a central concern of Schweitzer – finding ways for people in economic society to exist as more than just workers and consumers. Schweitzer and Leopold are then brought in to add moral weight to the call for a "fair distribution among *all* members of life's commonwealth" (Brown and Garver 2009, 86 [emphasis in original]).[71]

The way is now open to extend what Brown calls a "new story" that integrates scientific cosmology, religion, and economic theory, and establish with it a stronger connection to the academic domain of philosophy. This comes by way of Schweitzer's engagement of Nietzsche's own interpretation of natural science to support life-affirming cultural truths and an Ethical Mysticism. As I argue in chapter 3, Nietzsche is *the* most important and influential philosopher in academia today. By drawing on his unquestioned authority, and by connecting this to Schweitzer's advances (which make of Nietzsche's unfinished work a viable social ethic), the project of Brown and Garver would gain another invaluable inroad into the academic domain of philosophy, which hitherto has not been supportive of such figures as Leopold and Thoreau.

A Final Assessment: Appraisals and Criticisms

Schopenhauer's influence on Schweitzer has been well documented. But exactly how Schopenhauer's will-to-live theory grounded Schweitzer's philosophy was either not well understood or was presumed to have been a strategic error on Schweitzer's part. It was thought that Schweitzer's reliance on Schopenhauer pushed Reverence for Life into unsupportable metaphysical excess and made certain of his claims about non-human life appear to be romanticized imaginings based upon mere analogy. This investigation instead demonstrated that the analogy here is not about psychological transference but, rather, about the way Schopenhauer sought to escape the "lair of the skull" and to establish the independent reality of the natural world. Only then could he engage in an analysis of cosmological causality, posit the existence of a cosmological Will, and present the will-to-live as the Kantian essence of things in themselves. By using these techniques, Schopenhauer seeks to prove that phenomenal reality exists apart from Cartesian consciousness. And Schweitzer *needed* the will-to-live concept: only Schopenhauer could provide him with a satisfactory linkage between rational consciousness and the empirical world.

Schweitzer approaches philosophy by building his ethic around what he calls elemental truths. These are seen as permanent, unchanging aspects of human nature and existence: they include Schopenhauer's will-to-live theory and his universal cosmological Will. Schweitzer recovers these elemental philosophical truths from Schopenhauer because they are compatible with natural science. Yet, at the same time, he needs to divorce the will-to-live and the cosmological Will from Schopenhauer's greater metaphysical claims about Buddhist *samsara* and salvation. This is why he turns to Nietzsche and the naturalism found in his early works. Schweitzer views Nietzsche's Will to Power theory as something that is in agreement with modern biology: its naturalism more closely mirrors evolutionary theory than does Schopenhauer's Buddhist-inspired metaphysics of perception. And so, while Schopenhauer creates a way to demonstrate that the empirical world actually exists, Nietzsche, in turn, demonstrates that sensible reality is actually controlled by myriad competitive natural forces. The naturalistic Will to Power theory was an improvement that advanced Schopenhauer's theory of causality; it recast Schopenhauer's theories as purely biological phenomena for explaining physiological development and made them compatible with the scientific worldview. However, Schweitzer was not sceptical about empirical science like Nietzsche was, and so he instead held to modern cell theory to explain the emergence of order from the complex Will to Power biological processes. This is how he can present the will-to-live theory as biology, not as metaphysics.

It is through these two earlier thinkers that Schweitzer finds a way to give Continental philosophy a solid footing in the empirical world. He needs to be able to claim the will-to-live as an elemental truth for both natural science and rational consciousness. This is the first linkage he is after. The second is an elemental first principle for morality, which he finds in Schopenhauer's ethics of compassion. Schweitzer took Schopenhauer's work and improved on it by turning to Darwin's evolutionary understanding of social instincts. Then, with this moral principle now established in natural science, Schweitzer felt he could, with confidence, claim compassion as another elemental truth.

Schweitzer wrote that he sought to create a "mysterious combination" for the philosophies of Schopenhauer and Nietzsche. He would do this by combining the individualistic ethics of natural life-affirmation from the works of Nietzsche with the altruism found in the self-sacrifice (which is to say, life-renunciation) from the works of Schopenhauer. This produced a mystical worldview that envisioned other life as being cosmologically connected to the self such that personal fulfillment could be actualized through ethical service to others. This is why Schweitzer's project includes a curious worldview that is simultaneously dualistic and monistic. For Schweitzer, Reverence for Life "must have nothing to do with an ethical interpretation of the [natural] world; it must [instead] become cosmic and mystical" (POC 307). In his opinion, it is not permissible to see the world of nature as an ethical yardstick for human society. Perhaps in the poetic abstract, or with a selective and overly imaginative licence that obscures individual fates, Nature (writ large) can become a loving "mother" who provides for all her many children. But when one considers *exactly* what happens during predation, disease, and death, there is just too much needless suffering, and far too little to uphold a sense of justice for it all.

But Schweitzer's conclusion forces a problematic dualism between the nihilistic worldview of empirical science and the life-view of human rationality, which aspires to higher ideals for society and ourselves personally. His solution is to identify the core of ontological self-awareness as containing one element recovered from natural science (evolutionary social instincts) and one from rationalist ethics (compassion). Together with the specific influences of language and other cultural thought-forms, they collectively and pre-rationally inform the first fact of consciousness. The "I + will-to-live" nexus thereby becomes the ontological foundation for Schweitzer's New Rationalism. And it holds true for each and every person regardless of culture, time, or circumstance. In this one bold stroke, Schweitzer dispels the ethical anthropocentrism of Descartes and secures a solid foundation for his Reverence for Life ethic, which could now emerge as a cultural truth for all people everywhere, a philosophy of civilization for everyone.

That describes his elemental nature philosophy. It represents only the first half of his project. The philosophy, in turn, supports Ethical Mysticism, which *does* represent a poetic interpretation of the natural world. This is the secondary metaphysic emerging from New Rationalism, but it never subsumes the scientific worldview – at least not completely; rather, it takes the dualism of the scientific worldview and the life-view of rational consciousness and synthesizes them into the monism of the universal will-to-live. And so, while the *universal* will-to-live is a metaphysical concept in the Aristotelian sense of the term, the will-to-live concept for *particular* life was still seen as a physical truth in harmony with biological science. The two are connected by an epagoge that uses inductive reasoning to posit a general class for the particularized phenomena of perception. It is thus a very minimalist metaphysic.

The cultural values of Reverence for Life have their foundation in Nietzsche's synthetic a priori. While these values have their origins in natural science, this science is interpreted with a certain amount of artistic licence. That is Nietzsche's escape route from nihilism, and something Schweitzer evidently took to heart. He also takes from Nietzsche the focus on developing a strong sense of personhood. Schweitzer believes that the restoration of civilization is dependent upon the type of self-actualized and free-thinking persons that Nietzsche describes. They were to be the ones who must rescue it from the dismal conditions he saw at the dawn of the twentieth century. But Nietzsche's vision of personhood is selfish and solitary, and it lacks an ethical component. Schweitzer therefore takes Nietzsche's emphasis on developing true personhood and joins it to Schopenhauer's concept of the self as the mirror of the world: egotism can then be directed outwards for vicarious fulfilment through Ethical Mysticism. This combination of the two disparate philosophical systems produces for Schweitzer a very powerful and focused ethical orientation in a "this worldly" devotion to others.

Nevertheless, Schweitzer's work remains fragmentary and unfinished. What he was able to do consists of only an elemental morality of compassion, a very bare-bones beginning for a virtue ethic, the cosmological constant of the will-to-live (worldview), an ontological first principle of the "I + will-to-live" nexus (life-view), and an apophatic hermeneutic that explained the experience of compassion (essentialism). His aim is to bring these disparate spheres of human existence into a new ethical life such that *"reason and the heart must work together* if a true morality is to be established" (*APR* 7 [emphasis in original]) because "the true heart is rational, and the true reason is sensitive" (13). Promoting the fullest development for all life is what he sets before each rational moral agent as their duty. This holds true for both furthering one's own life and for the other life in the natural world – individually, collectively, and even evolutionarily.

The question of how Schweitzer can single out humans in an ethical system based on naturalism comes from the fact that people possess the unique combination of a Cartesian self-aware ego and the cosmological will-to-live. In human beings, the cosmological constant of the will-to-live becomes entwined with the Cartesian ego to form the core of their rational consciousness. This allows humans to become moral agents in a world otherwise deterministically controlled by instincts and natural laws. The elemental morality of compassion becomes the linkage between philosophy and religion. Schweitzer sees Christianity through the lens of Schopenhauer's philosophy. This is how he makes his faith intelligible to his scientifically trained mind. And because of this, it is not correct to say that Schweitzer disguises Christianity (or any other religion) as his philosophy; rather, his philosophy extends into mysticism, where it connects to the ethic of the historical Jesus. In the context of his own personal religious outlook, somewhere in the undefined middle ground between philosophy and religion, in a place where all deep thought becomes mystical, Schweitzer finds an understanding of Jesus that allows Christianity to coexist with philosophy and natural science. For Schweitzer, mysticism is the flower of philosophy, and devotion to an ethic of altruism is its cherished fruit – a fruit that can be plucked and shared within any culture or religion. It was not something meant to be palatable only to Christians; rather, it was to be a philosophy for *all* of civilization.

But there is yet another basic problem underlying the crisis in civilization. Schweitzer's diagnosis is simple: people are overworked and too exhausted by trying to make a living to do much of anything else. His prescription is also straightforward: people need the time, the inclination, and the educational background to be able to meditate on the meaning of life and to conduct their affairs with true moral character. Schweitzer wanted his elemental nature philosophy to step into the gap and give people the seeds of thought for self-reflection. But the original problem remains. How, in the midst of busy work lives, raising children, and simply maintaining a household, are working people to find the time and the energy to engage in reflecting on the larger social and political issues of the day?

Schweitzer does not address this problem, aside from a few comments about the distribution of wealth in society. And so the original problem remains. While he structures his arguments in a conversational style aimed at the educated laity and working families, these are the very people who for the most part do not have time for such heavy reading. Ironically, in trying to create a living philosophy for everyone, Schweitzer almost missed having any readers at all. But it is said a book will find its audience, and this is exactly what happened in an unexpected way. Schweitzer's *Civilization and Ethics* (vol. 2) was smuggled into Hitler's prisoner of war camps, where it was read by and gave comfort to the POWs (*Letters* 261). Schweitzer marvelled at this because his works were considered dangerous contraband, and yet many people later confirmed the story. Then, in the collective worldwide soul-searching after the war, Schweitzer emerged as a great moral figure with a powerful message of universal compassion. He was even recognized with a Nobel Peace Prize in 1952. But, with the anti-colonialism backlash that gained strength in the 1950s and the 1960s, both his acclaim and his works began to fade from public notice.

Schopenhauer and Nietzsche grew in their prestige even after their works were no longer read for enjoyment by the general public. The strength of their philosophical arguments is recognized in academia, and other thinkers emerged to carry their legacy forward. This has not happened for Schweitzer, at least not within the academic discipline of philosophy. This work here has sought to reveal that a coherent and inno-vative elemental nature philosophy does exist in Schweitzer's Reverence for Life ethic. It includes an essentialist ontology that he refers to as the New Rationalism, which is based in the hermeneutical analysis of being. From an academic perspective, this is perhaps the most engaging aspect of Schweitzer's work since it is an alternative to, and predates, a similar theory promoted by Martin Heidegger.

Schweitzer re-engages epistemology in such a way that it is possible to posit the existence of the non-human world. This may sound like a modest claim, but environmental ethics has been hamstrung by those philoso-phers who have drawn support from Heidegger to insist that wildlife, old-growth forests, and everything else that traditional environmentalists have sought to protect have no intrinsic value, that all the phenomena of the natural world take their very existence as *only* social constructions based in human rationality – which is to say the "world" that is presup-posed in the constitution of the *Dasein*. An extreme example of this is found in the work of those "strict constructionists" who deny both the independent existence of non-human nature and scientific facts. While it is possible to argue persuasively for environmental ethics from such a perspective, Schweitzer provides a way for the scientific worldview and the life-view of human consciousness to coexist without one subsuming the other. Put simply, this breathes new life into a whole host of important thinkers who have been marginalized due to the anti-essentialist turn in philosophy, including (but not limited to) John Muir, Aldo Leopold, and Schweitzer himself.

The only picture for environmentally sustainable communities in the life and works of Schweitzer comes from the construction and operation of his hospital. Yet because he keeps his philosophy rooted in elemen-tal principles, he does not stand in the way of such visionaries as Aldo Leopold. Schweitzer's philosophy can be used to support communitarian models that include the full biotic community: it is a lived philosophy with "calluses on its hands," resulting from making those tough decisions. Schweitzer just holds an absolute ethic over us lest we use the power of rationalization to excuse the inexcusable. What is necessary is not always right but may be still necessary (POC 317). Schweitzer was not afraid to make those tough and necessary decisions himself. The debt-based *Schuld* mentality was the means of keeping excesses in check and the collective soul-searching for how to reverence all life ongoing.

But perhaps most importantly of all, this investigation has shown how Schweitzer highlights the role of the individual in ethics. He insists that the work of creating an ethical society is not carried out by producing new and elaborate articulations of theory but, rather, by facilitating individual people to develop ethical personhood through elemental morality. Key to this project is ensuring that people have the educational background and economic security to be able to engage in the reflection necessary to build strong moral character. But Schweitzer is not an elitist. An ethical worldview ultimately comes from a pre-rational insight (the sublime of compassion) regarding the will-to-live, and so "the difference between learned and unlearned is entirely relative" (POC 308). Yet modern economic life stands in the way of ethical development. When this happens, "personalities and ideas are then subordinated to [those economic and political] institutions, when it is really these [ethical agents] which ought to influence the latter [social creations] and keep them inwardly alive" (16). But Reverence for Life holds the hope for something else to emerge.

Whether in colonial Africa or in the urban architecture of Europe, Schweitzer believes the only guarantee for the restoration of civilization lies in the elemental truth given in the will-to-live. Life is good. Moral character can develop from that simple elemental seed when a person comes to see his or her life to be equally present in the other through an apophatically informed analogy to the self. All life can then be seen as good and can be reverenced as such. Thanks to Schopenhauer, Schweitzer found a way to bridge the distance between self-interest and altruism. This can grow into a religious worldview through Ethical Mysticism, which further strengthens as a person engages in moral reflection – or it may remain limited to family and friends, which is also fine. Schweitzer believed the power of example from ethical geniuses coupled with the knowledge that the ethic is absolute would be enough to keep society on the right path.

Part of Schweitzer's project included the intention to propose a political framework for the ethical governance of society. In chapter 6, I reveal the complexity of Schweitzer's thought on this subject, and I offer an opinion on why the final volumes of *The Philosophy of Civilization* were never completed. Nevertheless, if democracy is to work, Schweitzer's commentary and concerns are as important today as they were in the times about which he wrote. It may be, as he himself declares, that democracy will always remain contradictory and incomplete. Yet this is advantageous for two key reasons. The first is that it keeps moral responsibility personal – that is, it does not permit a person to defer to an external codified ethical system that removes his or her ultimate responsibility. The second comes from the fact that, imperfect as it is, Schweitzer still provides a moral alternative to the straightforward clarity found in Nietzsche's political solution.

Being human with human failings is not a crime. Reverence for Life asks for perfection but only expects constant and earnest striving towards this end. This is its power. Falling short of these ideals has great mystical significance because compassion is stronger than love. The truth is love can become broken-hearted. Compassion already is. When a person learns the virtue of sincerity, which I believe includes compassion for the imperfect self, such failures are given an avenue for redemption through the other. Altruism brings the two separate lives together where the true essence of humanity is rediscovered, and healing is found. One's life then moves on with renewed determination and deepened sincerity. Reverence for Life draws its strength from embracing these elemental truths as a lived and very personal experience. Only then, Schweitzer believed, can a real and sustaining hope for civilization be carried forward for a better future.

Epilogue

At a distance never too far behind his scholarly work is the enigma of the man himself. Schweitzer is an exceptionally complex historical figure to study, and his thoughts were not always recorded in written texts for scholars to later analyze. Much of the man, and especially his inner devotional life, will always remain a mystery. The focus of my book has been on his philosophy, not the biographical questions about his own personal experience of Ethical Mysticism. It is my position that there is a difference between the two. The philosophy supports mysticism: the mysticism, however, does not determine the nature of the philosophy from which it originates. This is the advantage of an elemental nature philosophy. It is a one-way street that takes a person into an ethical relationship with the cosmos. But in my efforts to clarify the philosophical foundation of his ethic, important details about its fruition as a "living philosophy of the people" were pushed into the background. The picture I have created is therefore somewhat incomplete. My epilogue will attempt to remedy this situation, and that brings me back to the question of Schweitzer's own mystical outlook on the world.

In reflecting about this man who had created such a magnificently evocative ethic, I kept coming back to that Palm Sunday meditation mentioned back in chapter 5. There is something very significant and meaningful written there, that much is obvious. Evidently written in the midst of the experience, the all-too-short letter gives us a glimpse into what he felt that day, sitting alone in an overwhelming silence that was filled with ambient jungle sounds from insects, birds, and other wildlife – an obvious contradiction that somehow wasn't in that moment. It had become a tragic and alien psalm of sorts, and the way he described it makes the experience seem like some kind of communion. Yet it wasn't with Christ or God, but an inhuman timelessness encroaching into him from the wilderness. It is a very striking and powerful letter. I avoided writing too much about it in that chapter, knowing that any commentary I could give would quickly become increasingly speculative. It seemed appropriate to keep my comments minimal and to the particular academic points being made there. But here in this epilogue I feel I can now hazard a few lines of thought about the deeper significance of Schweitzer's letter – and in the process, perhaps add some additional insights into the man himself. This will also give me a chance to provide a few words of reflection about what he meant by saying Reverence for Life could become a *living* philosophy of the people.

I believe the Palm Sunday letter relates to the negative theology Schweitzer wrote about in the last chapter of *The Quest of the Historical Jesus*. Silence, it should be recalled from my discussion in chapter 4, was also the medium through which the Church Fathers experienced the ineffable Godhead. Schweitzer's letter therefore suggests, at least to me, that his inner spiritual life was perhaps apophatic in certain similar ways. This is not to say that the Patristic Fathers have an exclusive ownership over apophasis, or that Schweitzer's Protestantism was somehow derivative of the Hellenic Christianity he believed had gone astray from the religion of the historical Jesus and Apostle Paul. Rather, and to use a more contemporary example, Joseph Campbell (1988) believed that behind each world religion there was the very same transcendent absolute. He called it "a great silence" and claimed the particular and culturally distinct elements of every religion were all just attempts to enframe what was otherwise indescribable, for that sacred silence was ultimately an experiential reality (120–1).

Schweitzer's apophatic experience of mysticism, I believe, was similarly constituted and focused. The reason for this comes from something else I read in Campbell's book. A shaman from the Caribou Inuit once told him that "[true wisdom] lives far from [hu]mankind, out in the great loneliness, and can be reached only through suffering. Privation and suffering alone open the mind to all that is hidden to others" (xii). The sublime of suffering was a constant presence for Schweitzer; it became a doorway to experiencing an essentialism with all of existence, as I have argued in the previous chapters. But I also suspect that he might agree with that shaman about true apophatic wisdom as well.

I am thinking here of two incidents recounted by Melamed and Melamed. In the first, they mention that Schweitzer would occasionally take well-deserved breaks from tending to his patients. Curiously, instead of resting or doing something recreational, he would sit alone in silence next to the Ogowé River. It was not idle relaxation because there was evidently something about his countenance during these times that would make the native Gabonese very uncomfortable. Not that they feared that he would be attacked by wild animals or that he was about to take an ill-advised afternoon swim. Rather, there was something in his deeply contemplative demeanour that unnerved them greatly. They would find excuses to interrupt him and get him back indoors.

The second incident is even more revealing. Schweitzer one night was tending to a patient who was slowly dying. It was an advanced case of sleeping sickness and, as such, untreatable. Nothing could be done for him except to provide for his comfort, and even then, not much could be done. The nurses and other attendants had already left; their services turning to other patients, the ones who they could help. No relatives were at his bedside. Schweitzer however stayed, giving the man water when he asked for it, but otherwise not being able to do anything except be a silent witness to his lingering death. This is the tragedy of the human condition in microcosm but not in the abstract. A person was dying, a person he only knew as a patient. It was at this time that a local Gabonese man happened to be going by the hospice building and was able to observe surreptitiously. Schweitzer was at the dying man's bedside, staring silently into the night. What struck him was the unfathomable expression on Schweitzer's face. It hit him in some unexpected way, and it would have a lasting impact. Later he could only report that the unspeaking and unobserved encounter conveyed to him an insight into the true meaning of compassion. Something had changed him that night, something pre-rational.

"How much would already be accomplished toward the improvement of our present circumstances [in Western civilization] if only we would all give up three minutes every evening to gazing up into the infinite world of the starry heavens and meditating on it, or if in taking part in a funeral procession we would reflect on the enigma of life and death" (POC 62). He was speaking from experience with these words. And it was no idle remark since there evidently were profound insights he had received from these moments of communion with *das Irrationale*. Schweitzer had a special kind of relationship with apophatic silence, that much I can say.

In turn, that silence spoke to the core of his being in a way that escaped words. The Palm Sunday meditation is the closest he ever came to putting it in writing. In his publications he only hinted at these mystical experiences, mentioning once that, "In the *stillness* of the African jungle I have been able to work out this thought and give [mysticism] expression" (80 [emphasis added]).

If I were to try to describe what he meant by "stillness" and outline the inner processes of mysticism from a scholarly perspective, which obviously cannot do justice to something that is by its very nature indescribable, I would say that it appears he would linger in the "perpetual now" that opens up in the mind for rational reflection (*topos noētos*) while focused on the silence of eternity. Significantly it was a natural silence, one that was external to the experiencing self. Then, once in this contemplative state-of-being, something there would resonate in a primal way with the "I + will-to-live" nexus within. It appears that for Schweitzer these experiences were informed in some mysterious way by the same pre-rational intuitions that, when directed towards other beings, revealed that the self was connected to other life through the universal will-to-live and the infinite cosmological Will. But when contemplating "emptiness" in this way, some kind of communion would take place with the timeless inhumanness found in wild nature, or with the unspeakable ancient ache that arises from an awareness of death. I would therefore agree with Campbell that there is a kind of transcendent absolute here. But for Schweitzer it was in no way reified into an object of religious devotion because, for him, apophatic silence is the privative of all absolutes. It is an eternal emptiness, a grave stillness that somehow spoke to the soul.

This brings me to the last story about Schweitzer I'd like to mention, the one from my Introduction about the taxi and the homeless man. That incident in 1919 caught Schweitzer off guard. He could only watch in silence as the porter chased away the poor man who was just looking to help with the suitcases for a little spare change. The obvious hardships of his life left an impact on Schweitzer, and so did the guilt of not having spoken up. We can only imagine the uncomfortable feelings that ruminated in his conscience that night, being as he was indoors, warm, in fellowship with supportive friends, sharing a nice meal, and at the same time keenly aware that the homeless Parisian had none of these basic decencies everyone deserves. The memory of it no doubt stayed with him long after the sermon. It undoubtedly became part of his reflections about economic society for his Reverence for Life project. Perhaps that silent and momentary pre-rational connection with an anonymous man was only then given a voice, finally, in the pages of *The Philosophy of Civiliza-tion*. Perhaps he considered it a small and partial payment for the life-debt of not having spoken up when it really counted.

Nearly a century has passed since that cold, wet night in Paris. Home-lessness is still commonplace in Western societies. Many more, as econo-mists would say, are the "working poor" who are barely getting by. Much worse is seen on the nightly news. There are famines in far-away coun-tries and natural disasters that destroy entire cities, leaving families with nothing but their lives. Worst of all is the suffering people inflict on each other through war and persecutions of every kind. Life is suffering. Schopenhauer had written of this ancient truth of Buddhism, and he ad-vised his readers to psychologically detach from it all: give society over to Philosopher-Kings, but otherwise he said a person could do nothing but devote him- or herself to a philosophy of life-resignation. Schweitzer however testified to the power of a fierce *No!* in the face of these social injustices. Even if the poor will always be among us, as the Gospels say, Schweitzer sought to destroy our apathy about it. To be *human* means to never stop trying. That, he says, is what defines us as a species.

As of the date of this publication, it has been almost exactly one hun-dred years since Schweitzer set foot in Africa to begin what he must have thought was a hopeless battle against leprosy. This disease, I am embar-rassed to admit, meant very little to my modern sensibilities. I knew it was horrible, of course, but so is an untreatable cancer. Then I saw photo-graphs of some of Schweitzer's patients and read the painfully detailed ac-counts of a leper's life by Gregory Nazianzus (4th century) in his Oration, "On the Love of the Poor" (see pages 45–9). It was unimaginably tragic, an existence trapped in a grotesque and hideous parody of the human form, an unending suffering both physically and emotionally. Nevertheless, Gregory, like Schweitzer, passionately testifies against the innate response of revulsion their appearance would trigger in people, for "the opportun-ity to show compassion lies open to you even if the Alien One alienates you" (61). People have many pre-rational responses to the world, but only compassion makes us fully human – and compassion can be, *and needs to become*, a universal response to all suffering.

Silence is uncomfortable sometimes. There is something deeply sig-nificant about that too. Schweitzer, I think, would say discomfort is the stirrings of conscience looking for an articulation to make sense of the world. For Socrates that inner voice was divine. Apophatic theologians like Gregory believed the ineffable God could be encountered in this si-lent mystery, resonating with an "inner logos" such that fallen humanity could be transformed into our true destined selves (*theosis*).[72] Joseph Campbell believed similar "great silences" exist at the heart of the sacred in every world religion. And so I now turn back to the question that has framed this epilogue. The modern mystic Schweitzer had a lifelong relationship with this same kind of hesychastic silence in his own experience of Ethical Mysticism. He wanted his Reverence for Life ethic to become a living philosophy of the people, for each person to be empowered by his or her conscience to become true and moral persons. And he also wanted them to find *their own* experience of Ethical Mysticism. This is why, I believe, he did not address his readers as either a mystic or a theologian. Reverence for Life is an elemental nature philosophy that can become extraordinarily mystical as a lived experience, at least for some. This makes it problematic to neatly classify as either entirely secular or inherently religious. Mysticism is elusive that way. In the end the label is more a matter for academics.

The silence needs to speak for itself.

Notes

1 Schweitzer obtained advanced degrees in medicine (surgery), musicology, philosophy, and religion. But to be precise here regarding his religion doctorate, Schweitzer obtained a licentiate degree in Protestant theology and then completed a second qualifying dissertation on the New Testament (specifically, the depiction of the Last Supper in the Gospels, *das Abendmahlsproblem*) to teach at Strasbourg University. This is generally considered a distinction without difference, and it is usually referred to as a doctorate.

2 Matthew 25 presents a parable concerning the Kingdom of Heaven and the coming of Christ in His glory to judge the nations. The righteous are declared righteous for having clothed, fed, cared for, and even visited the person of Christ while He was in prison. This causes great confusion to the assembled people since none of them had actually done any of these things for Jesus, and so they ask Him what He means. The key verse is then given in Matthew 25:40. "The King will reply, 'I tell you the truth, whatever you did for one of the least of these brothers of mine, you did for me'" (NIV). The message is that Jesus commands those who love Him to care for the needy and poor in society.

3 The only available treatment for leprosy was a botanical extract called chaulmoogra oil which would take months or even years to show positive results. Schweitzer therefore had to build and look after separate leper colonies on his hospital grounds.

4 The intrinsic here is a reference to the Kantian "thing in itself" behind phenomena.

5 Schweitzer's contributions here are not limited to just the practice of tropical medicine and working with indigenous communities. Giordano and Pedroni (2007) take Schweitzer as being representative of a virtue ethic within the practice of medicine itself, in that "the reverence for the good of the patient is therefore [also] a reverence for the life and the world of that patient" (142). Giordano and Pedroni present Schweitzer as a counter-example to the modern ethos of medicine, wherein "medicine becomes [only] an instrumental good, competing with numerous other instrumental goods as commodities within a consumerist framework, the values of which are changeable and dictated by social demand and market variability" (143). Giordano and Pedroni turn to Schweitzer as a case study for restoring the doctor/patient relationship within medicine today from its current technocentric- and economic-focused morass (148).

6 This is the author's own translation from *Kulturphilosophie – Zweiter Teil: Kultur und Ethik* (*Vorrede* vii–viii). C.T. Campion was personally picked by Schweitzer for the English translation of many of his works, including *The Philosophy of Civilization*. Campion's is therefore considered the definitive translation of this work and, with few exceptions, will be utilized exclusively throughout. Campion's translation reflects Schweitzer's approach to philosophy – which is to say, to communicate simply and conversationally the essence of complex philosophical ideas. His approach, however, sometimes fails to capture some of the technical nuances of Schweitzer's words. Occasionally, therefore, I will be providing my own translation of key passages.

7 Nietzsche warned that: "industrial culture [...] is altogether the most vulgar form of existence that has yet existed. Here one is at the mercy of brute need; one has to live and sell oneself, but one despises those who exploit this need and *buy* the worker. Oddly, submission to powerful, frightening, even terrible persons, like tyrants and generals, is not experienced as nearly so painful as is this submission to unknown and uninteresting persons, which is what all the luminaries of industries are. What the workers see in the employer is usually only a cunning, bloodsucking dog of a man who speculates on all misery" (*GS* §40, 107 [emphasis in original]). Schweitzer listed the books by Nietzsche that he had read, including this one (*POC* 243n7).

8 Schweitzer specifically complained that students are not taught about the interconnection of the individual sciences. He anticipated David Orr (2004), who wrote that interdisciplinary science must be added to curricula because too many "students graduate without knowing how to think in whole systems, how to find connections, how to ask big questions, and how to separate the trivial from the important" (23).

9 See "The God of the Market Place: John Stuart Mill and Maximos Confessor on Economic Virtue" (Goodin 2010c) for the historical background on the claimed naturalistic foundation of economic utilitarianism.

10 Once he arrived in Africa, Schweitzer discovered that the absolute dogma of the Paris Missionary Society "played practically no part in the sermons of the mis-

sionaries" (*OLT* 142). Though he had come as a doctor only, "not many months after my arrival," Schweitzer writes, he was invited to engage in some missionary work, including examining candidates for baptism and preaching (143). Nevertheless, Schweitzer wanted to keep his work here very auxiliary to the work of others, and most of the local Gabonese never knew him to be anything other than a doctor (Wadlow 2007, 26). Schweitzer had come to understand that no one had a right to impose religion upon an indigenous culture (Melamed and Melamed 2003, 170–1). He would only perform baptisms for expatriates living in Gabon, never for the locals (170).

11 Schweitzer was rejected for missionary work in 1905 and, instead, arrived in Africa in 1913 as a medical doctor. The dates here are significant. The horrific abuses inflicted under the colonial rule of King Leopold II in the Congo region of central Africa only became widely known in Europe in November of 1905 (Hochschild 1998, 251). Leopold was eventually forced to divest himself of his personally owned empire and to give direct control to his Parliament: "Reports of abuses against gatherers of wild rubber in the Congo did drop off markedly after the Belgian takeover of 1908" (278). The final meeting of the Congo Reform Association was held in 1913, marking an end to that particular nightmare of murder, slavery, and torture (277). In its place a new economic regime was imposed on Africa, "a new method of forcing people to work that drew much less protest from missionaries and humanitarians: taxes" (278). Schweitzer, operating from the French portion of the Congo region, was an exception.

12 Ernst Georg Wilhelm Deecke (1831–1897) was a philologist by training.

13 The following discussion draws on Goodin (2010a).

14 David Hume (1711–1776) was the foremost materialist of his age and delivered a devastating attack on Cartesian rationalism. Hume chided Descartes' self-conscious "I" as a basis for personal identity, pointing out that in sleep a person becomes insensible to him- or herself and thus may "truly be said not to exist" under Cartesian logic (Hume 1973; *A Treatise of Human Nature*, Book I, Part IV, Sec. 6). For Hume there is no principle of personal identity and the experience of consciousness is only a consequence of sensory "impression" recorded in memory from external reality. The dissolution of the recursively aware self with sleep, and the re-emergence of self-awareness upon awakening, points to a wholly material basis for the experience of personal identity.

15 According to Friedrich Lange of Marburg (1828–1875) the objectivity of the natural sciences resides exclusively in the common sensory organization of the human brain, and this fact explains how different people can report similar observations for the same phenomena (1881, 177; also 202–4). The seeming mechanical materialism of the natural world is therefore, for Lange, not the result of its intrinsic properties but the categorization of sensible intuitions in the mind, as Kant described. So-called scientific objectivity, Lange concluded, is merely shared epistemological subjectivity through the Kantian perceptual manifold. But the mind and the Kantian soul were not limited by the empirical because

the mind synthesizes its own inner world through which humanity retains its special cosmological dignity. Lange attempted to bridge scientific empiricism with the more humanizing traditions of German idealism with his claim that natural science itself exposes "the same transcendental root of our human nature, which supplies us through the senses with the idea of the world of reality, and which leads us in the highest function of nature and creative synthesis to fashion a world of the ideal in which to take refuge from the limitation of the senses, and in which to find again the true Home of our Spirit" (364–5). Lange was arguing against the emerging spirit of scientific nihilism that threatened to disillusion society, a project later taken up by Nietzsche.

16 Schopenhauer externalized the Kantian forms of sensible intuition to prove that nature was not a mental phenomenon. He did this by extending the range of Transcendental Ideas that exist as the "unbounded extension of their empirical use," as Kant had described (Kant 1950, 81; §45).

17 *WWR*, the Supplements to the Fourth Book, Vol. 2, §41, 482.

18 See for example Escobar (1996), who notes that, "Post-structuralism focuses on the role of language in the construction of social reality; it treats language not as the reflection of 'reality' but constitutive of it ... For some, *there is no materiality unmediated by discourse*" (326 [emphasis added]). Poststructuralism, taking its cue from Heidegger's hermeneutic theory, understands external reality in strictly phenomenological terms and that the intelligible nature of the sense world is determined and constituted *in its very essence* by human language.

19 Today we would instead point to the role of DNA in controlling biology, something that was only discovered in the 1950s.

20 Heidegger (1993, 289, from the essay "Modern Science, Metaphysics, and Mathematics" §E) would go further and say it "does not exist." The there-beingness of existence is a projection of its own ontic-ontological structures, and "we come to terms with the question of existence always through existence itself" (54; *Being and Time*, "Introduction" §1.4). This would become a foundational claim for the existentialists.

21 Charles Darwin published in 1859, a year before Schopenhauer's death.

22 Notably and characteristically, Nietzsche would instead call this the "most mendacious minute" of history and argue that only the so-called clever animals (humans) could possibly mistake our own intellect as something of "such importance, as if the world pivoted around it" (*PN-TAL* 42).

23 Schopenhauer argued that the higher evolved animals also possessed a certain measure of Cartesian recursive self-awareness, and he mocks those who claim otherwise: "If any Cartesian were to find himself clawed by a tiger, he would become aware in the clearest possible manner of the sharp distinction such a beast draws between its ego and the non-ego" (*OBM* §19, 176). Schweitzer similarly mocks those who say that animals do not possess a consciousness like our own: "It seems as if Descartes with his dictum that animals are mere machines had bewitched the whole of European philosophy ... as if he had never seen a thirsty ox enjoying a drink" (*POC* 297).

24 Schopenhauer believed that this was in fact happening and points to the recent emergence of animal rights organizations and anti-cruelty laws, which were being enacted in Europe for the first time (OBM §19, 180–2).

25 It should be noted here that, in his 1929 work *The Mysticism of Paul the Apostle*, Schweitzer considered the mysticism of Ignatius (d.103 or 113) much inferior to that of Paul. According to Schweitzer, Ignatius set forth a too strong sacramental emphasis for achieving a mystical and metaphysical union with God (369), while Paul found it in an ethic of love born in an eschatological expectation of the Kingdom of God – "to live with the eyes fixed on eternity, while standing firmly on the solid ground of reality" (333). Mysticism, for Schweitzer, must be entirely this-worldly.

26 This third category refers to a pre-rational intuition of sympathy that enables a person to sense the inner being of another – a subject discussed in chapter 4.

27 For further discussion on this issue, see Saarikoski (2007).

28 Because of Nietzsche, Foucault would later say that "the search for descent is not the erecting of foundations: on the contrary, it disturbs what was previously considered immobile; it fragments what was thought to be unified; it shows heterogeneity of what was imagined consistent with itself" (Gemes 2001, 349; from the essay "Nietzsche, Genealogy, History"). Even Habermas, who takes a critical view of postmodern philosophy, concluded that "Nietzsche appeals to experiences of self-disclosure of a decentered subjectivity, liberated from all constraints of cognitive and purposive activity, all imperatives of utility and morality. A 'break-up' of the principle of individuation becomes the escape route from modernity" (94; from *The Philosophical Discourse of Modernity*).

29 Nietzsche recalls Schopenhauer here, who had said that "animals are already exposed to illusion, to deception" in understanding the intuitions from perception, but our uniquely gyrencephalic brains allow humans to create abstract concepts for reflection because "that complicated, many-sided, flexible being, man, who is extremely needy and exposed to innumerable shocks and injuries, had to be illuminated by a twofold knowledge in order to be able to exist" (WWR-2 §27, 151).

30 See Nietzsche's pun on Schleiermacher's name to characterize rational philosophers in the Kantian tradition as "veil makers" in *Ecce Homo*, The Case of Wagner §3, 321.

31 Heidegger (1993) denied the existence of any reality independent of human perception and claimed that the mind controls the appearance of empirical phenomena. He specifically mentions Galileo's famous experiment of dropping two weights of unequal mass off the tower of Pisa to prove they fall at the same rate. Heidegger alleged Galileo only saw this happen because this is what he *expected* would happen. "Both Galileo and his opponents saw the same 'fact.' But they interpreted it differently and made the same happening visible to themselves in different ways" (290). For Heidegger, scientists merely impose, albeit unconsciously, their expectations on their experiments and produce test results that their minds have actually created: "Insofar as every science and cognition is expressed in propositions, the cognition that is taken and posited in the mathematical project

is of such a kind as to set things upon their foundation in advance" (291). Heidegger is saying that there is no reality other than mathematical (meaning, rational) laws that are superimposed over experience to make phenomena appear to us in a predetermined way. Stated another way, he is saying that empirical science is in no way objective. This is because: "There is no such [empirical] body" for scientists to study (289). There is only the mind, which is what creates our entire social environment. Such claims, needless to say, are quite obviously and manifestly absurd. Otherwise, we could triumphantly announce throughout the world that hunger, disease, and poverty could be simply and immediately remedied through daydreaming alone. Notwithstanding, and despite the inadequacy of his ideas to serve as a philosophy of science, his works still stand unchallenged and foundational for delving into ontological questions on how human beings come to terms with their own existence. Because of this, in my opinion, Schweitzer's New Rationalism makes for a better starting point for dealing with subjects in environmental ethics.

32   Though the exact details of what happened on that day of his collapse (3 January 1889) are uncertain, it is believed that Nietzsche witnessed a horse being whipped mercilessly in the streets of Turin, Italy. He apparently ran to the horse and threw his arms around its neck to protect it from the beating, suffering a complete emotional and mental breakdown at the same time. What is noteworthy is that Nietzsche *despised* the ethics of compassion. It is tempting to remark here that this event could be interpreted as Nietzsche's admitting Schopenhauer was right all along when he interceded to stop an animal from being abused and that, by wrapping his arms around its neck, he really was embracing his old master once again. Could it be said that the philosophy of compassion destroyed the *Übermensch* with a broken heart? While that last claim is meant to be somewhat facetious, it is still ironic that Nietzsche, the champion of the Darwinian "beast" that devours without pity the human herd around him, spent the last years of his life unable to care for himself and was the recipient of altruistic pity from family and medical professionals.

33   For an in-depth study of Darwin's views on the emergence of social instincts through natural selection, see Richards (2008).

34   Schweitzer's description of the human species as a "herd" animal echoes Nietzsche, who, through his reading of Darwin, had interpreted human beings this same way.

35   Leopold (1966, 239) also believed that it was an "evolutionary possibility" for our species to extend ethics to include non-human life. This is where his thought resonates most closely with that of Schweitzer. But Leopold argues this point from a somewhat different perspective. He wrote: "The extension of ethics, so far considered by philosophers, is actually a process in ecological evolution. Its sequences may be described in ecological as well as in philosophical terms ... Animal instincts are modes of guidance for the individual ... Ethics are possibly a kind of community instinct in-the-making" (238–9). Leopold sought to bring human so-

ciety and non-human nature together in a communitarian ethic (Callicott 1987, 388–9), a subject to be discussed further in the final chapter.

36 Schweitzer makes a distinction between scientific knowledge about the world and the mystery of existence (*POC* 308). The key here is the will-to-live. Through Nietzsche, it is seen as a scientific truth in harmony with biology, and, as such, empirical science confirms "that in and behind all phenomena there is the will-to-live" responsible for its development. This creates a dualism between the scientific worldview and the life-view from the vantage of rational consciousness. But then through Schopenhauer this scientific "knowledge passes on into [personal] experience ... [whereupon this] forces upon me an inward relation to the world, and fills me with *reverence* for the mysterious will-to-live which is in all things" (308–9 [emphasis added]). This is the process by which dualism yields to become a mystical monism of the universal will-to-live.

37 Briefly, the image of God has been variously (and non-exclusively) described by the Church Fathers as freedom, dignity, virtue, an indwelling *logos*, the rational soul, and so on. To be clear here with respect to the rational soul, it is not the same as the mind of God. Being greatly informed by the neo-Platonist philosopher Plotinus, they invariably maintain there is an un-crossable divide between the discursive intellect of human reasoning (*dianoia*) and the perfect unity of the divine *Nous*. In the words of the Cappadocian Father Basil the Great (329–379): "Nothing is with God as it is with us" (2005, 34).

38 Because Schweitzer's New Rationalism is elemental, this allows for it to be combined with similar theories, such as the existential biology of Hans Jonas (1966). Jonas sought to expand Heidegger's hermeneutical *Dasein* to include non-human life. Schweitzer's work can further secure and expand Jonas's innovative ontology with an improved understanding of human consciousness and the will-to-live.

39 Jean-Paul Sartre famously declared "existence precedes essence," an anti-essentialist claim that set him at odds with Schweitzer. In a letter dated 2 May 1956, Schweitzer mentions this dispute and writes that, because of this, "We do not talk about philosophy" (*Letters* 266). In this letter to Professor Kurt Leese, Schweitzer writes that he has "become utterly unsympathetic toward existential philosophy" and describes his own work as *"Philosophia naturalis perennis*, the eternal philosophy of nature" (266).

40 Schweitzer's dissertation for his medical doctorate was a psychiatric analysis of the historical Jesus based on what could be identified as "historical kernels" of truth from the Gospels. Schweitzer considers the claim that Jesus may have suffered from some kind of epilepsy or another kind of mental disorder capable of manifesting the apparent symptoms of pathology (e.g., visions, delusions, etc.). Schweitzer concludes that the eschatological worldview of Jesus was not out of place for his time and that "the only symptoms to be accepted as historical and possibly to be discussed from a psychiatric point of view – the high estimate which Jesus has of himself and perhaps also the hallucination at the baptism – [all] fall far short of proving the existence of mental illness" (*PSJ* 72).

41   The ambiguity of these terms has been previously documented by Mike Martin and James Brabazon. I am also indebted here to my friend and fellow scholar, Robin Lutjohann, for his insights as a native German speaker into the development of the examples given here, which show the full linguistic range of this word.

42   From the essay "Nietzsche, Genealogy, History" (Foucault 1984, 87–8).

43   This phrase is borrowed from Benedict Anderson (1991, 35), who uses it with regard to Hegel (although in a different context than that discussed here).

44   Husserl explicitly presented his theories as a "first philosophy" in an academic course at the University of Freiburg during the 1923–24 school term; it was his specific intent to appropriate and transform Aristotle's project for the modern era (Marion 2002, 13). Heidegger, a student of his at Freiburg, sought to advance this project further by recasting empirical science as being subsumed under the domain of his own philosophy (see note 31 above).

45   For example, Bruno Latour (2004) wrote that those who promote an essentialist metaphysics of nature are anti-democratic authoritarians who position themselves as the only qualified spokespeople to represent the non-human world (128–9). He instead calls for a "political epistemology" that holds all truth claims, even those of the natural sciences, to be on equal terms for democratic debate (13). He believes that the empirical world does not exist apart from human ontology and that, consequently, there can be no such thing as a scientific fact; values and scientific facts therefore cannot be distinguished and so neither should have a privileged status for political decision making (187, 198). Latour only acknowledges power relations between political forces (238). He seeks to put an end to the "*incontestable form of authority that would stem from things themselves*" manifested by those "militant" ecologists who claim to speak for the mute world (14, 20 [emphasis in original]). Non-human nature only exists as "collectives" not fully assimilated into society (238). While his argumentation is anything but clear, he appears to be envisioning these social constructions as pieces of the world caught up in a Heideggerian unfolding of human essence (i.e., the "ek-sistence" of the *Dasein* projection towards the truth of Being) through technological creation (cf., Heidegger's *Letter on Humanism* and *The Question Concerning Technology*). Latour seems to be aware of the sensational and unsupportable nature of his claims, particularly those about empirical science and the non-independent existence of the natural world, since his book constantly rails against an unnamed "epistemology police" whom he fears will attack his work (17, 241).

46   Schopenhauer cautioned that "cause" (*Ursache*) as an explanation of changes for inner and outer phenomena cannot be understood as "cause" in terms of analytical reasoning (*Grund*). There is "a clear distinction between requiring a reason as the ground for a conclusion, and asking for a cause for the occurrence of a real event" (*FFR* §6).

47   That said, the hallmark of any hermeneutic philosophy, and what makes this field so intriguing for academics, is how it can continually be elaborated upon

to bring forth new insights into the human condition. For example, what does Schweitzer's work mean for understanding the experience of one's own aging, or our foreknowledge of having to die someday? Also, how does the "I + will-to-live" nexus interplay and respond within ourselves during an encounter with a stranger, an old friend, a lost love, or a bitter rival? And what are its implications for art and aesthetic theory? Et cetera. All these questions are far beyond the scope of this present work. They will have to be addressed in further publications by myself and others.

48 Metaphysics in this sense, what Heidegger called onto-theology, is considered today as a poor foundation for philosophical inquiry. The problem here is a conception of a transcendent basis for existence that removes the study of being qua beings from direct examination. This is seen as problematic for several reasons. The first (and foremost) is the Nietzschean deconstruction of the Kantian transcendental subject whose simple essence was a priori time. The second is that, in rejecting metaphysics and preferring to instead study the immediate experience of existence, philosophers are, in a very real sense, trying to emulate scientific methodology by examining "the empirical *me*" rather than a transcendental *I*. Marion (2002, 45) describes the difference this way: "I specifically draw this conclusion in challenging the pretension of any *I* to a transcendental function ... In other words, the *ego*, deprived of transcendentalizing dignity, must be admitted as it is received, as *adonné* [given]: the one who is itself received from what it receives ... The *ego* keeps, indeed, all the privileges of subjectivity, save the transcendental claim to origin." The claim here is that the experience of sensation is what actually produces the experiencing self; the external world is what produces the "person" who we think we are (a claim similar to that of David Hume). All this is being maintained because Nietzsche had seemingly destroyed the claim to a simple Cartesian ego and because of the perceived need to find theories and methodologies that can study the empirical in a scientific manner – albeit under a phenomenological understanding of what is claimed to be "empirical" (admittedly, this is a very circular affair). In all this, it should be noted that Schweitzer is only claiming the will-to-live as transcendental, not the Cartesian ego. Furthermore, as a metaphysical claim, the will-to-live concept is an epagoge extrapolated from the particulars of sensory experience; it is no more metaphysical than the Aristotelian idea of a "secondary substance" such as the genus name "canine" for all dog-like creatures and the class name "mammal" for placental animals. In addition, the Universal Will is not a deified "unmoved mover" in the Aristotelian understanding but simply a name for cosmological causality. The philosophical objections to onto-theology should not therefore cause Schweitzer's proposals to be rejected outright. They deserve serious consideration.

49 Schweitzer, the uncompromising historically critical scholar that he was, evidently doubted the Catholic and Orthodox Christian understanding of Jesus' cry of lament from the cross (Matthew 27:46), which is that He was reciting the first line of Psalm 21 (LXX). Schweitzer apparently believed this was a later scriptural

alteration that concealed a kernel of historical truth. Notwithstanding, tradition holds that Jesus' words "My God, My God, why have You forsaken Me?" expressed not a moment of doubt but one of utmost piety. He was reciting a Psalm: even while dying on the Cross, Jesus still worshiped God. Psalm 21 is a lament, perhaps the most powerful and moving one in the whole palmistry. But as with all laments, faith and trust in God is finally and definitively affirmed in the end: "I will declare Your name to my brethren; in the midst of the Church I will sing to You" (21:23, LXX).

50 As an aside, this letter was his response to the director of the Paris Mission after being rejected for missionary work. This uncharacteristically angry response by Schweitzer reveals the strength of his faith in the face of being challenged on this exact point.

51 Schweitzer made an impassioned defence of the Christian faith in *Christianity and the Religions of the World* (1923). This work was published in the same year as *The Philosophy of Civilization* and was based on lectures given at the Selly Oak theological colleges (University of Birmingham) in February 1922 – which explains its strong apologetic character in attacking other religions. Its intended audience was seminary students, and its aim was to show that the Christian religion was not inferior to what some have contested were the intellectually superior religions from India and China. The tone of the work comes across as a "pep talk" to seminarians demoralized by the attacks of historical critics on the sacred texts of the Christian faith. Schweitzer himself was to blame for a good part of that scholarly deconstruction with his *The Quest of the Historical Jesus*. This context must be kept in mind when considering the uncharacteristic and almost polemical language he sometimes employs in this book – it is not a text for respectful interfaith dialogue. The upshot of his arguments is that Christianity and the historical Jesus should be seen as promoting a philosophical understanding of the human person with a particularly strong ethical mandate aimed at the present world. The philosophical grounding for Christianity is, not surprisingly, in harmony with the ethical worldview of his secular Reverence for Life ethic.

52 In a latter work, Barsam (2008, 24 [emphasis in original]) emphasizes Christianity as the hidden thread in Schweitzer work: "The influence of Jesus in Schweitzer's thought, and Schweitzer's belief in the activity of the Will-to-Love to transform the will-to-live to a will-to-reverence, is the unacknowledged yet integral *theological* presupposition throughout his philosophical work." Barsam's book goes on to provide a thoughtful treatment of Reverence for Life in terms of Christian ethics with continued relevance today – an analysis that certainly stands in its own right as *one* possible theological exposition on Schweitzer's Ethical Mysticism. But this cannot be considered a limitation on Reverence for Life as something exclusive to Christians alone.

53 Schopenhauer described the intellect as a slave (*Sklave*) bound in service to its demanding master, the will-to-live (*PP-IBG* §50; see also *PP-OPI* §22). Only if the people – i.e., the "serfs" (Latin: *glebae adscripti*) – can break free of their control-

ling impulses to conform to the common nature of the community can true artistic, poetical, and philosophical achievement be achieved; otherwise, "*das gemeine Wesen bleibt ein gemeines Wesen*" (*PP-IBG* §50).

54 Nietzsche describes the World of the Last Man very cryptically in *Thus Spoke Zarathustra*: "The earth has become small, and on it hops the last man, who makes everything small. His race is as ineradicable as the flea-beetle; the last man lives the longest. 'We have invented happiness,' say the last men ... [for] one still works, for work is a form of entertainment" (*PN* 130–1). Nietzsche's unpublished notebooks further explicate this vision of the World of the Last Man and speak of it as a future society completely dominated and administered by a global economy. To be able to function, a globalized society would need to instil economic and "machine virtues" into its populace so that each citizen "must learn to experience as most valuable those [inner] states in which he [or she] works in a mechanically useful way" to society as a whole (*WLN* 10[11], 176). But to do this, the very psyche of its citizens must be controlled, even though this would lead to a danger of *ressentiment* due to the accumulation of "boredom" and "monotony" in the population of workers (176). The way to address both problems, he indicates, would be to use educational institutions to create a psychological sense of pleasure mingled with what is presented to each person as his or her civic duty. Each student must "learn to see boredom lit up by a higher charm ... [by] learning something that does not concern us [e.g., uninteresting but required subjects]; and feeling that our 'duty' lies precisely there, in that 'objective' activity" (176). The school experience prepares the future workers of that society for tolerating the monotony of menial jobs, their having been inculcated with the "machine virtues" of unquestioning obedience and diligence through repetitive but intellectually unengaging school assignments. Such a worldwide economy would need to destroy the intrinsic potential of humanity for *becoming* and even *being* because "this miniaturisation and adaption of men [and women] to more specialized usefulness" would make them "ever more finely 'adapted' cogs" in an aggregated mechanical whole, the singular and soulless Last Man (*WLN* 10[17], 177). The Last Man thus becomes a kind of Hobbesian Leviathan, a single ontological collective comprised of cells of specialized workers trained to keep functioning an abstract institutional body – which is to say, the economy itself. The Last Man "stands upon them, lives off them ... in moral terms, this total machinery, the solidarity of all cogs, represents a maximum points in the *exploitation of man*" (177 [emphasis in original]). This will all be done in the name of job specialization and increasing economic efficiency. People will thereby be made to serve the greater good of the economy rather than having an economy that caters to social well-being and the needs of the people. This inversion of purpose that causes the individual to be subjugated to a reified creation of thought called the economy was the height of horror for Nietzsche. Combating this monstrosity had to become part of his project. "It can be seen what I'm fighting is *economic* optimism [as a form of social progress]: the idea that everyone's profit [i.e., the greater

good] necessarily increases with the growing cost *to everyone* [in the loss of self through economic life]. It seems to me that the reverse is the case: *the costs to everyone add up to an overall loss*: man becomes *less*" (177 [emphasis in original]). Nietzsche's words here presage David Orr (2004), who extends this same concern over human meaning in economic society (140) to its ecological ramifications. He writes that by subjugating educational institutions solely for the purpose of creating a "world class" labour force (26), we are equipping "people merely to be more effective vandals of the earth" (6).

55 Nietzsche does note that Napoleon made democratic nationalism possible (*WLN* 10[31], 181) but says this is just another case where "every fruitful and powerful movement of [hu]mankind has also *produced alongside it* a nihilistic movement" (*WLN* 10[22], 180 [emphasis in original]).

56 In one of history's most bizarre twists, Propaganda Minister Joseph Goebbels saw an opportunity for a public relations coup. He invited Schweitzer to return to Germany and teach Bach at a university (this was the only aspect of Schweitzer's work they liked). Goebbels signed his letter with the Nazi salutation, "*Mit Deutschem Gruß*," a very particular phrase now forbidden by §86A of the Federal Republic of Germany's penal code (*Strafgesetzbuch*). Schweitzer, naturally, declined the invitation and brazenly signed his response, "With Central African Greetings," an unmistakable rejoinder that showed his intense distaste for Nazism by altering their salutation this way. Schweitzer had declared the African races his brothers (*EPF* 131–2).

57 See also "God of the Market Place" (Goodin 2010c) for a discussion of economic historian Karl Polanyi regarding Aristotle and the Greek distinction between true wealth (*ousia*) and mere possessions (*euporia*).

58 For further discussion, see Goodin (2010c).

59 Perhaps Schweitzer was overly unfair regarding the moral character of Schopenhauer. While he did indeed have a reputation as a lifelong and notorious seducer of women, it would be far too dismissive to characterize Schopenhauer, as some have, as an unfeeling sexual predator. Biographer Helen Zimmern (1876) instead presented him as a victim of his own desires and as just too susceptible to the power of female beauty (70). Admittedly, this is an overly generous portrayal. But she then goes on to document a most revealing event in Schopenhauer's life. At an art gallery Schopenhauer once became lost in contemplative reflection while gazing at a painting of Armand Jean le Bouthillier de Rancé (1626–1700), the founder of the Trappist Cistercians (a contemplative order that emphasizes physical penance through manual labour). Schopenhauer became visibly pained and said to an onlooker that harmonizing one's nature into a state of pure asceticism was "a matter of grace" that had been denied to him (171). Nevertheless, on his deathbed he still hoped to attain Nirvana, yet feared it would be withheld from him (246). It may be that he was greatly troubled by his lifelong treatment of women for, as a final act of compassion and contrition, he bequeathed the majority of his wealth to societies devoted to the care of the hated Prussian soldiers disabled in the 1848 revolution and to their orphans and widows (249).

60 For further discussion, see Goodin (2007).

61 The time of Schweitzer's life leading up to this event is depicted in a 2009 film entitled *Ein Leben für Afrika*. The screenplay was developed by James Brabazon and it reveals how the CIA investigated Schweitzer as a potential threat to US interests.

62 Schweitzer never lost his innate childhood conviction about the sacredness of all life, and he made special note of the need to educate children through the power of example so they would not grow to fear being seen as sentimental by their peers: "even [if you] make yourself look ridiculous in front of thoughtless people ... [they too] will also be more moved than they would like to admit by the elementary truth in that which touches them in such unfamiliar ways" (*APR* 26).

63 See Melemed and Melemed (2003) for a full account of this incident as well as for an account of Schweitzer's positive and collaborative work with the indigenous medicine practitioners of Gabon.

64 Schweitzer did choose to respond to one piece of the nuclear industry propaganda: the so-called "clean" environmentally friendly (low fallout) nuclear weapon. Schweitzer deconstructed this claim by pointing out that these unjacketed hydrogen bombs contained a Hiroshima-sized fissionable trigger and that these show-piece weapons were only meant as a distraction to the real menace – the new Cobalt H-Bombs designed to destroy entire ecosystems and sterilize the soil for decades by salting the earth with lethal Cobalt-60 fallout (Cousins 1985, 179; see also *PAW* 7–8). These sinister weapons were designed to destroy the agricultural lands of the American Midwest and the Soviet Steppe, respectively. As another aside, the paranoia of the Cold War led the US government to become concerned that Schweitzer's work was actually being produced by Soviet agents, but a secret investigation revealed that all the manuscripts were in Schweitzer's own handwriting (Wittner 1995). See also endnote 61.

65 Norton (2003, 15) notes the full context from Hadley's work here: "The criterion which shows whether a thing is right or wrong is its permanence. Survival is not merely the characteristic of right; it is the test of right." The Pragmatists rejected a priori reasoning and unchanging universal truth; they instead sought experiential and contingent truths, and they drew heavily upon Darwinian theory and the scientific method (Langston 2003, 156–7). They believed that such truths revealed "a world still open, a world still in the making," to use Dewey's expression (156). Leopold (1966) employs the same terminology when he writes that "ethics are possibly a kind of community instinct in-the-making" (239). Because Schweitzer's ethics are based in elemental thinking, not in elaborate a priori metaphysics, it is possible to support cultural truths such as those confirmed by Leopold's scientifically informed pragmatism.

66 Very notably, in this essay Leopold (1991, 72) says that the writer of the Book of Job should be recognized as "the John Muir of Judah" for his rich and detailed descriptions of the wonders of the natural world.

67 Duncan was inspired in part by Karl Polanyi's work. Polanyi however could only point to worker cooperatives as a model for a new departure to preserve society

in the face of self-regulating international markets. Specifically, he identified the nineteenth-century Owenite "villages of cooperation," which were capitalist ventures aimed at promoting the well-being of the employees and their families. And they made a profit too. Polanyi considered Owen a visionary. "One man alone perceived the meaning of the ordeal [posed by self-regulating markets], perhaps because among the leading spirits of the age he alone possessed intimate knowledge of industry and was also open to inner vision. No thinker ever advanced farther into the realm of industrial society than did Robert Owen ... The organization of the whole of society on the principle of gain and profit must have far-reaching effects. He formulated them in terms of human character. For the most obvious effect of the new institutional system was the destruction of the traditional character of settled populations and their transmutation into a new type of people, migratory, nomadic, lacking in self-respect and discipline – crude, callous beings of whom both [the stereotypical] laborer and capitalist were an example. He proceeded to the generalization that the principle [of social organization] involved was unfavorable to individual and social happiness. Grave evils would be produced in this fashion unless the tendencies inherent in market institutions were checked by conscious social direction made effective through legislation" (Polanyi 2001, 133). Duncan advances Polanyi's thought, but, by his own concession, the exact economic reforms required still need to be developed further. He writes that his work "may usefully suggest, but cannot absolutely specify, what social institutions might be more suitable for that [economic] activity ... [and to argue that] some of what we need and want could actually be fairly easily made more abundant, and that it is liable to become scarce in some absolute sense only if we destroy certain fundamental supports of our living environment" (Duncan 1996, 199, see note xxxv).

68 For further discussion, see Goodin (2010b).

69 Paul Taylor developed an ethical framework supporting bio-centric egalitarianism in his *Respect for Nature* (1986), a project that was inspired in part by Schweitzer. Taylor, however, based his arguments in large part on evolutionary science (99–100). Since humans emerged within a biotic community, this is where our creaturely self-identity should be grounded. He writes that, "once we do grasp [this realization] and shape our world outlook in accordance with [this fact], we immediately understand how and why a person should adopt that attitude [of respect] as the only appropriate one to have toward nature" (90). Taylor is an intellectual forerunner of Peter Brown's conception of a commonwealth of life.

70 While Schweitzer would not support the global governance regimes advocated by Brown and Garver, as my chapter 6 makes clear, this does not mean the moral force of his philosophy cannot still be used to call for international economic reforms in support of their proposals.

71 A noteworthy element here is the International Clearing Union proposal to temper predatory trade imbalances that lead to ecological degradation in vulnerable nations – a proposal developed by Brown and Goodin (2008, 192–3; see also Brown and Garver 2009, 120–1).

72 Vladimir Lossky (1976), a neo-patristic scholar, described created beings as the *thelemata logoi*, or the willed-ideas of God: " ... the divine ideas ... are to be identified with the [divine] will or wills (*thelemata*) which determine the different modes according to which created beings participate in the creative energies [of God]" (95). He also points out that the Greek Fathers of the Eastern Orthodox tradition hold that: "Every created thing has its point of contact with the God-head; and this point of contact is its idea, reason[,] or *logos* which is at the same time the end toward which it tends" (98). It should also be observed that the participation in and transfiguration through God's grace is not limited to humans alone, but is open to the entire cosmos, as these quotes reveal.

References

Abelsen, Paul. 1993. "Schopenhauer and Buddhism." *Philosophy East and West* 43 (2): 225–78.

Anderson, Benedict. 1991. *Imagined Communities: Reflections on the Origin and Spread of Nationalism*. London: Verso.

Arendt, Hannah. 1988. "Nietzsche's Repudiation of the Will." In *Nietzsche: Critical Assessments II: "The World as Will to Power – and Nothing Else?,"* ed. Daniel W. Conway and Peter S. Groff. New York: Routledge.

Aristotle. 1999. *Nicomachean Ethics*. Trans. Terence Irwin. Indianapolis: Hackett Publishing Company.

Atwell, John E. 1995. *Schopenhauer on the Character of the World: The Metaphysics of the Will*. Berkeley: University of California Press.

Aurelius, Marcus. 1966. *Meditations*. Trans. Maxwell Staniforth. Aylesbury, Great Britain: Penguin Books.

Babich, Babette E. 2004. "Nietzsche's Critique of Scientific Reason as Scientific Culture: On 'Science as a Problem' and Nature as Chaos." In *Nietzsche and Science,* ed. Gregory Moore and Thomas H. Brobjer. Hampshire, UK: Ashgate.

Barsam, Ara Paul. 2002. "Albert Schweitzer, Jainism, and Reverence for Life." In *Reverence for Life: The Ethics of Albert Schweitzer for the Twenty-First Century,* ed. Marvin Meyer and Kurt Bergel. New York: Syracuse University Press.

– 2008. *Reverence for Life: Albert Schweitzer's Great Contribution to Ethical Thought*. New York: Oxford University Press.

Barth, Karl. 1961. *Church Dogmatics* (vol. 3, pt. 4). Edinburgh, UK: T&T Clark.

Basil the Great. 2005. *On the Human Condition*. Trans. Nonna Verna Harrison. Crestowood, NY: St Vladimir's Seminary Press.

Baum, Gregory. 1996. *Karl Polanyi on Ethics and Economics*. Montreal and Kingston: McGill-Queen's University Press.

Berry, Thomas. 2009. *The Sacred Universe: Earth, Spirituality, and Religion in the Twenty-First Century*. New York: Columbia University Press.

Bookchin, Murray. 2007. *Social Ecology and Communalism*. Oakland, CA: AK Press.

Brabazon, James. 1975. *Albert Schweitzer: A Biography*. New York: Putnam Press.

– 1976. *Albert Schweitzer: A Biography*. London: Victor Gollancz Ltd.

– 2000. *Albert Schweitzer: A Biography*. 2nd ed. Syracuse, NY: Syracuse University Press.

– 2002. "Schweitzer at the Beginning of the Millennium." In *Reverence for Life: The Ethics of Albert Schweitzer for the Twenty-First Century*, ed. Marvin Meyer and Kurt Bergel. New York: Syracuse University Press.

Brown, Peter G. 2001. *The Commonwealth of Life: A Treatise on Stewardship Economics*. Montreal: Black Rose Books.

– 2008. *The Commonwealth of Life: Economics for a Flourishing Earth*, 2nd ed. Montreal: Black Rose Books.

Brown, Peter G., and Geoffrey Garver. 2009. *Right Relationship: Building a Whole Earth Economy*. San Francisco: Berret-Koehler.

Buffon, Comte. 1969. "Discourse on Studying and Treating Natural History." In *The Age of Enlightenment*, ed. L. Crocker. New York: Harper and Row.

Callicott, J. Baird. 1986. "Moral Considerability and Extraterrestrial Life." In *Beyond Spaceship Earth: Environmental Ethics and the Solar System*, ed. Eugene C. Hargrove. San Francisco: Sierra Club Books.

– 1987. "The Conceptual Foundations of the Land Ethic." In *Companion to a Sand County Almanac: Interpretive and Critical Essays*, ed. J. Baird Callicott. Madison: University of Wisconsin Press.

Campbell, Joseph. 1988. *The Power of Myth*. New York: Anchor Books.

Carson, Rachel. 1962. *Silent Spring*. New York: Houghton Mifflin Company.

Cavendish, Richard. 2003. "Albert Schweitzer's Nobel Prize: October 30th 1953." *History Today* 53 (10): 57.

Clark, Henry. 1964. *The Philosophy of Albert Schweitzer*. London: Methuen.

Cordero, Luis Alberto. 2007. "Controlling the Arms Trade." In *Reverence for Life Revisited: Albert Schweitzer's Relevance Today*, ed. David Ives and David A. Valone. Newcastle, UK: Cambridge Scholars Publishing.

Cousins, Norman. 1985. *Albert Schweitzer's Mission: Healing and Peace*. New York: W.W. Norton.

Dansdill, Timothy. 2007. "'A Boundless Ethics': Reverence for Life versus Divine Dominion." In *Reverence for Life Revisited: Albert Schweitzer's Relevance Today*, ed. David Ives and David A. Valone. Newcastle, UK: Cambridge Scholars Publishing.

Darwin, Charles. 1882. *The Descent of Man, and Selection in Relation to Sex*, 2nd ed. London: John Murray.

Descartes, René. 2006. *René Descartes: Meditations, Objections, and Replies*, ed. and trans. Roger Ariew and Donald Cress. Indianapolis: Hackett Publishing.

Dewey, John. 1898. "Evolution and Ethics." *The Monist* VIII: 321–41.

Duncan, Colin. 1996. *The Centrality of Agriculture between Humankind and Nature*. Montreal and Kingston: McGill-Queen's University Press.

Epicurus. 2010. "Principal Doctrines." *The Internet Classics Archive*. Available at http://classics.mit.edu/Epicurus/princdoc.html (viewed 19 February 2012).

Escobar, Arturo. 1996. "Construction Nature: Elements for a post-structuralism political ecology." *Futures* 28 (4): 325–43.

Foucault, Michel. 1984. *The Foucault Reader*, ed. Paul Rainbow. New York: Pantheon Books.

Gelven, Michael. 1989. *A Commentary on Heidegger's Being and Time*, rev. ed. DeKlab: Northern Illinois University Press.

Gemes, Ken. 2001. "Postmodernism's Use and Abuse of Nietzsche." *Philosophy and Phenomenological Research* 62 (2): 337–60.

Giordano, James, and Julia Pedroni. 2007. "The Legacy of Albert Schweitzer's Virtue Ethics to a Moral Philosophy of Medicine." In *Reverence for Life Revisited: Albert Schweitzer's Relevance Today*, ed. David Ives and David A. Valone. Newcastle, UK: Cambridge Scholars Publishing.

Goodin, David K. 2007. "Schweitzer Reconsidered: The Applicability of Reverence for Life as Environmental Philosophy." *Environmental Ethics* 29 (4): 403–21.

– 2010a. "On First Principles: Arthur Schopenhauer and Bridging the Science/Religion Divide." In *How Do We Know? Understanding in Science and Theology*, ed. Dirk Evers, Antje Jackelen, and Taede Smedes. London, UK: T and T Clark International.

– 2010b. "Social Insecurity and the No-Avail Thesis: Insights from Philosophy and Economic History on Consumerist Behaviour." *Ethics, Place and Environment: A Journal of Philosophy and Geography* 13 (1): 15–18.

– 2010c. "The God of the Market Place: John Stuart Mill and Maximos Confessor on Economic Virtue." *World in the World: Concordia University Graduate Journal of Theological Studies* 3 (1): 15–35.

Hadot, Pierre. 2006. *The Veil of Isis: An Essay on the History of the Idea of Nature*. Tran. Michael Chase. Cambridge: Belknap Press of Harvard University Press.

Hartmann, Eduard. 1931. *Philosophy of the Unconscious: Speculative Results according to the Inductive Method of Physical Science*. London: Kegan, Paul, Trench, Trubner and Co. Ltd.

Hay, Peter. 2002. *Main Currents in Western Environmental Thought*. Bloomington: Indiana University Press.

Heidegger, Martin. 1993. *Basic Writings*. Ed. David Farrell Krell. San Francisco: HarperSanFrancisco.

Hochschild, Adam. 1998. *King Leopold's Ghost*. New York: Houghton Mifflin Company.

Hume, David. 1973. "Of Personal Identity." In *A Modern Introduction to Philosophy*, 3rd ed., ed. Paul Edwards and Arthur Pap. New York: The Free Press.

Ice, Jackson Lee. 1994. *Albert Schweitzer: Sketches for a Portrait*. Lanham, MD: University Press of America.

Jonas, Hans. 1966. *The Phenomenon of Life: Toward a Philosophical Biology*. New York: Harper and Row.

Kant, Immanuel. 1950. *Prolegomena to Any Future Metaphysic*. Ed. L.W. Beck. New York: Bobbs-Merrill Company.

– 2007. *Critique of Pure Reason*. Trans. Norman Kemp Smith. New York: Palgrave Macmillan

Kizima, Sergy A. 2007. "Albert Schweitzer: The Influence of His Life and Ideas on Eastern Slavic Countries." In *Reverence for Life Revisited: Albert Schweitzer's Relevance Today*, ed. David Ives and David A. Valone. Newcastle, UK: Cambridge Scholars Publishing.

Lange, Friedrich Albert. 1880. *History of Materialism and Criticism of Its Present Importance*. Vol. 2. Trans. E.C. Thomas. Boston: Houghton Osgood and Company.

– 1881. *History of Materialism and Criticism of Its Present Importance*. Vol. 3. Trans. E.C. Thomas. London: Trubner and Company.

Langston, Nancy. 2003. *Where Land and Water Meet: A Western Landscape Transformed*. Seattle: University of Washington Press.

Latour, Bruno. 2004. *Politics of Nature: How to Bring the Sciences into Democracy*. Trans. Catherine Porter. Cambridge: Harvard University Press.

Leopold, Aldo. 1966. *A Sand County Almanac*. New York: Random House.

– 1991. *The River of the Mother of God and Other Essays by Aldo Leopold*. Ed. Susan L. Flader and J. Baird Callicott. Madison University of Wisconsin Press.

Lindroth, Sten. 2004. "The Two Faces of Linnaeus." In *Linnaeus: The Man and His Work*, ed. Tore Frängsmyr. Sagamore Beach, MA: Science History Publications.

Lossky, Vladimir. 1976. *The Mystical Theology of the Eastern Church*. Crestwood, NY: St Vladimir's Seminary Press.

Marion, Jean-Luc. 2002. *In Excess: Studies of Saturated Phenomena*. New York: Fordham University Press.

Martin, Mike W. 2002. "Rethinking Reverence for Life." In *Reverence for Life: The Ethics of Albert Schweitzer for the Twenty-First Century*, ed. Marvin Meyer and Kurt Bergel. New York: Syracuse University Press.

– 2007. *Albert Schweitzer's Reverence for Life: Ethical Idealism and Self-Realization*. Hampshire, UK: Ashgate.

Melamed, Steven E.G., and Antonia Melamed. 2003. "Albert Schweitzer in Africa." In *Culture, Ecology and Politics in Gabon's Rainforest*, ed. Michael C. Reed and James F. Barnes. New York: Edwin Mellen Press.

Meyer, Marvin. 2002. "Affirming Reverence for Life." In *Reverence for Life: The Ethics of Albert Schweitzer for the Twenty-First Century*, ed. Marvin Meyer and Kurt Bergel. New York: Syracuse University Press.

Mikkelson, Gregory, M., A. Gonzalez, and G.D. Peterson. 2007. "Economic Inequality Predicts Biodiversity Loss." *Public Library of Science* 2: e444. doi:10.1371/journal.pone.0000444.

Mougin, Damien, and Claudine Mougin. 2007. "Reflection on Albert Schweitzer in Africa." In *Reverence for Life Revisited: Albert Schweitzer's Relevance Today*, ed. David Ives and David A. Valone. Newcastle, UK: Cambridge Scholars Publishing.

Nazianzus, Gregory. 2006. *Gregory of Nazianzus*. Ed. and trans. Brian E. Daley. New York: Routledge.

Nietzsche, Friedrich. 1967. *The Birth of Tragedy and The Case of Wagner*. Trans. Walter Kaufmann. New York: Vintage Books.

– 1967. *On the Genealogy of Morals and Ecce Homo*. Trans. Walter Kaufmann and R.J. Hollingdale. New York: Vintage Books.

– 1968. *The Portable Nietzsche*. Trans. Walter Kaufmann. New York: Viking Press.

– 1968. *The Will to Power*. Trans. Walter Kaufmann and R.J. Hollingdale. New York: Vintage Books.

– 1974. *The Gay Science*. Trans. Walter Kaufmann. New York: Vintage Books.

– 1986. *Human, All Too Human*. Trans. R.J. Hollingdale. Cambridge, MA: Cambridge University Press.

– 1990. *Twilight of the Idols and the Anti-Christ*. Trans. R.J. Hollingdale. London: Penguin Books.

– 1997. *Untimely Meditations*. Trans. R.J. Hollingdale. Cambridge, UK: Cambridge University Press.

– 2002. *Beyond Good and Evil: Prelude to a Philosophy of the Future*. Trans. Judith Norman. Cambridge, NY: Cambridge University Press.

– 2003. *A Nietzsche Reader*. Trans. R.J. Hollingdale. New York: Penguin Books.

– 2003. *Writings from the Late Notebooks*. Ed. R. Bittner, trans. K. Sturge. Cambridge: Cambridge University Press.

Norton, Bryan G. 2003. *Searching for Sustainability: Interdisciplinary Essays in the Philosophy of Conservation Biology*. Cambridge: Cambridge University Press.

Orr, David. 2004. *Earth in Mind: On Education, Environment, and the Human Prospect*. Washington: Island Press.

Polanyi, Karl. 2001. *The Great Transformation: The Political and Economic Origins of Our Time*. Boston: Beacon Press.

Richards, Robert J. 2008. "Darwin's Theory of Natural Selection and Its Moral Purpose." In *Cambridge Companion to Darwin's Origin of Species*, ed. Robert J. Richards and Michael Ruse. Cambridge: Cambridge University Press.

Richardson, Dennis J. 2007. "Schweitzer's Legacy in Public Health." In *Reverence for Life Revisited: Albert Schweitzer's Relevance Today*, ed. David Ives and David A. Valone. Newcastle, UK: Cambridge Scholars Publishing.

Roetz, Heiner. 2003. "Albert Schweitzer on Chinese Thought and Confucian Ethics." *Journal of Ecumenical Studies* 40 (1–2): 111–20.

Saarikoski, Heli. 2007. "Objectivity and the Environment–Epistemic Value of Biases." *Environmental Politics* 16 (3): 488–98.

Salter, William MacKintire. 1915. "Nietzsche on the Problem of Reality." *Mind* 24 (96): 441–63.

Schopenhauer, Arthur. 1889. "The Fourfold Root of Sufficient Reason." In *Two Essays by Arthur Schopenhauer.* London: George Bell and Sons.

– 1889. "On The Will in Nature." In *Two Essays by Arthur Schopenhauer.* London: George Bell and Sons.

– 1965. *On the Basis of Morality.* Trans. E.J.F. Payne. New York: Bobbs-Merrill Company.

– 1969. *The World as Will and Representation,* vol. 1. Trans. E.F.J. Payne. New York: Dover Publications.

– 1970. *Essays and Aphorisms* [Parerga et Paralipomena]. Ed. and trans. R.J. Hollingdale. New York: Penguin Books.

– 1988. "Der Intellekt überhaupt und in jeder Beziehung betreffende Gedanken." In *Parerga und Paralipomena II, Band 6, im Sämtliche Werke.* Mannheim: F.U. Brockhaus.

– 1994. *Manuscript Remains* [*Nachlasswerke*] *of Arthur Schopenhauer: Philosophical Writings,* edited by Wolfgang Schirmacher. Translated by E.J.F. Payne. New York: Continuum.

Schweitzer, Albert. 1923. *Christianity and the Religions of the World.* Trans. Johanna Powers. London: George Allen and Unwin Ltd.

– 1923. *Kulturphilosophie – Zweiter Teil: Kultur und Ethik.* Bern, GR: P. Haupt.

– 1923. *Kulturphilosophie – Erster Teil: Verfall und Wiederaufbau Der Kultur.* München: C.H. Beck'sche Verlagsbuchhandlung.

– 1931. *On the Edge of the Primeval Forest.* Trans. C.T. Campion. New York: Macmillan.

– 1931. *Memoirs of Childhood and Youth.* Trans. C.T. Campion. New York: Macmillan.

– 1936. "The Ethics of Reverence for Life." *Christendom* 1 (2): 225–39.

– 1949. *Goethe: Four Studies.* Trans. Charles R. Joy. Boston: Beacon Press.

– 1949. *Out of My Life and Thought.* Trans. C.T. Campion. New York: Henry Holt and Company.

– 1950. *The Animal World of Albert Schweitzer.* Ed. Charles R. Joy. Boston: Beacon Press.

– 1953. *The Mysticism of Paul the Apostle.* Trans. William Montgomery. London: Adam and Charles Black.

– 1954. "The Problem of Peace." Nobel Lecture for the 1952 Peace Prize, delivered on 4 November 1954, Oslo University, Norway. Available at http://www.nobelprize.org/nobel_prizes/peace/laureates/1952/schweitzer-lecture.html (viewed April 2012).

– 1958. *Peace or Atomic War?* London: Adam and Charles Black.

– 1965. "Philosophy of Religion." In *A Treasury of Albert Schweitzer*, ed. Thomas Kiernan. Trans. Kurt F. Leidecker. New York: Gramercy Books.

– 1965. *A Treasury of Albert Schweitzer*. Ed. Thomas Kiernan. New York: Gramercy Books.

– 1966. *The Essence of Faith: Philosophy of Religion*. Trans. K. Leidecker. New York: Philosophical Library.

– 1969. *Reverence for Life*. Trans. Reginald H. Fuller. New York: Harper and Row.

– 1975. *The Psychiatric Study of Jesus: Exposition and Criticism*. Trans. Charles Joy. Gloucester, MA: Peter Smith.

– 1987. *The Philosophy of Civilization*. Vol. 1, *The Decay and the Restoration of Civilization*. Vol. 2, *Civilization and Ethics*. Trans. C.T. Campion. Buffalo, NY: Prometheus Books.

– 1988. *A Place for Revelation: Sermons on Reverence for Life*. Trans. David Larrimore Holland. New York: Macmillan.

– 1992. *Letters: 1905–1965*. Ed. Hans Walter Bähr. Trans. Joachim Neugroschel. New York: Macmillan.

– 2000. *Die Weltanschauung der Ehrfurcht vor dem Leben: Kulturphilosophie III, Werke aus dem Nachlass*. München: C.H. Beck.

– 2000. *The Quest of the Historical Jesus*, ed. John Bowden. Trans. W. Montgomery, J.R. Coates, Susan Cupit, and John Bowden. London: SCM Press.

– 2002. "Letters, 1902 – 1905." In *Reverence for Life: The Ethics of Albert Schweitzer for the Twenty-First Century*, ed. Marvin Meyer and Kurt Bergel. New York: Syracuse University Press.

Taylor, Paul W. 1986. *Respect for Nature: A Theory of Environmental Ethics*. Princeton: Princeton University Press.

Trefon, Theodore. 2003. "Libreville's Evolving Forest Dependencies." In *Culture, Ecology and Politics in Gabon's Rainforest*, ed. Michael C. Reed and James F. Barnes. New York: Edwin Mellen Press.

Wadlow, René. 2007. "The River to Ngomo: Albert Schweitzer in the Galoa Heartland of Lambaréné." In *Reverence for Life Revisited: Albert Schweitzer's Relevance Today*, ed. David Ives and David A. Valone. Newcastle, UK: Cambridge Scholars Publishing.

Wittner, Lawrence S. 1995. "Blacklisting Schweitzer." *Bulletin of the Atomic Scientists* 51: 55–61.

Zimmern, Helen. 1876. *Arthur Schopenhauer: His Life and His Philosophy*. London: Longmans, Green and Co.

Index